THE TRAINING INVESTMENT
BANKING ON PEOPLE FOR SUPERIOR RESULTS

THE TRAINING INVESTMENT
BANKING ON PEOPLE FOR SUPERIOR RESULTS

Margaret Rahn Keene

BUSINESS ONE IRWIN
Homewood, Illinois 60430

Project editor: Ethel Shiell
Production manager: Bette K. Ittersagen
Jacket designer: Renee Klyczak-Nordstrom
Compositor: Eastern Graphics
Typeface: 11/13 Century Schoolbook
Printer: Arcata Graphics/Kingsport

Library of Congress Cataloging-in-Publication Data

Keene, Margaret Rahn
    The training investment : banking on people for superior results / Margaret Rahn Keene.
       p.   cm.
    Includes index.
    ISBN 1-55623-318-3
    1. Bank employees—Training of. 2. Employee motivation.
3. Career development. I. Title.
HG1615.7.T7K44 1990
332.1′068′3—dc20
                                         90–35839
                                          CIP

Printed in the United States of America

1 2 3 4 5 6 7 8 9 0 K 7 6 5 4 3 2 1 0

To my patient and
understanding husband, Allan

PREFACE

The entry of the 90s brought winds of change of such magnitude that their impact will undoubtedly affect the political and economic landscape for the duration of the decade. An era of dictatorship, greed, and self-serving excess is now being followed by an era of focus on fundamental social issues and concerns: the "me" generation has been succeeded by the "we" generation.

Especially gratifying is the renewed emphasis in this country on education, particularly in light of our declining competitive edge vis-á-vis other industrialized countries. Slowly we are beginning to realize that as a nation we have wasted great talent and potential by systematically denying those from lower social strata access to good education. There is now a greater sense that reversing that attitude will pay off handsome dividends in the form of a better life for all.

This book draws its basic premise from that spirit. Bankers have learned through the deflation of the thrift industry, the sharp reversals in the investment banking and brokerage industry, and the write-downs in the commercial banking loan portfolios that success in the financial industry cannot be achieved through balance sheet gimickry or taking on overvalued assets. Rather, success must be achieved the old-fashioned way—by a slow building of financial strength through carefully considered strategies executed by highly capable employees.

The book's focus is on establishing a systematic and integrated approach to developing a bank's employee base to its highest level of capabilities. It emphasizes the "long haul" over the "quick-fix," the whole organization over parochial interests, and direct involvement over delegation. The book addresses the "new realities" of the 90s—the flattening of the organizational hierarchy, resulting in a redundancy of managerial staff, as well as the emergence of the "baby bust" generation, resulting in a shortfall of qualified entry-level workers.

We have all discovered that societal problems are best addressed by banks (or any business entity) when the ultimate solutions make good business sense as well. The highly competitive financial industry especially cannot afford to consider any new venture that does not have a mutual pay-off—to the worker and to the bank. This book rests it case on a fundamental premise—that if a bank develops its employees to their fullest potential, then the individuals in turn will "repay" the bank through increased productivity and loyalty. In turn, society will benefit through a higher standard of living.

In short, this book aims to assist banks in developing skilled and enthusiastic employees who willingly take up the competitive challenges facing the institutions they work for. Creating such a workforce requires more than inspirational phrases on cafeteria walls or rah-rahs at annual meetings. Human resource policies must be established that naturally encourage and develop employee motivation—such as through empowerment, developmental and succession planning, job posting, incentive systems, "personal best" achievement awards, and other aspects of job satisfaction. Nearly every developmental policy requires the intense involvement of training and education. Banks shouldn't merely want employees who are just trying their hardest; banks need employees who have a firm understanding of how to achieve their goal.

Many financial institutions in this country have already taken these issues to heart. They have redesigned or expanded their programs to incorporate broader concepts to create a better workforce. These new approaches, and the impact they have had on the success of the bank, are presented in the book. One theme runs throughout each of these success stories—the direct involvement of the banks' senior management. It was their breakthrough "vision" that allowed others to "see" the value of emphasizing—almost making an obsession of—the development of human resources. The credit goes to them. They had the foresight to realize that the future of any organization is in the hands of the employees and that an executive, therefore, cannot pay too much attention to meeting their real needs—namely, deriving the satisfaction from being able to do a superior job, having a fair opportunity to be personally successful, and being a valued member of the organization. Cleverly worded mottos on corporate pencils are not enough. Only specific actions count.

This book deliberately shied away from interviewing those at the largest "money center" institutions. Too often, smaller banks think that "it's easy for money-centers to do all that training—they've got the necessary money." Instead, we mainly chose larger community and regional banks to demonstrate that at every institution of size, training is not only affordable but perhaps is even more critical from a competitive point of view.

Overall, the book reflects the current evolution-revolution in the approach to training and development. It disputes the long-held notion that training is a function that, like the company cafeteria, is important but does not warant attention at the highest levels. Rather, it shows that a highly trained and motivated workforce, combined with a solid strategy, is the only way to assure success—and therefore should be a "top of the pile" item on every bank executive's desk.

Margaret Rahn Keene

ACKNOWLEDGMENTS

It would be very wrong for me to suggest that I was the sole author of this book. Yes, I *wrote* it in its entirety, but the true authors are those whose fundamental ideas form the basis of this book.

Unfortunately, there were more superior ideas than could be adequately handled in this book; many thoughts and refinements were left for future editions. We hope to give justice to everyone's contribution over time.

I would like to express special appreciation towards those whose efforts really made this book come into existence, not only by providing excellent insight, but also by assisting in doing the necessary legwork. In particular, I would like especially to point out that the best ideas are wasted unless they are effectively executed. The following people are as exceptional in executing ideas as they are in conceptualizing them.

At the risk of denying them full credit for all their abilities, I would like to highlight the significant areas of contributions of my "coauthors," all of whom are or were training directors or managers at the time of writing this book.

Edward Zinser (National State Bank) and William Schoel (SouthTrust Bank) have created overall training programs that truly take into account the needs of the "whole" bank. Robert Albright (Huntington National Bank) and Barbara Phillips (Seafirst Bank) helped develop the continuous learning concept even more intensely with the creation of the Huntington Institute and the Seafirst College. William Donahue (First American Bankshares) and Robert Schoonmaker (Provident National Bank) successfully keyed in on the executive-level training, an area that has been traditionally underattended.

Robert Hamilton (Sovran Bank) and Connie Ruhl (Mellon Bank) respectively, placed their focus on operations and technical training with outstanding results.

Jill Flynn (First Union Bank) and Charles Lussenhop (Southeast Bank) furthered sales-training programs at their banks, successfully integrating all aspects of the selling function to create a bankwide culture.

Jeff Judy (Norwest Bank), Rodney Cornwall (Seafirst Bank), and William Barksdale (South Carolina National Bank) have established especially insightful credit training programs that go well beyond the normal cut- and dried-approach for developing analysts.

Amy Rego (American Savings Bank), Gail Snowden (Bank of Boston), and Joan Ustin (National Westminster Bancorp) have demonstrated special sensitivity to needs of the employees when developing programs, with their efforts yielding a wide array of human resources dividends.

Others in a nonbank training role also deserve our sincere thanks: specifically, Bruce Johnson and Diana Osinski at the American Bankers Association, Jerry Halamaj at the Bank Administration Institute, Clarence Reed at the Robert Morris Associates, and Roger Raber at the National Council of Savings Institutions, for providing insight, statistics, and other backup data.

Special thanks go to my editor, Jim Childs, for his patience in guiding me through this project.

The knowledge and enthusiasm that these people have shown in support of my effort cannot be understated, and I wish to thank each of them for their personal contribution to this book.

M. R. K.

CONTENTS

CHAPTER 1

MANEUVERING THROUGH THE TRAINING MAZE

"Find the best people and train them well—that's the Merrill Lynch philosophy."—*Copy from a recent Merrill Lynch ad campaign.*

It's a typical business day in the 90s. A meeting of the executive committee of a regional bank has begun. The agenda and supporting materials have been passed out. A cursory glance of the items under review reveals:

- A slow erosion in earnings as retail marketing efforts continuously yield less profits from an already over-banked area.
- A competitor bank just announced a new thrust into the primary middle market lending territory.
- The strategic committee avidly recommends expanding in the capital markets arena even though the official staff is unprepared to take any initiatives.
- The branch managers are complaining that teller turnover is approaching 75% a year.
- The human resources (HR) department is pulling together an expensive "golden handshake" program to weed out the "deadwood."
- The bank's recruiters are rejecting 50% of the nonexempt people they interview, up from 40% the year before.
- Approximately 30% of the new management training class left within six months after the program was completed, at a cost to the bank of over $250,000.
- A lawsuit from an employee for wrongful dismissal.

- The market value of the bank's stock is slowly slipping, leaving the door wide open to acquisition by the giants from the neighboring states.

After three hours of discussion, decisions on the "next step" for all of the issues were made. Afterwards, a committee member commented to a colleague, "You know, I realized as we were talking that not one of the 'next steps' we decided on was a *solution*. We don't really have a handle on dealing with any of it. We're just taking potshots and hoping that one of them will hit the mark. What I can't figure out is where did all these problems come from? Have they been around all these years and we simply ignored them until they finally boiled over, or are these new issues?"

BANKING WAS DIFFERENT THEN

As inconceivable as it is now, in the 60s the word *competition* was unknown in most bankers' lexicon. The banking world played by several rules of gamesmanship: (1) you rarely sought to steal any business from a competitor bank, and (2) you never ever stole any business from a friendly bank. If the customer decided to do business with your bank, such occurrences most often were attributed to relationships formed on the 19th hole, not to the perceived quality of service.

The 3-6-3 of the 60s

This apparent lassitude on the bank's part was actually almost justifiable. The prevalent economic situation during the 60s discouraged banks from bringing in additional customers. The Vietnam War and the War on Poverty, combined with recessions in the beginning and end of the decade, had engendered a serious credit crunch that did not abate until the 70s, when money became easier and banks had found new ways of funding. For the most part, banks were stretched just to meeet their current customers' demands.

Why even bring in new business if the answer to any loan requests would basically have to be no?

Attracting more depositors was also not a major concern. Hamstrung by Regulation Q, which determined the interest rate that could be offered on deposits, banks expanded their deposit base by cleverly locating branches. Knowing that most individuals' choice of a bank is predominantly based on convenience, the strategic plan for expanding a bank's customer base was to track the developing neighborhoods and select the right giveaways at the branch opening ceremonies. Service quality and customer satisfaction were non-issues, particularly since most banks were indistinguishable in the public's eye. All bankers knew the basic tenet of branch banking: that toasters got people in the door and inertia kept them there.

Thus, there was little reason why bankers shouldn't be proponents of 3-6-3 banking, that is, pay depositors 3%, lend to them at 6%, and hit the golf course by three in the afternoon.

What Did Bank Personnel Need to Know to Perform Effectively?

Not much.

But then, what was there to know? Memorizing the bank's product list was not a demanding chore. Throughout the 60s, bank products became increasingly more complex, although by today's standards most would now fall into the plain vanilla category. For instance, the certificate of deposit (CD) did not even exist prior to 1961 and was only universally adopted during the latter half of the decade. Bank-backed credit cards, which made their debut in the 50s, were just beginning to be commonly offered and were not expected to outpace auto loans, installment lending, or mortgage financing.

As for commercial credit, the two mainstays were the seasonal working capital line of credit and the equipment term loan. The structure of the revolving credit was introduced in the late 60s, hitherto a type of credit facility that was used only in asset-based transactions. One major money center bank recently noted that there were so few term credits offered, they did not even have a term loan department until 1972.

Training, of course, did exist. But considering the near complete lack of differentiation between banks, generic-variety training, provided by banking schools or self-study manuals, was entirely adequate. A foundation of knowledge learned in the early years would suffice for an entire career, and skills learned in one institution would be completely transferable to the next.

PATCH AS PATCH CAN

But seeds of change were being sown in the 60s, and harvesting began in the 70s. The credit crunch pushed the large corporates into dumping the banks in favor of commercial paper. The subsequent scramble by the banks for replacement business pushed the banks into having to market their services. The bank's reliance on depositor inertia was foiled by rising interest rates, which ultimately drove billions out of the banks and into money market funds. To counter the trend, new deposit services and instruments were developed, leading to the dismantling of interest rate regulation in the 80s. The slow transformation of a bank from a monolithic repository of funds to a dynamic entity had begun.

Employee development followed suit. In some cases, new strategic initiatives incorporated training issues and concerns, which were resolved with the selection or design of a program addressing the need. But more frequently, training was ignored until it occurred to someone, often a line manager, that perhaps the poor showing in an area might be the result of the staff's lack of knowledge and/or skills. A training program would be the quick-fix solution.

Thus, a patchwork quilt of training emerged. Training for individuals was usually self-selected, haphazard, and ill-timed at best. Even those who were privileged enough to receive formal training in the management training program were not necessarily exposed to all the right elements. As reported in one of the many books about problem banks published in the 80s, a group vice president at a large bank noted that "the people on the line didn't have a clue as to what they were supposed to do." His comments were based not only on his own impressions but those of the bank's clients as well, who had reported their comments to a market research group. Nonetheless, that bank had pushed to increase loans by 10% a year for the previous five years, despite the fact that "turnover was far too high and training was inadequate."

Another story tells of a bank chief executive officer (CEO) who once gave a pop quiz to attendees at a staff meeting on their knowledge of the bank, such as how many overseas offices the bank had, their location, and so forth. As expected, the test results were disastrous—but scores vastly improved on the quiz given a month later.[1]

THE 70s: IF IT AIN'T BROKE, DON'T FIX IT

Should employees be treated like school children in order for them to realize they must stay informed, as the conventional wisdom of the 70s suggested? True, responsibility rests with the individual to assure that he or she is well trained. Learning does not occur unless the student reaches out to accept it. But two things must also exist: first, the training must be available (if not in-house, then through the American Institute of Banking (AIB) or others' programs), and then there must be an incentive to use it.

But where were the incentives? Little if any note of the effort was reported in the annual performance appraisals (presuming a formal one even occurred), much less reflected in a salary hike. With the exception of the CEO's surprise quiz, it was unlikely that the employee would be tested on the knowledge or skills.

If anything, the training system of the 70s created disincentives. Lost time would be penalized with a work pileup. And attending a seminar with less inexperienced people could cause embarrassment over the apparent need for remedial training. Besides, if one's superior hasn't said it's a problem, why fix it?

It's Your Job—You Figure It Out

In essence, banks expected employees to come to understand the changes within their jobs virtually without any guidance. One executive compared the process to going to a peculiar kind of school.

> It's as if the teacher walks in on the first day and hands out a copy of an old test and says, "Here's what you needed to know to pass the test last year. I'm going to give you a different test this year, but I'm not going to tell you what topics it will address. Furthermore, it'll be up to you to figure out what you have to know to pass. In other words, I won't be giving you much information, but at the end of the year I will be rigorously grading your tests."

"Suddenly" Employees Are Deadwood

With few incentives to utilize what little training was available, employees often lacked the knowledge and skills needed to do their jobs efficiently. If you asked a bank president if there were any "deadwood" employees in the bank, and the answer is invariable: "Are you kidding? Everywhere." You'd hear stories of 20-, 25-, and even 30-year veterans who just weren't pulling their weight. Blame was generally placed on the bank's previously unrealistic or paternalistic attitude, or on the bank's changing culture, or a different strategy being introduced, and so forth.

But who was really to blame?

Did the employees ever know that they were not adequate contributors? What was their incentive to change? Were the opportunities for appropriate training or development available? Granted, the responsibility to remain current lay with the employee. But it also lay with the bank to provide the opportunities to do so. But when neither accepted the responsibility, the situation became entirely lose/lose for both the bank and the employee.

The Learning Curve

For many years, training within the banking industry occurred within the first two years of an employee entry into the industry. The length of the program depended on the type of position: proof operators might receive one day; tellers, two weeks; while "management trainees" in formal programs, typically 18 to 24 months. If an individual moved from one bank to another, the knowledge of the job was presumed, and rarely was there any follow-up training. Thus a typical "learning curve" looked like the one in Figure 1–1.

An exception was made for those who moved on to supervisory or managerial positions—they generally received additional training relating to managerial work within a few months of the promotion. But that too rapidly fell off after the initial stage was completed.

FIGURE 1–1

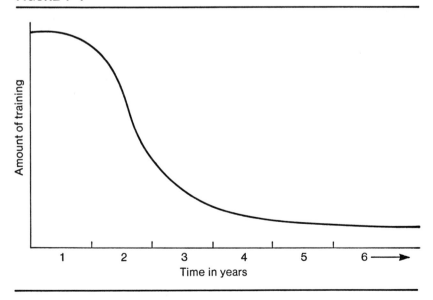

THE 80s: THE TRAINING WAVE

The 80s brought a new attitude towards training. The rapid changes in the industry—the loan loss experiences in the early part of the decade combined with the rise in competition fostered by the deregulation of banking—sparked a new interest in developing employees who could meet the new challenges. Management saw that the "if it ain't broke" attitude of the 70s was coming back to haunt them. Their employees had great gaps in their knowledge of the financial product, poor sales skills, sloppy analytical techniques, and a terrible sense of what quality service encompassed. In short, they discovered the hard way that something *was* broke, and had been broken all along.

Training and development solutions soon emerged as panaceas. Training needs and related programs were implemented with a vigor, often descending on the employees as a tidal wave. "Everyone within the retail area will go through a sales training program." Or "the entire wholesale banking division will be subject to a complete relationship banking curricula of programs." The learning curve of the employee changed to the one shown in Figure 1–2.

Line-Driven

To meet the sudden surge of training needs, banks expanded the size and function of the training areas. Commonly, but not necessarily, the department's place on the organization chart reflected the bank's own philosophy of the organization structure. In some banks, the training function became centralized at the corporate level, sometimes even forming an "academy" or "college" for professional training, where career-tracked training was concentrated, with all the systems' unit banks depending on it for training.

Other banks were reluctant to centralize training, mainly for fear of losing the essence of urgency and relevance that having the training nearer to the point of need can bring. Instead, it created or expanded training areas within the division, relying on the corporate level only for

FIGURE 1–2

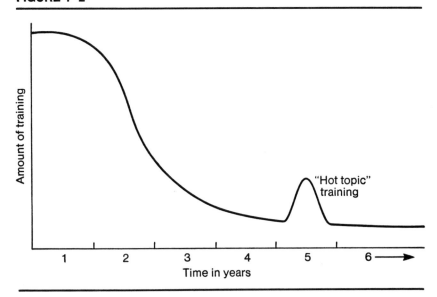

"human resources" type training, such as supervisory and management skills training.

In any case, training took on a new aura, and the need for training specialists became apparent. For the most part, the lax attitude towards training in the 70s left the industry without people who were as competent in banking skills as they were in training and development skills. Banks commonly compromised by either hiring those who had training competencies, with the expectation that they would "learn" the banking industry or designating someone within the bank who was an expert in the subject matter with the expectation that they would "learn" the training discipline.

A new term began to be applied to the training effort: line-driven. All the designs were related to, and driven by, line needs. Training now sought not just to "educate," as might be the case in the entry level training, but specifically to aid the divisions in goal achievement. The training specialists sought or developed courses that the line managers determined were needed either because of an evident shortfall or because of an embarkment on new business strategy. Training specialists began to perceive and, in some cases, officially describe managers as their "clients" and themselves as "consultants." An era of "you tell us what you need, and we will help you find the solution" prevailed.

The greater involvement of the line management represented a substantial improvement over the previous approach, where training often met line needs through a combination of luck and guesswork. However, the shift of reliance on the line managers to determine training needs left a major gap in the training scenario.

Managers naturally sought programs to solve the problems they perceived. Not necessarily being human resource specialists, they reached for apparent solutions, not ones that were generated through a systematic analytical approach. Soon training was expected to solve a whole slew of "problems"—reduced productivity, poor sales atmosphere, falling revenues—whether the problem was training related or not. The focus is typically short term: "fix this problem and fix it now." In line with the immediacy expectation, future developmental needs are ignored or dealt with haphazardly.

WHERE WE ARE NOW

While this book will offer up many ideas and approaches, unfortunately, none of them will reveal a simple or a one-shot solution. Instead, it will show that development is a long-term involvement that must track the individual through many stages. We have come to learn that development and personal growth are life-long processes, not just something that can be dealt with once in the early stages.

Similarly, banks and the banking system are in a constant state of change. Developmental programs cannot be established on the assumption that they are the sole solution to the immediate problem and therefore can be left in place indefinitely. Constant reevaluations are needed; otherwise, banks fall into the trap of assuming that the programs of the previous decade are adequate.

With each passing year, the competitive environment has forced banks to reassess nearly every aspect of their business plan. Reasonably, such retooling of the business line in turn requires reassessment of all the qualifications needed by employees to meet that plan.

Nonetheless, the perceptions of job qualifications still tend to be mired in the ideas of previous decades, when the skills needed were less formidable. As a demonstration of this, list on a piece of paper all the job qualifications that would be appropriate for a commercial account officer in order to handle just the relationship management aspect alone (ignoring credit and technical skills). A typical answer might be "ability to determine customer needs." How many qualifications did you come up with?

Now, compare your list with one below drawn up by the San Francisco training consulting firm, Omega, Consultants to Bank Management, as part of the research they conducted for developing their bank training systems (Figure 1–3). Chances are your list was slightly shorter and more appropriate for a time when a less competitive environment prevailed. (This might be an interesting question to put to the senior executive in charge of the commercial banking effort.)

FIGURE 1–3
Competencies for Relationship Managers and Sales Managers

From the analysis of data gathered from relationship and sales managers, competencies were synthesized, then grouped into clusters.

The high-performing relationship manager:
Maintains a value-added attitude about the sales role:
- Demonstrates effective interpersonal sales skills in gathering information, explaining information, explaining product solutions to customer or prospect business problems, and differentiating self from competition.
- Creates an image of personal value to the customer or prospect through knowledge of and experience with middle-market businesses.
- Stays self-motivated by understanding the intrinsic rewards of the relationship manager job.
- Remains proactive and initiates prospecting and customer-oriented activity.
- Demonstrates an interest in the customer by acquiring knowledge of the customer's or prospect's business, responding promptly and offering recommendations and advice.

FIGURE 1–3 (continued)

Diagnoses customer's current and future needs:
- Conducts research to understand customer's business plans and financial situation in terms of capital structure, current debts, banking products used or under review, etc.
- Anticipates customer's primary business needs, based on experience with similar customers or business situations.
- Employs effective questioning and listening skills to elicit the customer's personal perception of business direction, goals, intentions, and attitudes toward a bank relationship.
- Evaluates customer's goals and intentions from business/banking perspective and influences customers and prospect to differentiate wants from needs.
- Demonstrates consultative role in discussing business and financial issues by recommending suggestions, supplying technical resources and financial education, and offering reasonable alternatives.

Applies product and service solutions:
- Constructs a "portfolio" of products for potential use for each account situation as the account grows.
- Clearly links product's features and benefits to improvements in customer's perceived needs and business situation.
- Uses experts to help explain or qualify products and services.
- Differentiates between the bank's products and services and the competition's products and services.
- Presents creative, flexible alternatives to customer needs, including doing without a loan or service for business growth reasons.
- Advocates appropriate products and services based on the customer's current business and financial situation without suggesting more than is required.

Develops account plans and strategies:
- Isolates key accounts and specifies their potential based on their status (existing/new), size, growth potential, and industry segment.
- Anticipates long-range problems and opportunities based on customer business plans.
- Structures long-range account strategy in accordance with bank's objectives and other priorities.
- Identifies the competition's position in the account and anticipates their potential strategies.
- Establishes and maintains rapport with the customer through a regular calling program.

Manages internal bank relationships:
- Educates internal people to priorities and issues in different accounts.
- Builds positive personal relationships with internal people.
- Establishes self as locus of control and contact for the account.
- Involves internal people with customer calls when feasible.
- Demonstrates an understanding of internal people's priorities and problems in getting work done.
- Informs customers as to what to expect in doing business with the bank.

FIGURE 1–3 *(continued)*

Manages time and personal organization:
- Uses support systems and people to share the work.
- Differentiates between and prioritizes opportunities based on potential business or relationship.
- Develops activity plans based on business goals using a variety of time-planning techniques.
- Actively monitors time usage and employs ground rules to avoid time waste.
- Regularly reserves time for specific high-payoff activities.

Monitors account/bank relationship:
- Updates personal knowledge or current account activity and status of apparent trends on a regular basis.
- Identifies new product and service opportunities as well as current product and service problems.
- Demonstrates commitment, interest, and responsiveness to the account by continuing to add personal value to the relationship.
- Explains to the customer how the bank functions and thinks.
- Maintains a consistent program of visiting accounts, depending on the relationship with the bank.
- Establishes relationships between the customer and others in the bank to demonstrate commitment and continuity.

Coordinates territory planning and prospecting:
- Conducts ongoing research to define market opportunities, isolating growth industry segments in need of capital.
- Develops a hit list of high potential target accounts by industry segment and by company within industry segment.
- Identifies both the bank's and the competition's strengths and vulnerabilities within the marketplace.
- Creates a referral network of existing customers, attorneys, CPAs, and others in the business community who know he/she is interested in doing business.
- Responds immediately to inquiries and rapidly follows up leads.
- Regularly spends a specific and significant amount of time prospecting by following up network referrals, writing prospecting letters, and calling for initial appointments.

The high-performing sales manager:
Sets goals for individual performance:
- Develops mutually agreed on, high-expectation goals through a participative process.
- Directly links the bank's goals and direction to individual's contributions.
- Clearly states and documents goals in terms of measurable outcomes, indicating acceptable and superior performance.
- Adapts performance expectations to individual's skills, capabilities, and potential.
- Creates a number of specific goals reflecting both activity and financial outcomes in several categories.

FIGURE 1–3 *(continued)*

- Reviews performance regularly and adjusts goals if indicated.

Establishes performance standards and tracks performance:
- Specifies standards for performance appropriate to the setting as part of goal-setting process.
- Establishes standards for different accounts according to their needs and potential.
- Personally reviews progress reports (call reports, pipeline sheets, target account plans, etc.) to track the development of specific deals with individuals responsible on a regular, scheduled basis.
- Conducts frequent sales meetings to review status, develop new strategies, and acknowledge successes.
- Ensures that, at any given time, individuals know where they stand vis-à-vis their sales goals.

Analyzes market potential and develops strategies/priorities:
- Conducts active research using personal and bank resources to define the territory and the market.
- Targets specific primary areas of potential business in the defined market according to what direction the bank wants to take.
- Remains sensitive to changes or movements in the marketplace.
- Analyzes the competition's activities to identify areas of strength and vulnerability.
- Develops a business development plan indicating who and how the market will be addressed.
- Matches available staff with potential prospects and customers.

Establishes mission/direction and management role:
- Explains how individual efforts fit into overall bank objectives.
- Demonstrates persistence by reinforcing belief in goals and by ensuring that everyone knows that their selling activities play a crucial role in achieving goals.
- Establishes self as an active member of the team by trying to exceed goals, remaining involved and informed, being results-oriented, even assigning self a sales quota.
- Endorses the direction mandated by top management.
- Assumes personal responsibility for the success of individuals.
- Provides operational ground rules and systems support.

Organizes and allocates staff:
- Designs an organizational structure that reflects a team, senior-junior, hunter-skinner, or other sales philosophy.
- Assigns individuals to specialized functions to facilitate and support the sales process.
- Matches individual's skill and experience with the requirements of different accounts and markets.
- Selects and hires relationship managers who appreciate the requirement for selling to both new and existing accounts.
- Conducts frequent, short sales meetings on a regular basis.

Trains and motivates staff:
- Displays personal energy and enthusiasm to encourage and stimulate the staff.

FIGURE 1–3 *(concluded)*

- Uses a variety of rewards and recognition techniques for motivation.
- Identifies the potential intrinsic motivators in the relationship manager's job and emphasizes these as rewards.
- Establishes mentor relationships with relationship managers as appropriate to the setting.
- Identifies what motivates each relationship manager as an individual.
- Endorses and supports training activities by conducting frequent clinics, sales meetings, and product presentations and assigns individuals to formal training.

Makes effective joint sales calls:
- Ensures call is focused on the relationship manager.
- Carefully determines the objectives and tactics for each joint call ahead of time with the relationship manager.
- Identifies the various uses of joint calling and employs these as strategy and the sales situations dictate.
- Spends a majority of time on joint calls of different types to demonstrate continuity, aggressiveness, and commitment to prospects, customers, and relationship managers.
- Provides feedback, coaching, and strategy recommendations after the call.

Provides coaching and feedback on performance:
- Maintains involvement by staying close to where the performance is taking place.
- Employs a wide range of techniques for providing feedback on performance.
- Provides frequent, immediate, and focused feedback directed to the behavior, not the individual.
- Conducts formal performance appraisal discussions at regular intervals throughout the year.
- Anticipates obstacles to achieving goals and remains prepared to develop alternative approaches.
- Provides frequent praise publicly and privately.
- Gives negative feedback constructively, not punitively.

Source: © Omega Performance Corp.

Given that set of qualifications, is it reasonable to assume that individuals holding the position of relationship manager had all the necessary talents to perform the function without formal training? Clearly, no. Yet, in a survey on Bank Personnel Policies and Practices completed in 1986 by the Bank Administration Institute (BAI) in Rolling Meadows, Illinois, a full 32% of the 636 respondents indicated that their budget for sales training was "minimal." Another

51% stated it was "moderate," and only 18% said it was "large."

As unnerving as that statistic is, the surprise is even greater when we compare it to the data on credit training, which nearly every banker would point to as the foundation of banking business. With 462 respondents, an astounding 39% indicated a "minimal" budget allocation. (I suppose that accounts for some of the credit headaches and write-offs banks have been experiencing lately.)

Ozzie and Harriet Don't Live Here Anymore

Change has not been limited to the business of banking or to the industry. To compound the complexity of the situation, the composition of the workforce has also been changing over the decades, as have the employees' attitudes towards the corporation as the paternal institution. The familiar stereotypical white middle-class worker has been replaced by an increasingly diverse group. Experts estimate that over the next 10 years only 15% of the work-force entrants will be native-born white males. Only 7% to 10% of the U.S. families will fit the traditional "Ozzie and Harriet" model of a father who works and a mother who stays at home and has 2.4 children. It's not just native-born females and ethnic minorities who will fill the void: by the year 2000, look to 23% of the workforce being comprised of immigrants.

Each entering group comes in with far differing expectations about what the employer should be providing than its predecessors. The Bank Administration Institute surveys employees at dozens of banks each year to determine their attitudes towards their employer. Over the years, it has tracked the comments by employees and now holds a data base of over 400,000 responses.

The summary of the attitudes reflects the growing perception we all have that the working world is a different place. Yet, for most of us, the perception has still lagged behind reality—we still expect to see respect for authority and a linear life pattern (school, work, marriage, raising children, etc.).

The social situation of today reflects a less loyal, more demanding employee, whose education doesn't necessarily match the type of employment and whose marriage has a 50% chance of dissolving. But while bankers tempted to shake their heads in dismay over the lost past, they must recognize that their own institutions are contributing to the unrest; certainly, they are no longer offering the lifetime of employment opportunities that once were synonymous with the industry. The promise of job security that brought applicants to the banks' doors now have been replaced by the fear of downsizing, mergers, relocation, competition, and continuous change. Ozzie and Harriet are gone, but so is the neighborhood they lived in.

The shift in employee attitudes is measurably different. Comparison of survey data in even relatively short periods shows significant changes. Between 1984 and 1988, the BAI records a decline in nearly every single major category that it tracks. Below is a category listing and the comparison of favorable responses:

	1984	1988
Orientation training	77%	71%
Work satisfaction	80	72
Personnel policies	69	67
Perception of manager performance	63	58
Bank image	67	59
Growth and advancement opportunities	67	65
Communication	45	43
Pay	40	36

Kan Yu Reed Dis

Employee attitudes notwithstanding, just getting competent employees will be a major issue. The American Bankers Association (ABA) in Washington did a study on "Basic Skills in Banking," which focused on literacy skills deficiency in "at risk" areas in the bank, such as teller, bookkeeper, loan clerk, and so forth. A survey of 391 bankers showed that over

80% of the respondents stated that 23% of their banks' employees in these at-risk positions experienced basic skills problems. In addition, the banks indicated that over 35% of job applicants in 1988 were turned down because of a perceived lack of basic skills.

What couldn't the respondents do? Adding, balancing the cash box, counting money and verifying, mistaking $75.00 for $750.00, not being able to follow basic balancing procedures—all were typical errors of respondents seeking teller positions.

The litany of communication errors is longer for all the basic positions: can't express an idea carefully to customers, can't communicate with supervisor, doesn't speak English properly, as in "I seen" and "I done." Written communication is even more maligned: *wright* for *write*, not using capital letters at the beginning of sentences, spelling, and poor grammar. The ABA goes on to note that outside studies have shown that reading ability alone accounts for 8% to 13% of variance in job performance.

A Heartbeat and an Opposible Thumb

The first tempting response of most managers to all this is simple: *If they can't read and write, we won't hire them!* We'll improve our selection process so that they are screened out prior to even getting in the door. Well, not so fast. Even ignoring the Equal Employment Opportunity Commission (EEOC) considerations, the problem is one of a diminishing workpool: A 1987 U.S. Department of Labor-Hudson Institute report "Workforce 2000" forecasted a critical shortage of skills in the coming decade due to a collision between a declining pool of skilled labor and an increased demand for more highly skilled workers.

A 1988 BAI published report on "Teller Management, Policies, and Practices"[2] showed that 25% of the teller positions turn over each year. (In inner-city areas, the number approaches 100%.) Thus, four years from now, the average bank will have a completely new set of people standing behind the counter.

"We hire anyone with a heartbeat and an opposible thumb," noted one personnel manager in a low unemployment state. Facetiousness was only part of the sentiment: banks in many areas have found out that they have to rely on inner-city workers in order to meet even the lowest headcount requirements. Some banks in the big city areas have a startling rejection rate of a *24 out of 25 applications* for a teller position, and even the accepted ones are reduced by another 10% the first day on the job after the drug test results come back.

Further complicating the situation is the finding that general literacy education does not improve the performance on the job—that job literacy requires an instructional focus on the reading communications, reasoning, and math skills demanded by a particular job. Special training programs specifically for the banking industry must be employed. A bank can't rely on generic training to fit the bill.

Fewer Chiefs-per-Square Indian

The workforce issue becomes even more complex in light of an emerging national trend to streamline the corporate organization by flattening the hierarchy—eliminating unnecessary layers of management. While the move should be applauded if banking wishes to maintain its competitiveness, it cannot be viewed as simply weeding out excess personnel. The survivors will be faced with new challenges: managing 100 people is not like managing 10, particularly when the workforce will not be the homogeneous entity of the past.

The tradition of promoting the most capable or most senior worker to be manager will be severely threatened as it becomes obvious that the traits required in *managing* are not the same as the traits required in *doing*. Banks have been notable in their reluctance to do nontechnically oriented training, barely buying into managerial training beyond the most basic. "You mean that 'touchy-feely' stuff. Sure, we do some of that," commented one senior executive when asked about the extent of their managerial training. No, I didn't mean touchy-feely; I meant the very specific information any manager will need to know to be able to guide, motivate, and develop subordinates while maintaining productivity, reducing costs, tackling problems, creating teamwork, supporting new innovations, forging interdepartmental relationships, and strategizing for the future skills that the typical nonmanagerial employee, not even the most experienced, could be expected to have possibly developed during his role as an "Indian."

Lava Lamp Syndrome

All these growing trends will be demanding more attention of the training and the human resources function. With limited resources, banks are prone to fall prey to what I call the "Lava Lamp Syndrome." Lava lamps are those elongated ovals lit from inside and filled with liquid, in which blobs of an unknown substance float. The training problems and emerging issues are like the blobs—whichever blob floats to the top of the lamp becomes the problem of the day.

So very often, training dollars are thrown at the problem issues—such as improving the sales and service culture— frequently at the expense of the more fundamental programs. Overstated, perhaps, most banks do have well-established teller, platform, supervisory, and credit training programs. But what happens to the employees past entry level is yet another issue.

Programs are started, only to be stopped when funds dry up or are canceled for lack of attendance. Or quick-fix programs are offered instead of well-executed ones whose impact on the attendees is often deemed more of an incursion on their time than a worthwhile effort.

THE MIXED MESSAGE SYNDROME

The impact of a constantly shifting focus on the importance and role of training can have an insidious impact on its value. The message sent is that training is sometimes important, sometimes of dubious value. Employees soon acquire a cynical attitude about the role of training in their own development. It ultimately leaves them more wary about the role of training, further undermining future efforts. The ultimate result is one of a slow erosion of the quality of the employee. Further, the bank finds itself without an effective system to effect change. The core of the problem is the blurry view of the meaning of basic training concepts—putting them in the right context and relevance.

Training areas with ill-defined roles suffer from more than just a poor image. The way the bank uses training and development (T&D) sends out a powerful message about how an organization regards its human resources. In some banks, an officer who is chosen to attend a special development program may be regarded as a fast tracker. In other banks, training is primarily used for remedial needs, with all the stigma attached there.

Why Confusions Abound: Part One

The problem lies in the unspoken expectations that the word *training* carries. Training, to most, means that the participant is being taught a skill that can be applied to a job. Thus, the person who attended an accounting course (assuming no work-related exercises were included) was not truly being "trained," but rather "educated." Similarly, the individual who had to rappel up a cliff in the hills was being "developed," not trained. If either of them had expected to come back better prepared to do the job at hand, they probably came back disappointed.

Training is for the present—someone can do something better now. Development is for the future—someone will be more capable of achieving a goal as he or she progresses in their careers. Education is background for both—someone will better assimilate the training or teaching with the foundation that was laid.

Thus, part of confusion as to what the purpose of "training" is lies with the expectation that is connoted even prior to the individual signing up for the program. Admittedly, training associations and T&D departments carry some of the blame, as they too blur the distinctions. For instance, wording taken from a bank training catalog reads:

> *Basics of Financial Planning:* More than ever, the ability to assess your client's needs and deliver appropriate financial services to meet those needs is a critical skill. This self-instruction course introduces you to the financial planning process and the array of products you can draw upon to meet client needs. Key topics include bonds and government issues, common stock, mutual funds, life insurance, and annuities.

What the description omits is that the course will not truly provide any of the skills necessary to do financial planning. It is an "educational" background, and the individual who took the course in an attempt to get the necessary skills will be disappointed. That, in turn, leads to confusion of purpose.

Despite our plea that the right word always be used, we will generally be using the word *training* when we wish to suggest either just training or all three—training, development, and education. Only when either *education* or *development* is more appropriate will we use the specific word.

Why Confusion Abounds: Part Two

Far more serious than the semantical issue is the one relating to the underlying purpose of training in the first place. Even if the participants know *what* the purpose of the training is, they may not know *why* they are there. Even those organizing the program may not be entirely certain. Continuing with the above example, the program is designed to educate someone about financial planning. And with additional training, that person may indeed be a good financial planner. But, is creating a core of financial planners one of the goals of the bank?

Note that the course description says that *"the ability to assess clients' needs and deliver appropriate financial services to meet those needs is a critical skill."* It doesn't say, or even imply, that the bank's goal is to support, develop, and reward those who can successfully expand the bank's business through financial planning. Those considering selecting this course would have to wonder whether the effort is worthwhile. Thus, a second reason for the confusion is general inability to communicate the true purpose of the training.

THE TRUE PURPOSE OF TRAINING

The true purpose of training is to support the short- and long-term strategic goals of the organization.

OK, you think, everyone *knows* that; they just don't think to phrase it that way. But, if that's the case, why then are all the key concepts missing? The example of the financial planning course did not suggest that financial planning is a major goal of the bank—nor did it indicate that the participant would be expected to take a more advanced course or otherwise demonstrate mastery of the topic. As a result of not having the point of the training fully articulated, its role remains murky. It ends up being reduced to something that simply exists, that one expects to be there—like the company cafeteria.

George S. Odiorne, the organizational development guru, calls it the Activity Trap: the situation that people find themselves in when they start out for what once was an important and clear objective, but in an amazingly short time they become so enmeshed in the activity of getting there that they forget where they are going.

Thus, when training programs are designed, the objectives most always list the obvious points, such as in-depth knowledge of retail products, improvement in attendees' ability to do sales calls, and so forth. Less frequently is the program listed within the context of an even greater strategic or goal-setting picture. Part of the problem lies in the blur between creating immediate worker capabilities and developing longer-term producers. In short, training is caught in the activity trap.

The Way Employees See Training

As a result of too much unfocused activity, or on-again, off-again training, or no effort at all, banks have done themselves a major disservice. From its compilation of data from numerous employee attitude surveys done in banks of all sizes, BAI ranks the employees' own feelings about how effectively they were trained. On the average, only 72% of the employees believed that they "had enough information to do their job well." An even lower number, 69%, felt satisfied with "the training which the bank had given them." (Surprisingly, there was hardly any statistical difference between the different sized banks.) In essence, 30% of the employees did not have a decidedly favorable opinion about how well they were trained.

In other words, about one third of the banks' employees do not believe that they were adequately prepared for the position they are in. *One third!* Are banks missing the point of training—that training is done ultimately for the banks' sake and that money consistently and effectively invested in training is returned in the form of higher productivity?

A Clarifying Comment

We refer to the training and development department, but the terms *training* and *development* are often confused. For sake of clarity, the *training is designed to assist the bank in achieving its short-term goals.* Development, on the other hand, deals primarily with the future. Its effect is to create those who could be considered generalists—those who can see the big picture, but not necessarily perform any one of the job functions. Its purpose is to insure the creation of a cadre of thinkers and achievers that can adequately meet the new challenges that arise. *Development is designed to assist the bank in achieving its long-term business strategies.*

Without training, a bank will slip behind in current productivity; without development, a bank will slip behind in its long-term ability to compete.

Putting T&D into Its Proper Context—The SouthTrust Example

There are many banks that do systematically include training and development as an integral part of their strategic thrusts. These initiatives most often gel when they accompany a major decision point. Julian Banton, CEO and President of SouthTrust Bank of Alabama, noted that his bank was at that point several years ago. "The decision to expand our training was simple. It was made simultaneously with a decision we took several years ago to expand our marketing territory."

For SouthTrust, the need for training was based on a three-part analysis: First was the new business goal; second was the status of the available resources; third was the strength of the competition. Banton explains:

> We were after at least a 15% year-to-year increase in profits, but we had already saturated the local markets and trimmed the fat from our expenses. We could have kept the status quo, but that would have put us in a weak stance vis-à-vis the acquiring bank. To retain our independence, we had to keep our stock price high; to do that we had to improve our profits; to do that we had to grow. So growth had to come from markets outside Alabama. But the locations that were the most appealing were also being heavily banked by our competitors.
>
> On the other hand, our workforce is drawn locally. Being in Alabama, we don't have the advantage of the New York and Chicago locations, which can more readily attract top-quality people. We knew our weakness versus the competition—but we were not going to rely on luck to see us through. We established a training plan to overcome our limitations.

Not surprisingly, training is very well received at South-Trust. Since the primary focus is to make an individual more effective on the job, it has aided SouthTrust in achieving higher earnings. In 1988, SouthTrust, the 169th largest U.S. bank, in terms of assets, ranked 14th in overall performance and 11th in overall asset and profitability growth rates based on a *United States Banker* magazine report. In addition, the system averaged a 17% plus growth in net income over the previous five years. Banton continues:

> We always had a good training culture here—line managers are always open to accepting new program and development ideas. *I think that's partly because we have always known what we were trying to achieve, and we established an orderly system to achieve it.* We've also made sure that we have the right professional in the training director's job—in our case, Bill Schoel—who can carry out the goals. We don't consider the training area a place to send a failed banker to pasture. We have too much riding on our T&D concerns. We don't want a case of a brilliant idea but lousy execution.

In the Loop

SouthTrust made certain that the critical training and development aspects were the strategic planning loop from the earliest points, allowing it to be *reactive to the strategies, proactive with the solutions.* Left outside the loop, the T&D areas can only be reactive to problems created by the strategies—firefighting rather than fire prevention.

Certain criteria must be present for effective involvement of T&D in strategic planning, amply demonstrated by the SouthTrust example:

1. Management at all levels must appreciate the importance of the training and development function and be willing to accept the recommendation of the area.
2. The process must elicit the opinions of the training area early enough so that the appropriate adjustments to the strategy can be made before final commitments have occurred.
3. Those representing the training area should have an adequate experience, knowledge of the banking industry, problem-solving and decision-making abilities, and interpersonal influence skills to be effective in the role.

Lacking any of the these three criteria, the training area's involvement in the strategic process will revert to something ineffective and meaningless. Either management will listen indifferently to the training recommendations, or they will come too late to have impact, or they will not show adequate depth of thought to be taken seriously. The vicious cycle recurs: If T&D is deemed irrelevant in the early process, it ends up having to fight the fires caused by half-baked strategic thinking. If failure occurs, it has to take the blame, and ultimately it loses further credibility. It is then even less likely to be brought into the process in the future.

We Call Them Our Most Important Assets

When the perception of training declines, the group that loses the most is, not surprisingly, the employees. We've all heard it said, "Our employees are our most important asset." And they are, especially in the banking industry, which has precious little else (except for certain technological systems) to distinguish one institution from another.

Yet if the care and treatment of employees continues to be treated in a scattershot manner, the persistent problems in employee apathy, of low morale, and of diminishing productivity levels will continue. Banks cannot continue to lay the blame on the "vanishing work ethic" or the "lousy school system." Banks must first point any accusatory finger at their own approach to human resources management.

Admittedly, banks, like all corporations, are under continuous short-range pressures, dictated by quarterly income statements, which often force knee-jerk reactions in the predominantly variable-cost training arena. To compound matters, few successful managers are in their positions long enough to see their long-term investments in people pay off, minimizing the motivation to allocate resources in that direction. In any case, the executive compensation systems rarely reward for the investment efforts in human resource development.

Experts have decried for years this nation's undue emphasis on the short term at the expense of the long term, usually pointing to Japan as a model of corporate patience. But the sorry truth is that a bank must "produce" every year: it must sell so many accounts within one year, bring on a new transfer network system in two years, and so forth, to retain its appeal to investors. Unfortunately, banks cannot realistically place a time schedule on creating a superior workforce or changing a cultural attitude. The inability to predict success within a certain time frame dissuades managers from underwriting the long-term effort. It also leads to a reliance on "quick fixes," which only serve to further debase the search for real solutions; for, when they fail, management loses further interest in continuing to try.

The banking industry now must deal with the new realities of changing organizational structure, the composition of the workforce, and continuing competition. *Doing so requires a systematic, long-term approach, led by senior management, supported by the line managers, and implemented by the training and human resources areas.* More resources, including time and money, will have to be allocated to this issue than ever before. But for those who follow the regimen, the payoff can be enormous—from simple improvements in the bottom line to salvation from the oblivion of being a victim of a hostile takeover.

REFERENCES

1. Hector, Gary. *Breaking the Bank: The Decline of Bank of America.* New York: Little, Brown, 1988.
2. "Teller Management, Policies, and Practices," Rolling Meadows, Ill.: Bank Administration Institute, 1988.

ADDITIONAL READINGS

Abboud, Robert A. *Money in the Bank: How Safe is It?* Homewood, Ill.: Bank Administration Institute/Dow Jones-Irwin, 1988.

McGill, Michael E. *American Business and the Quick Fix.* New York: Henry Holt and Company, 1988.

Zweig, Phillip L. *Belly Up: The Collapse of the Penn Square Bank.* New York: Crown Publishers, 1985.

CHAPTER 2

BRAVE NEW WORLD: CHANGING THE MANAGERIAL GUARD

"We don't train our managers. If they were smart enough to get this far, then they should be smart enough to keep going. We believe in sink or swim."—*Comment made by a president of a money center bank that has since been acquired by another institution.*

Change is evident everywhere in banking: in the types and services banks offer, in the way the services are delivered, in the technology of integrating the information, in the internal organizational structure of the bank, in the composition of the workforce, in the number and mandates of banking entities, in the makeup of the competitive forces, and in the external environment. It occurred throughout the 70s and 80s and will continue for at least another decade.

So many years of calm waters had existed prior to those decades that banks were notoriously unprepared for the buffeting of the global banking environment. The banks' responses to the challenges they faced were handled more like a series of earthquakes where the movements of great masses create major dislocations, rather than like a continuous series of very small tremors that the environment can absorb more readily. Stories of large write-offs and massive mergers resulting in major layoffs were prominently featured in many business periodicals. Usually accompanying the articles were interviews with the newly unemployed who spoke of sudden and tactless dismissals.

One bank story revolves around an executive who called a subordinate manager into his office and said, "I gathered a number of your staff in a conference room. Go in and tell them that everyone in that room has been let go." Although daunted, the manager nonetheless followed out orders. After the announcement, one employee noted that the manager was also in the room. Did that mean that he too was fired? The manager returned to the executive's office to press the question. The executive responded, "Well, I did say *everyone* in that room."

MANAGING CHANGE

Turning the pattern of change from large earthquakes into small tremors is very much a managerial responsibility. However, of all the management disciplines, it is the least well addressed. Statistics show that stress-related insurance claims have tripled from the beginning of the 80s to the end of the decade—a sign that situations have moved beyond employees ability to effectively deal with them. Managers must be able to address:

- Change as it impacts the business—what new financial products, delivery modes, or sales methodology will be needed?
- Change as it impacts the organization—how will the departmental structure, reporting lines, and staffing requirements be changed?
- Change as it impacts the employee—what jobs will be eliminated or changed, how will productivity be affected, how will career expectations change?

What the Future Will Bring

Experts predict the bank of the future may have little resemblance to the current structure. The teller with the bank drawer full of bills and coins is giving way to the automatic teller machine (ATM) and the credit/debit card. The corporate loan even now is becoming only a backstop facility. And the contact officer making customer calls may be replaced by a "loan purchasing" agent, as banks move increasingly towards being buyers and sellers of loans.

Whether these changes will come to full fruition or will fall by the wayside like many other financial predictions is unclear. What is more certain is that customer expectations will expand considerably with the continuous broadening of the financial arena. Just as banks no longer are bound by their immediate geographic area, they may soon no longer be bound by time and space.

The concept of "9 to 5" time has long since been eroded by the ATM, with wholesale money transfer systems rapidly following. Voice and electronic mail allow incoming information to occur at any time. Cash management systems allow data to flow out at any time. "Zero-based" time for all delivery services is approaching. Whenever the customer needs the product or service, it will be immediately available—not just during 9 to 3, or 9 to 5, or during money transfer hours, or whenever a representative is free—but immediately.

The concept of place is also shifting. The worker who was previously bound to headquarters now does work at home with the blessing of computer modems and fax machines. Remote work centers are increasingly common. Several insurance companies ship claims processing work *overseas* to locations where the labor pool better fits their needs.

The managerial skills required to deal with all aspects of change cover a broad ground: sensitivity and analysis to trends, strategic thinking, problem solving, interpersonal negotiation, and communication and persuasion skills being the basic ones.

For years, banks have relied on these qualities being innate (at least among those selected to move up to managerial career ladder) and therefore not requiring any further honing. While true for a select few, for the majority of managers and executives, this lack of preparation aggravated, if not precipitated, many of today's banking problems. Unexpected or negative trends crept up on banks without being perceived early enough, and when they were finally perceived, the solutions were often inadequate, in turn leading to radical realignments, resulting in sharp downsizing and restructuring, causing lowered morale and productivity decline.

The More Things Change, the Fewer the Managers

Faced with all the issues relating to these changes, the banks, it would seem, would create a greater number of managers to help the employees face the new situations. The opposite is true. Most banks are reorganizing their organization charts to flatten the hierarchical pyramid. Yet, despite the impact the new organizational structure will ultimately have on a bank's viability through this evolutionary period, the attention given it, either in the boardroom or cafeteria, rarely exceeds a comment or two. The issue warrants better attention: the quality of the managers' skills will be a crucial factor in determining the effectiveness of the bank.

I'm not advocating more managers; I'm advocating better trained ones. Banks that have traditionally promoted the most senior or the best-performing individual to manager level stand to find themselves with diminishing productivity levels at best and unexpected personnel issues at worst.

Unfortunately, these same banks will not have a clue as to the root cause of the problem because they will not be able to see the relationship between unhoned managerial skills and organizational ineffectiveness. To further complicate matters, banks (as do many companies in other industries) tend to shun organizational development experts ("too vague, too much mumbo-jumbo"), leaving them without a resource to provide the needed insight.

Managing Productivity, or Managing People to Produce

These necessary skills will have to go well beyond those that newly promoted managers were able to readily pick up by osmosis or one-day seminars when the structure and workforce were less complex. In reality, the "sink or swim" managers were charged with a responsibility that *is* different from the one that will be expected of them in the future. Those managers were expected to maintain a level of productivity and sales among their subordinate staff—that is, they *managed productivity.* They were not necessarily *managing people to produce.*

The two are not the same. One can have a relatively

smoothly functioning department, yet be a terrible manager. Even though the work gets from here to there, the manager may not delegate well, provide good feedback, give direction, develop expertise among subordinates, and so forth. The Peter Principle flourishes in such a situation—highly competent workers are promoted to management positions where they eventually flounder. Alas, Peter is less articulate with the solution than with describing the problem. But he is right in pointing out that a good worker is not necessarily a good manager and that promotions should not automatically follow.

But Isn't Productivity What We Want?

Certainly. Who can argue it? But many companies, such as International Business Machines Corp. (IBM), have discovered that the true key to superior productivity is having individuals work at their maximum level. If the main focus is on work flow and the individual is treated as secondary, productivity may reach acceptable levels. However, when the main focus is on developing a superior workforce, then high productivity follows.

To assure that the development of the individual comes first, managers are judged by their ability to manage people in addition to departmental effectiveness. Granted, workflow management is much easier to measure—you count the number of money transfer items handled less the number of errors. Guidelines for measuring people management is much more complex, but not impossible. IBM and other companies use such yardsticks as the amount of subordinate training, the number of requests for transfers, and level of voluntary turnover. Other measures include the number of times an individual utilizes a company's "open door" policy, which allows subordinates to circumvent managers if they feel they have a poorly handled grievance.

It's What the Banks Needed at the Time

The lack of attention to management skills is the outcome of where a bank places its priorities. A bank that judges success by the number of timely completions of the proof sheet will create a manager whose sole interest is in closing the proof on time. If turnover, absenteeism, disgruntled employees, and undeveloped potential are not criteria for judgment, those factors will be ignored.

In fact, the managerial approach was actually quite appropriate for banks, given the market characteristics that used to prevail. Up until the last decade, banking was still a growth market, the product line was regulated and protected, and competition was low key or even nonexistent. A manager, to be effective, needed only to focus on assuring that the bank *"did things right."* Accordingly, most of the effort was directed at implementing good controls over internal processes and efficient processing of internal information. This is very different from taking a broader focus on the goals of the bank, where the manager strives to *"do the right things,"* and creates a department that will be successful in the long term.

Basic Management Training (Refocused)

A number of banks have taken the lead in structuring systems that address managing employee performance over managing work flow. Frequently, the system is designed around the use of an assessment tool, usually the performance appraisal form.

True, performance appraisal forms are as old as merit increases, and, when first used, managers did use them as a basis for objectively discussing the employees' strengths and weaknesses. But over time, their use became perfunctory. Particularly since annual merit increases were based on the review, many managers simply stuck in comments that were designed to support the intended increase. The objectivity diminished, and worse, the appraisals did little to motivate the individual to work more productively.

Most banks have since expanded the form to include a future work plan to eliminate subjectivity and to stimulate improvement in the employee's work habits. For instance, National Westminster Bancorp restructured its performance appraisal form to also include development objectives for the exempts (a reiteration of job responsibilities for the nonexempts) and quality control objectives. The new process is called Performance Leadership Systems.

The system is designed to focus the manager on the employee's potential to contribute. It integrates performance and quality objectives that the employee could reasonably achieve, as well as a development plan necessary for meeting future objectives. Interim follow-up dates are scheduled to review performance to date. The ultimate achievement of the objectives lays the basis by which the future salary increases are judged.

"The whole focus of the program is to get managers to set goals for the employees, which they then jointly become responsible to meet," noted Joan Ustin, VP of Training and Development, "not just an overall goal for the department for which no one has particular responsibility."

The bank's core training programs deal not only with the effective use of performance management systems, but also with the other basic elements of management skills, such as communication, coaching, team building, and dealing with difficult situations. The bank has made the core management skills training mandatory for all supervisors and managers, even those who have been with the bank for a number of years. "We need to keep reinforcing the manager's knowledge and skill base. It's easy to lose sight of the main goal—developing people—when your desk is loaded with work-flow problems."

IBM mandates that every manager take 40 hours of managerial development training *per year*. That many of the programs fill up only in December as managers scramble to meet the requirement is irrelevant. The point is that managers are continuously reinforced in the philosophy of managing people.

Flattening the Pyramid

Dealing effectively with employees on a one-on-one basis is complex enough. But the impact of the flattened hierarchy will only add to the complexity. Many supervisors and managers who handle only 15 people are seeing their jobs eliminated, leaving the higher-level manager to deal with as many as 100 people and more. Managers will be charged with having to apply their skills to a greater number of individuals.

"It's different managing 30 people when you've been previously managing 10. Ten people can still be essentially assistants; the manager has the time to give them direction every day. With 30 people, everyone must already know what to do—they only come to you with exceptions," noted one CEO who had found that many managers were unable to cope effectively when the bank changed the organizational structure. "And when you step up to 100 people, you don't want them to come to you even with exceptions; you want them to be able to handle the problems themselves."

Organizational delayering, for all its value, will exacerbate the managerial skills shortage: the "on-the-job" training (OJT) that did occur as one moved up the managerial ladder will be further diminished as the rungs in the ladder are reduced.

Don't Blame Us; Blame COLA
The abundance of middle-management positions that existed previously, allowing for small work groups, was not entirely caused by ill-conceived planning. The fast pace of asset growth the banks experienced during the 70s and 80s, the increasing complex array of new bank products, along with a relatively high number of new, inexperienced employees, created a need for a greater degree of managerial overseeing than might have been required in more placid eras.

Some of the blame for the banks' overindulgence in job titling should be placed on the pay-scale issue, compounded by the inflationary environment, forcing cost-of-living adjustments (COLA). Banks found themselves with individuals who warranted pay increases—partly for merit, but most certainly for increased cost-of-living reasons—but who had reached the top of the pay scale for a particular official level. What alternative was left but to create another official level? The head of the money transfer department who was a "supervisor" in the 60s, a "manager" in the 70s, and a "vice president" in the 80s, is now a "senior vice president."

Also, if the individual was given a different level, he or she had to have different job responsibilities. With similar reasoning, the banks simply added more managerial layers into the department, reducing in turn the actual revenue producing capacity that they had in the lower positions.

However, the combination of retrenchment and cost squeeze has simply begun to invalidate this approach to the promotion question. The fat that the title inflation system created has now reached a point of obesity. It must be trimmed or reshaped into muscle.

Defining Success through Management Positions
Just as banks were rapidly expanding the managerial positions available, employees were just as eagerly awaiting the tap on the shoulder. The mark of success came through the quite visible promotion announcement. Typically, the point of progression begins immediately after college. After the usual 18-month training course, the trainees are placed in functional areas around the bank with stepped promotion prospects. Getting promotions ahead of schedule generally bestows one with considerable respect from peers and a goodly amount of self-satisfaction. Likewise, failing to move along with the peer group is a sign of serious deficiency—a mark of shame. Many "left-back" employees have suffered much angst, either in private or more assertively in their manager's office, begging for reconsideration.

Ultimately, the route leads to a managerial position. A transfer to a staff position, no matter how mutually rewarding to the individual and the bank, generally is viewed as a signal that that person's career is "on hold" (unless, with luck, it is perceived as the rotational process the bank reserves for its best executive candidates—the peer respect is then likely to be doubled).

A step-ladder approach to grooming future management is entirely appropriate. Where the system falls down is that everyone wants to be pushed up to the management level *in order to feel fulfilled.* That the job in and of itself is not an appropriate one for the individual, ergo, not rewarding, is irrelevant. Maslow's hierarchy of needs wins out—external peer respect over internal self-satisfaction.

Brokerage Houses Have Done It This Way for Years

The Merrill Lynchs and the Dean Witters have long known that rewards can be in ways other than the usual ladder progression. Stock brokerage houses also know that organizations invite serious problems by automatically promoting the "top of the class" into a position that has managerial responsibilities. Those who are managers of a branch operation hold very distinct interests and rewards from the members of the sales force (or producers). Few who join a brokerage firm aim for (or even want) the branch management position, and it certainly does not follow that the top performer will be the one chosen.

Branch managers are selected because they derive their satisfaction from being the motivator, not the doer. The branch managers' skills are substantially different from the direct producers'—as is their incentive base. The better the group performs, the better the reward. The brokerage houses take steps not to confuse the two sets of skills or to structure the rewards so that the management position will carry greater "psychic" weight than the sales position.

The Endangered Species

Job enlargement will be substituted for promotion. Revenue production will again become the primary focus of the job. The problem of the pay scale ceiling is being addressed with more creative incentive pay structures—based on productivity rather than position (except at the most executive levels). The job responsibilities will be structured along functional lines vis-à-vis customer service or relationships, rather than reporting levels.

The manager who managed other managers is an endangered species. The Team VPs who reported to Group VPs, who reported to Executive VPs (sometimes just the opposite, since title definitions varied from bank to bank) all stand to have their pictures hung on the wall next to those of pandas and snow leopards.

A typical restructuring example is evidenced by Seafirst Bank in Seattle, which reduced its platform official staff hierarchy to three levels in its commercial banking area (relationship officer, senior relationship officer, and team leader).

It's Really the Work Flow That Is Changing

The new organization experts such as Peter Drucker predict that work flow will be "knowledge based" and accordingly that the workforce will be "specialists" in their own areas. Thus, the workforce will be largely directing and disciplining their own performance through organizational feedback from colleagues, customers, and headquarters. In short, they will be empowered.

Drucker uses the word *information* in the way we use the word *work* as a noun: "I have a ton of work to do" translates into "I have a ton of information to process." In his mind, the distinction lies in who has access to the information. In the present form organization, the manager commands and controls the flow of work. Thus the work comes into a central source, or manager, who is in charge of "doling" out the work. A subordinate may not be adequately familiar with what other subordinates are doing and have to refer back to the manager in order to appropriately interact with them.

In the "information" based organization, access to the information by the subordinate is immediate—the work flows directly to that individual's desk. As a "specialist" that person then is not only in charge of processing the information, but also in knowing who else to contact should issues or problems arise. He or she deals directly with customers, internal or external.

The flow of work then is not sequential—it does not go to one person who passes it to the next and so forth. "Work" or "information" flows simultaneously. The result is a type of synchrony, where specialists from all the various functions work together as a team from inception of research to the product's establishment in the market. Thus intervention in the flow by a manager will be superfluous in the context of normal situations, only needed for directives and exceptions.[1]

To function effectively, the new information-based organization must have a clear, simple common objective that translates into particular actions. The business must be structured around goals that state performance expectations and provide feedback. The individual should always know who he or she depends on for information, how much information is necessary to perform the job, and who is dependent on that individual for the finished processed information.

The role of the manager is that of maintaining a high performance level of the subordinate in processing the information, making certain that he or she is capable of performing the function, providing feedback and support and developing their talents. In other words, the job of the manager is to make sure that the "specialist" is indeed a "specialist" and is truly motivated to function as one.

More Than Backs of Heads and Elbows

The statistics and information skirt the intangible emotional issue that cannot be quantified and accordingly cannot be tested for. It is an intense sense of "not belonging" that accompanies those whose social integration throughout his or her life has been shortchanged.

One bank training director, in doing a needs analysis of a highly paper-processing-oriented back office department to create a managerial skills program, came across a statistic that he couldn't understand. The turnover data for a particular department had listed the "quits," the "transfers," the "sick and maternity leaves," and the "no shows." What were "no shows"? It turned out to be people who simply never showed up for work one day. The training director pursued this: did the manager call the individual's home to determine why the individual was a no show? No. Did the manager ask other members of the department about the absent co-worker? No. Didn't the manager worry about their well-being? No—if they don't show, they must have quit.

This attitude is commonly called "backs of heads and elbows," referring to what managers ideally want to see on the occasion they bother to look up from their desks. It will be a recipe for a human resource's nightmare if applied on the coming workforce, whose social integration will have been stunted by the diminished family lifestyle. Worker loyalties, already stretched thin by their personal environment, will decline even further, and their malaise will manifest itself in sharply increased absenteeism, substance abuse, and turnover. (See Chapter 4 on Career Pathing for more discussion of today's work force.)

New Level of Expectation

Clearly, our expectation of how the new workforce should contribute to the bank's success (and with what level of enthusiasm) will also have to change. The new hires out of college and into the managerial program are typically not representative of the average worker and cannot be used as guides. The ambitious college grad who stays late to finish a work project before catching a beer with his colleagues has little in common with the assistant branch manager who runs home after the office to start supper for the kids and do a late night load of laundry.

An interesting example of the shifting of work habits and attitudes follows. One bank designed a new self-study training program for retail products—basic information that can be easily absorbed in that format. They handed it out to the platform staff with the expectation that it would be reviewed at home or during lunch hour. Conceptually, the training format was excellent: the platform people who would use the books were entering the job at different times, they were starting from different levels of knowledge, and they worked at various locations. For the bank, it solved both the logistics and timing of training a diverse group of employees.

What they had neglected to consider was the true motivation and lifestyle of the typical platform worker.

They were primarily women and mothers. Their evening hours, even their lunch hours, left them little time to sit and study. Even when they knew they would be tested on the material, they just couldn't "get around" to it.

The participants displayed few qualms about not being able to complete the study books. To them, the priorities of home came before the priorities of work, and no further justification was needed. The bank ultimately had to ditch the whole self-study system and return to the more conventional stand-up training.

Profiling the 90s Manager

The selection of managers will require much greater attention than merely picking the top performer. The manager of the 90s will be *re*introduced to several "new" responsibilities. Lester B. Korn, a noted headhunter, recently surveyed 1,500 executives (conducted with Columbia University) to determine what managerial skills they believed the managers of the future would need. The results, summarized in a May 22, 1989, *Fortune* article revealed that the new manager would need to have increased ability to:

- Convey a strong sense of vision and ethics.
- Manage a larger, more diverse and complex workforce.
- Communicate more frequently with employees and customers.
- Motivate employees (mainly by linking compensation to performance).
- Place a greater focus on strategic thinking.
- Deal with poor performers.

Those that the executives rated notably *lower* in the future manager's bag of skills:

- Making all major decisions.
- Accounting and marketing knowledge.

- Knowledge of production.
- Computer literacy.

Bob Albright, VP at the Huntington National Bank in Columbus, focuses on this issue when he points out that increasing diversity in the workforce will require more *high-touch* managers. He recommends more sensitivity and interpersonal skills training as well as the development of a caring and concerned cultural attitude. Managers will have to view their job as a shared endeavor, working *with* rather than *over* subordinates, sharing a common department vision that all members can appreciate and internalize.

The Old Nice-to-Knows Are Now Need-to-Knows

Experts in management development list specific skills that should be in any training program to effectively create a manager with that profile. Broken down between human and conceptual skills, they are:

Human Skills

- *Decision-making skills*—Many decisions in the past were just choosing the best course of action with *known* facts. But the broadening of the markets has created many more unknowns and, accordingly, the need for more complex decision-making skills.
- *Team-building skills*—Since much will rely on group and committee decisions, the manager will have to be able to motivate and guide both individual and team abilities.
- *Communication skills*—Beyond the technical skills such as report writing, the new manager specifically needs the ability to communicate *persuasively*, both in writing and orally.
- *Leadership skills*—Beyond simply knowing various skills, the new manager must be able to integrate them into a consistent and coherent pattern of behavior.

Conceptual Skills

- *Trend-analysis skills*—The manager needs the ability to identify relevant environmental forces, sensing the strength and direction of these forces and interpreting trends and cycles.
- *Strategic analysis skills*—The manager needs the ability to take the environmental analysis and effectively compare it to the area's capabilities to determine the appropriate alternative.
- *Change management skills*—The manager needs the ability to understand the whole process of change and its impact on an organization.
- *Organization design skills*—The manager needs the ability to change the organizational structure to achieve the customers' needs, not just the bank's goals.[2]

It's not so much that these human and conceptual skills are "new"—but rather that there is a change in the level of emphasis now being placed on them. Developmental training programs addressing these issues were frequently deemed to be "nice-to-knows" as compared to "need-to-knows." Translated into reality, it meant that developmental training would occur (1) if the T&D department had been given the resources to develop a decent program, (2) if the manager was in the mood to take the program, and (3) if the bank was *not* having a bad year, which generally resulted in such programs being axed.

More to the point, the problem with the "need" and the "nice" is that they are more often distinguished by the immediacy of the impact rather than their relative value to the organization. Thus, the program that taught someone how to deal with a problem employee (short-term impact) was more important than a program that taught someone how to think strategically (long-term impact). These policies are the result of generating the highest quarterly earnings, the bane of many corporations that mortgage the future strength of their organization for the current net income.

Do You Put Your Car in the Garage?

Provident National Bank in Philadelphia (affiliated with PNC Financial Corporation) is a bank that believes in the importance of developmental training that stresses skills with long-term impact. Their philosophy is one of strengthening the organization through strengthening the individual. They have created a training curriculum offered to every employee whose core function is the development of the individual as an integral part of the organization. The further up the career ladder an employee is, the broader the scope and the more intense the developmental training. Thus, the senior manager has a more in-depth program dealing with, say, the management of change than the new hire does, yet all will be exposed to the underlying concepts in some form.

Why the emphasis on the organization? When the question was put to Robert E. Chappell, Provident's Chairman, he answered rhetorically:

> Do you put your car in the garage? If so, you are willing to spend now for expected long-term benefits.
>
> We are not being altruistic. We created a more extensive training curricula for the sake of the bank. Our long-term goal is to improve productivity—both for the sake of the customer and the sake of the shareholder. We believe that the more the employee knows about the bank and understands how he or she fits in, the more that employee will be willing to contribute. Committed people are productive people—it's as simple as that.

Living, Breathing Organism

Chappell described the bank as a living, breathing organism: it is constantly undergoing change and struggle for existence. He noted that if bankers are trained only once as if the bank were a static operation, they will miss the point. They will not only be ill-prepared for the change, but they will not have the necessary skills, either technical or managerial, to deal with it.

Provident's training programs do not stop at certain grade levels or ranks. "We don't presume that one needs to be trained in management issues as a junior officer," Chappell commented, but that the need ceases as soon as one becomes a vice president." Naturally, Provident alters the type and scope of the materials, but as much attention is placed on the program crafted for senior management as the program for new managers. If anything, added Chappell, "the skills of the senior managers are more critical to the health of the organization. To assume that these skills innately exist and require no further honing would be folly."

We Know What We Want

The curricula that Provident National Bank conceived has very specific goals and themes. Bob Schoonmaker, who was then in charge of developing the concept, explained: "Our overall goal is to raise productivity and to strengthen the organization's ability to be a provider of financial services. But first, we had to figure out what was necessary to achieve that."

Provident determined that the individual must be able to:

- Manage himself or herself.
- Manage the business.
- Manage productivity.
- Be integrated throughout the organization.
- Be responsive to the external environment.

Accordingly, the curriculum has three main learning tracks: technical skills (such as credit training), organizational/managerial skills (such as understanding the financial services industry or first-line supervision), and personal skills (such as report writing). The tracks are administered at four different levels: the employee level, the supervisor level, the manager level, and the senior manager level. The intensity and breadth of each changes as the employee moves up through the levels, although no track ever entirely disappears.

Throughout the entire curriculum, Provident has woven certain general themes: a high degree of customer focus, a need for diversity, the importance of being proactive and contributing, self-responsibility, and the ability to deal with change.

The ideal is to be able to match each person's abilities to handle (deal with) these activities (needs) and place him or her in the position that best maximizes these abilities. Moving through various career paths is encouraged, although it is the employee's responsibility to seek out new avenues of opportunity.

"Our goal is to make our employees happiest by putting them in positions that fit them best," added Schoonmaker. "It's not philanthropic on our part at all—a happy worker is a productive worker."

Not for Middle Managers Only

Exposing all the middle managers to new and continuous training is exemplary. But what good is having a highly developed and raring-to-go middle level if the upper level is still the same calcified "my way or the highway" group. If the bank's average middle manager is 35 and the average top one is 55, the bank will have to wait 20 years for the middle group to rise to the top, assuming that they don't quit out of frustration first.

Thus, development programs for upper management are equally critical. More commonly called *leadership development* (if only to distinguish it from the more straightforward managerial curricula), much of the developmental training occurring at the higher levels of management tends to be erratic and subjectively offered, frequently as a "good-year bonus perk" to an Ivy League university program or a group of on-again, off-again seminars presenting the latest in "hot" topics. So haphazard are the leadership development programs at many banks that most senior managers would be at a loss to concisely describe the development program laid out for them (assuming there is one at all).

The Touchy-Feely Factor Whoo-Whoo's

The fuzzy perception of upper management development is exacerbated by ill-considered programs that appear and disappear as management became enthusiastic and then disillusioned with the results. To some CEOs, the very words *leadership training* cause their eyes to glaze over when the issue is broached. Visions appear to corporate funds drifting down the drain while employees sit in circles learning how to devise toy helicopters to escape hypothetical jungles, all in the name of advanced creative thinking.

Despite the merits of such training, even the T&D profession tends to be less than generous with its comments about some of the more esoteric mind-bending programs that have been conjured up. It leads to an outright rejection of the overall development concept, returning to the comfort zone of only competency-defined skills training. The ultimate result is an erratic pattern of development programs that lose credibility at each juncture.

Systematic Approach

In a sense, it is unfair to single out banks; other industries also have shortchanged leadership programs. Harry B. Bernhard and Cynthia A. Ingols point out in a *Harvard Business Review* article, "Six Lessons for the Corporate Classroom," that their research shows that few corporations actually effectively integrate training and development into their strategic planning or even their human resource philosophies. They add that although most executive officers state that the development of executive talent is a major priority, corporate training and development are rarely used to assist them in identifying or developing future managers.[3]

As in all other training, banks that have the most success with their leadership development programs are those that have taken a consistent and well-considered approach. Leadership training is integrated into their strategies and is a continuous thread through the bank's mission and philosophy. It is neither erratic or whimsical, nor does it wax and wane with the bank's fortunes.

Getting Out and About

At the basic level of leadership development, some banks have consistently sent star performers to an advanced management school, such as those run by the trade associations and universities. The programs at these schools commonly have education-oriented curricula (as compared to curricula designed to develop specific behavioral traits), and, since they gather attendees from various sources, these programs are not customized to the sending bank's particular situation. But these "shortcomings" are also their strong points. Rather than either being precisely focused on an individual's attributes or offering another rehash of a bank's own internal programs, they can run in a slightly different direction. These programs can provide the attendee with:

- New conceptual approaches to thinking.
- Cross-fertilization of ideas.
- An opportunity to size up the competition.
- Fresh insights into dealing with challenges.
- An awareness that there is no one "right" answer.

Even banks with strong, positive cultures benefit from having their senior manager exposed to other attitudes. Banks that think that "we've got it knocked" while others are still groping for answers are exposed to becoming smug. Eventually, smugness leads to a deterioration of the very values banks prized the most—openness and creative thinking.

Every bank then should take advantage of off-site advanced banking schools to develop senior talent. Ideally, the manager sent should be one who can impact the organization upon return. But too often the one attendee returns to the bank as the "voice in the wilderness," preaching to an uninterested group, either because the bank's culture isn't open to change, or the other senior managers themselves are not educated and skilled enough to understand the issues involved.

A Program or a Perk?

These programs, however, bring with the aura of prestige and a suggestion that the participant is on a special "short list," particularly if the program is at an Ivy League school. However, some programs may be so broad and distant from the banking industry, that they may not meet the participant's or bank's needs at all. (Worse, the anticipated promotion may not come through, diminishing their value on two counts.) In fact, unless a majority of executives are routinely sent to off-site programs, the program should be viewed more as a perk than a serious training initiative.

Another approach is to organize an in-house program aimed at developing the leadership skills and behaviors identified as needed at that particular bank. However, these programs are frequently offered across the board, that is, everyone at a certain level must attend. Often, then, some modules will be very beneficial to certain participants but unnecessary for others, leaving the latter group annoyed by a sense of wasting time.

Tailoring the program to each manager's profile is another option—which is easier at the smaller institutions—and certainly appropriate if the managers come from different backgrounds. But for the larger institutions, it can be a recordkeeping hassle and perhaps more complex logistically than the program warrants.

No matter which program approach is chosen, all the trainers contacted agreed that one critical factor had to be present before any serious leadership program could be successfully implemented—the commitment of the top bank officials.

As one senior training manager noted, "Several times we had proposed a leadership program to line managers, only to be greeted with glazed-over eyes. It wasn't until our CEO recognized the need for higher-level training did the managers support the effort. Undoubtedly his vision and ability to verbalize our mission had a great deal of impact on the leadership program's acceptance."

Don't Underestimate the Asset

First American Bancorp headquartered in Washington, D.C. is a bank which realized that (1) it would be inadequate to send merely one or two people a year to an advance school for additional leadership education, and (2) the CEO had to be enthusiastically behind any serious leadership training thrust. Senior management certainly was aware of the need for advanced level training. In the early 80s the banking company had been through several years of a merging/acquisition process, leaving the company with a mixed bag of leadership skills and corporate cultures.

Rather than sending the whole managerial team to a variety of banking schools, they decided to combine the best of off-site training with in-house training by undertaking designing a curriculum in conjunction with the Wharton School that specifically addressed the particular situation. They felt that in doing so the bank system's senior managers would get:

- Exposure to broader economic, banking, and business concepts provided by the Wharton faculty.
- A curricula tailored to their needs.
- An opportunity to blend the varying corporate cultures into a unified one, reflecting the new management's values.

In 1989, they established The First American Management Institute, an in-residency program held at the Wharton School. The curriculum there was customized specifically for First American, designed to develop leaders with applied knowledge of that bank, not just generalized banking theory.

Participation is limited to First American vice presidents and above. The highest performing executives, subsidiary bank presidents, and so forth, were chosen to go first because the greatest reliance was placed on them to help meet goals. The program has four one-to-two week academic residencies at the Wharton School over the period of five con-secutive quarters, with intermittent seminars on the bank's premises. During the nonresidency periods, attendees must do major management projects and writing assignments.

"No 'hand-warming' is allowed here," noted Bill Dona-hue, training director at First American. "This is not meant to be a perk, with somebody going off to the Caribbean is-lands to listen to a clever speaker in the morning and play golf in the afternoon. It's tough stuff, both inside and outside the classroom."

In general, the program starts with broad theory and nar-rows to First American's particular situation. The presenta-tion, predominantly by the Wharton faculty covers strategic initiatives, industry trends, risk analysis, organizational the-ory, marketing concepts, and financial evaluative concepts, which are all ultimately applied to the bank's own situation. The faculty uses case studies, exercises, and bank simulation games. Attendees do the management projects on the bank premises and present them at subsequent in-residency ses-sions.

As Donahue notes, "It has the discipline of an off-site school and the applicability of being an in-house program. Everyone is very excited—and candidates' proposals for fu-ture attendees are stacking up on my desk. It's what people needed. More than that, we are providing it to them in a setting in which they can simultaneously feel challenged and comfortable."

Choosing the Right Program

Not every bank can afford creating a major leadership program. Many prefer to select executives to send off to an already established program. While most any execu-tive would feel flattered at being selected, actually the issues surrounding the selection are more complex.

Experts point out that the bank should consider the following items before sending someone off:

1. Appropriateness. Is the program chosen really right for the individual? What are the individual's particular strengths and weaknesses and how will they be addressed in the program? Mary Stuckart, a management consultant from Greenwich, Conn., recommends spending time with the executive, as well as the executive's superior, to determine his or her particular needs. This has to be handled with some sensitivity. Stuckart notes, "Rarely do executives state 'Oh, I'm terrible at strategic planning and need help.' At that level, they cannot afford to admit their shortcomings. Concerns of that nature have to be drawn out. I usually get the executives to tell 'war stories,' from which I can infer where their weaknesses are. I also chat with their superiors, who, of course, are generally more forthcoming."

2. Relevance. Will the program provide information that can be applied to executive's work needs? Or is the program too general to be adequately applied? We tend to think that any advanced education program will be a plus, particularly if it's at a famous university. But if the executive is in a program that primarily addresses manufacturing, not financial services, the executive may eventually think "what am I doing here?" It's best to make sure that the program really fits. Select from several schools, especially those sponsored by banking associations when making a choice.

3. Positive stress. While they may be flattered, many executives see spending three weeks or longer at a school a period of high stress. First, most programs are intense and often physically demanding. Not everyone is ready to go "back to school." Some executives may have worked their way up and would be very uncomfortable in a university environment. Second, the programs will take time away from the job, time which already is in short supply, causing more pressure when the executive returns. Thus, not only must the program be right, the timing must be right as well.

4. Expectations. Many executives see being selected for such a program like a tap on the shoulder—an intermediate point before the next promotion. If the bank's goal is to make the executive more effective in the current job, not provide a pre-promotion perk, then that must be made clear from the very beginning. Preferably, all executives at a certain level should be exposed to a certain amount of advanced education, so that everyone is aware that this is intended to raise the whole group's level of effectiveness, and not be a reward for the stars.

5. Environment. Sending executives off to a school is one thing. Having them apply what they learn is quite another. The return environment must be right, allowing, actually expecting, the executive to rise to new heights rather than return to the old habits. Otherwise, the efforts will be wasted. This is the responsibility of the bank as a whole—making certain that the right culture exists so that all the new ideas can be effectively adopted.

What the World Needs Now

The increasing movement of the banking industry to market saturation, undifferentiated product lines, and intense competition has been the driving force behind the required change in the organizational structure of banks. Most banks have reduced the layers of the hierarchical structure, particularly in the middle management area, causing more reliance to be placed on the remaining managers to meet productivity gains. In addition, the changing diversity in the workforce as well as the customer's expectations for service have restructured the work flow from being manager centered to employee centered. As a result, the characteristics of a successful manager must now have a different profile. Previously, the manager only needed to manage the work flow, that is *"doing things right."* Now, the focus must be on developing and implementing ideas in response to competitive change, achieving results through management of people, and increasing effectiveness by *"doing the right things."*

Accordingly, banks can no longer assume that employees have the skills, knowledge, or attributes to assume the managerial position simply because they were experts in a specific function. Training and development will be necessary if the bank wants a truly professional staff of managers. Clearly, not every skill will be required with the same degree of emphasis at all levels of management. Those managing high productivity areas will have a different set of skills than those managing a team of financial specialists. A manager heading the money transfer area may be highly dependent on good delegation and coaching skills, while the manager of the mergers and acquisitions area will be more reliant on motivational training and creativity.

Nonetheless, it would be wrong to believe that the money transfer manager does not need to grasp creativity or motivational concepts, or that the mergers and acquisitions team leader does not need to understand delegation or coaching theory. Periods of intense change demand an even greater need for managers well trained in every facet of management skills. In the long run, only those managers who are prepared to handle change will be able to keep the bank on an even keel.

REFERENCES

1. Drucker, Peter F. *The Frontiers of Management: Where Tomorrow's Decisions Are Being Shaped Today.* New York: Harper & Row, 1982.
2. Donnelly, James H., Jr., and Steven J. Skinner. *The New Banker: Developing Leadership in a Dynamic Era.* Homewood, Ill.: Dow Jones-Irwin, 1989.
3. Bernard, Harry B., and Cynthia A. Ingols. "Six Lessons for the Corporate Classroom," *Harvard Business Review*, Cambridge, Mass., September/October 1988.

ADDITIONAL READINGS

Gilbert, Thomas F. *Human Competence: Engineering Worthy Performance.* New York: McGraw-Hill, 1978.

Korsvik, William J., and Hervey A. Juris. *The New Frontier in Bank Strategy: Managing People for Results in Turbulent Times.* Homewood, Ill.: Dow Jones-Irwin, 1990.

Peters, Thomas, J., and Robert H. Waterman. *In Search of Excellence: Lessons from America's Best-Run Companies.* New York: Warner Books, 1982.

Walter, Ingo. *Global Competition in Financial Services.* Cambridge, Mass.: Ballinger Publishing, 1988.

CHAPTER 3

WHO WILL BE NEXT?: BEYOND THE PETER PRINCIPLE

"I want such a perfect blend between education and development that there will be no demarcation. There will be no end to education."—*Ronald E. Compton, President, Aetna Life & Casualty.*

Picture a college grad sitting at the desk of a interviewer during campus recruitment during the early 70s. The recruiter is saying

We'd like to hire you now, but there's something we should alert you to. Chances are, you probably won't be in your dream position by the time you're in your 40s. In fact, chances are, we won't need you at all. And if we merge or are acquired, you'll be out of this bank for sure.

Now, this is nothing against you: we think you're as good as the next highly qualified college grad. But unfortunately, you were born at the wrong time. There will be millions of baby boomers graduating from college just as you are getting ready to stake your career claim, and they'll have almost as much ability to do your job as you do. If we use one of them to replace you, we'll be getting a highly motivated and energetic person at a much lower cost.

Now, we expect this trend to continue until the year 2005 or so, at which time the last of the baby boomers will have hit their 40s. After that, the trend will reverse. Of course, by then you'll be in your 60s—too old for consideration. Just thought we'd let you know.

Of course, no bank has said that—not because they wanted to be unfair, but rather because they didn't know it themselves. But now it is becoming painfully obvious that banks (or any company for that matter) cannot assure positions up the corporate ladder; indeed, they cannot assure positions on the ladder at all. Demographics, the ones that futurists have been foretelling to deaf ears for years, are beginning to catch up with the front-runners of the baby booming generation.

Corporate life used to be structured to readily provide a medium for moving up the needs ladder. The "organization man," as defined in the 50s, had a built-in model for reaching the high point. Success was defined in terms of career advancement, and the rapidly expanding corporations of the post-war period could readily accommodate all talented comers.

SURPRISE, SURPRISE

However, today the current market structure and demographics are working against that model. Many banks are actively engaged in downsizing, either through lay-offs or attrition. Many of those that are not actually shrinking staff are limiting personnel growth to increase the per-person productivity from current staff. In addition, almost all banks are looking to flatten their hierarchical pyramid. The result is fewer managerial openings, fewer promotions.

The demographic situation is even less encouraging. For people born between 1945 and 1964, the future will be marked with frustrated expectations, at best, and job loss, at worst. This is true not only because the number of people available for positions is growing (versus the shrinking number of positions), but also because the positions are being readily filled by those at the younger end who tend to display more energy, yet are still satisfied with a lower salary. The baby *bust* situation will begin to affect banks through the 90s at the lower end of the scale, but the middle-management level will still be impacted by too many people for too few jobs.

SVP BY 33 OR BUST

Banks that once reserved the title of senior vice president (SVP) for those who had finally entered into the lofty heights of senior management now expect that level to be attained by the managerial candidates by the time they reach the age of 35, or at least within five years after that. Such expectations put the handwriting squarely on the wall: either make the grade by 40, or you're a candidate for the out-placement department (aptly called the "aloha room" by one New York bank).

Several bank executives, when interviewed for this book, noted that the "up 'n out" scenario was the only honest career path they could offer to plateauing managers. One executive commented that since they were only looking for "stars," this was an excellent way to winnow out mediocrity. Another noted that even if his most highly qualified managers asked him about their future, he would have to recommend leaving the bank; there just wouldn't be enough rewarding slots. "But I'd get those people's forwarding addresses, so that I can reach them if we ever want them again." Yet another grimly added that the "days of being put out to pasture are over. We simply don't have a big enough pasture to hold everyone."

The presumption that such events will only have a negative impact on the "losers" is illusory. The individuals born between 1945 and 1964 are in for a shock. They were taught "if you study hard, work hard, then the sky's the limit." Yet aside from the outstanding few, many may see that American dream disintegrate well before they've "hit their stride."

Senior managers who expect that the effect of creating a "make it or break it" culture is greater productivity are in for some rude surprises of their own. They will encounter a greater degree of stress, burnout, and psychological withdrawal from those who can make the grade but are worn down by the struggle and enforced competitiveness. Uncertainty caused by the fear of mergers only compounds the problem. Loss of productivity and unwanted turnover will result. In short, people will not find any value in loyalty if that loyalty is not likely to be rewarded.

The Survival Hop

Statistics that support the reduction in productivity or the rise in stress-related symptoms due to job concern are hard to come by. Nonetheless, corporations in other industries are already seeing the impact of the demise of corporate loyalty. When the Du Pont Company offered a generous early retirement plan to its 113,000 domestic employees, the chemical giant was overwhelmed: 11,200 elected to leave, about twice as many as the company had expected. In California's Silicon Valley, employee turnover at 231 electronic companies averages 27%, more than five times the departure rate for all U.S. manufacturing. Overall, average job tenure fell from 12 years in 1981 to 8.8 in 1987. Managers will soon hold 7 to 10 jobs in a lifetime, up from 3 to 4 in the 1970s.[1]

We'll Cross that Bridge When We Get to It

The "problem" of having an abundance of managerial talent combined with a reduction in need sounds like a boon to the banking industry. *But it isn't.* It only serves to mask an increasingly complex situation of staffing. No matter what the labor availability, banks must have the right person in the right job at the right time.

The problem with a large pool of resources to choose from is that banks lull themselves into believing that preparation is not necessary. They see at least two candidates for every slot, presuming with those odds that at least one will fill the bill more than adequately. What the thinking does not encompass is:

• *Are the candidates really ready for the proposed position?* Do they have the appropriate background for the new position? Do they know the broader banking industry environment or just the more narrow aspects required in their current job? Have they had any exposure to the managerial aspects of the job, or will that be a new discipline? If they are being transferred from another area, will the technical aspects be different? Do they even want the promotion or career change?

• *What will be the impact on the candidates not selected for the position?* Will they leave the bank when their hopes are frustrated? Or will they stay at the bank because other positions are hard to find, yet become apparently frustrated and underproductive? In either case, will the bank lose out on expertise? Who is available to replace them, and are they fully prepared for the change? Will their actions demoralize others around them? Will the bank's culture turn from positive to disenchanted?

Banks that fail to take these issues into consideration are relying heavily on luck. The newly promoted are plopped into positions without the bank having any assurance of their capacity to do the job, nor having taken any precautions against failure. It is the very situation that Laurence Peter warns about in his book, *The Peter Principle*.

The book theorizes that individuals are promoted to their level of incompetence (and accordingly left there). The theory is specious. More correctly, individuals are promoted to positions for which their competency is not assessed, and they are not trained to improve any shortcomings. That they might be competent in a position with training is, if at all, only casually addressed and most commonly after the fact, when habits and mistakes are already established. (Then, despite their shortcomings, they are left in those positions because they benefit from the devil-you-know versus the-devil-you-don't-know.) All of these pitfalls in selecting and promoting managers can be avoided with succession planning: *determining managerial needs and assuring that the internal supply of talent is adequately developed when the needs arise.*

Not Planning to Fail; Rather Failing to Plan
"Succession planning? We didn't set out to do it consciously. We just set out to make sure that we never again have a black hole in our senior- and middle-management team."

The comment was from William Lillis, President and CEO of the $4.5 billion American Savings Bank in White Plains.

> You see, we learned the hard way about management holes. In the early 80s, when we first created American Savings through the merger to three medium-sized banks, we expected to have the best of all worlds. After the merger, we would select the most outstanding employee from the three banks to manage the newly created departments. For instance, we chose the person who we deemed to be the best controller, the best retail branch administrator, and so forth. We figured that of all the problems we were likely to encounter in the merger, staffing would be the least of them.
>
> We didn't reckon on several factors. One was the fact that an entity that is 3 times larger is 10 times more complex. The controller was a "hands-on" manager. He used to have a staff of five assistants, but basically he managed the books himself. After we merged, he had 30 people who had to be managed, not merely acting as assistants. In this case, he wasn't prepared for it and failed.

This is an example of the Peter Principle in action—the bank had promoted the controller to his level of incompetence.

American Savings found out that not only was its staff not ready for the new positions, but that they were also not ready for the changes in the procedures and systems that the new entity required. The supervisors or managers were not experienced or trained to implement them. The bank discovered departments running tandem operations—the new way "for show," but the old way as the main system. Of course, the old systems eventually broke down, leaving the bank exposed.

Lillis noted that another factor was the change in the way the bank did business.

> When we had decided on merging, deregulation had just been mandated. But by the time the merging process was completed, we were in the high interest rate scenario of the early 80s. So we were faced with the situation of creating and developing new business on the one hand while interest rate reversals were draining out profits on the other. This combi-

nation attack-siege situation required a very specific type of managerial talent throughout the organization. When we looked around the bank, we realized we didn't have it.

Bringing in outsiders was the obvious solution, but it proved even more disastrous. A number of the new managers did not work out, and in some cases the bank was left further behind than where it started from. To worsen the situation, the morale of the current staff was declining, while many promising staff members left.

"After five or six years of this," Lillis continued, "we had 'enough.' We designed an extensive program to develop the managers we needed. Then we would be able to draw on the talent in our own organization. We would no longer be left high and dry."

Lillis added that just as ignoring the situation before had many surprising downsides, the program to develop management skills yielded many surprising benefits. "The staff's morale has shot way up; they can see their future more clearly. They're willing to take on greater risks and challenges. The 'old-timers' embrace it because it helps them overcome the threat of the younger generation. We sense that the organization itself is much more open and dynamic."

The Right Person at the Right Time

In essence, American Savings backed into succession planning. It's a concept that has been discussed in the planning literature for over 20 years, yet still remains a virtually ignored procedure.

For the most part, it is viewed as something that is only in the domain of the highest executive levels: Selecting the person who will succeed the president should he fall off a ladder cleaning out the rain gutters on his house (a tragedy that befell a former executive at Morgan Guaranty). It's almost as though one is saying that others in the lower echelon are expendable: ergo, no need to worry about replacement. American Savings' experiences, by no means unique, suggest otherwise.

Since the phrase *succession planning* means different things to different organizations, definitions are warranted. There are several levels of succession planning—ranging on the continuum from simplistic to very complex.

At the most *basic* level of succession planning, a manager merely selects a likely succession candidate. The senior management is informed, but the candidate isn't. Few specific steps are taken to groom the candidate for the future assignment.

At the middle level, the candidate is selected, often by a committee, and informed of the projected career path. The candidate has an opportunity to respond, and if he or she agrees that the move is appropriate, the bank begins a grooming procedure.

At the advanced level, several backup people are designated, not only for the most immediate likely opening, but for several positions further down. Their projected career track is discussed with the candidates, with likely variations that may emerge depending on openings. Grooming is more broadly based, reflecting the likelihood of unexpected openings occurring at different times.

Unfortunately, most organizations that do succession planning rely on the easiest succession planning routes: that is, a succession candidate is noted somewhere in a black book, and nothing further is done. In fact, an Association of Bank Trainers and Consultants (ABTAC) survey in 1989 on succession planning revealed that approximately 40% of the respondents operated in that fashion, while another 45% indicated that they didn't do any succession planning at all. Only 15% of the respondents indicated that they were at an advanced level, that is, a backup person was designated and developed.

Why Succession Planning Isn't Done

Banks routinely put their managers through the extraordinary effort of putting together a forecasted budget for the following year, with all of the attendant strategizing meeting, rewrites, variation justifications, and so forth. Yet when a much lesser effort regarding personnel planning is proposed, everyone shakes their head with an "who the hell's got time for this" eyeroll.

One ABTAC survey respondent noted: "Some succession planning is being done, but not in a formalized manner. While there is a great deal of lip service given by line management to the need for such a program, there appears to be little desire to go through the agony of determining necessary skills, measuring where people are, and delivering training to close the gap."

In short, "Don't bother us; we're already busy."

Another respondent to the survey added: "Our organization is not ready yet for a formal succession planning system. Moreover, our corporate culture is such that when we are ready, the system will need to appear simple and almost informal (i.e., not be paper intensive).

That respondent is probably stating a universal attitude: Unless the introduced system looks like it can be easily accomplished, the managers won't even deal with it. And that respondent is right—managers will scuttle any plan, most commonly by providing poor or off-handed data, if they feel put upon.

It's Not That Hard, Really

A good system should incorporate relative ease of implementation in order to surmount the hurdle of inertia. Sometimes a complete system can be approached on a step-by-step basis so that the senior managers acclimate themselves to addressing future needs and the middle managers to the need for assisting in their own development.

Bill Schoel, head of the HR Development at SouthTrust in Birmingham, Alabama, is using that tack to bring the senior managers in line with the bank's more forward thinking. They have established a Professional Development Program that has many of the basic elements of succession planning: determining and filling the gaps in the quality of the middle managers. Added Schoel, "It's not that we hadn't developed our managerial level before—but it was most commonly done on an 'as-needed' basis. As we've grown, though, we realized that we could no longer 'shoot from the hip'—we needed an objective and orderly approach to determining the managers' strengths and weaknesses and providing the necessary training."

The program is jointly administered by the HR Development Department and the Personnel Department. They introduced an assessment instrument designed by an outside firm. In using it, the manager, his or her superior, and five peers respond to a series of questions about the manager, which are then compiled and sent back to the manager to review. Then he or she meets with the program's administrator and counselor to discuss this data, as well as the manager's own concerns and needs. They lay out a course of training and development that addresses both issues. The HR Development Department offers a separate listing of courses, training materials, books, and other development media for the manager to select from in order to improve their soft spots. The manager has the option to review the results regarding the recommended training path with his or her senior manager. Most do.

Taking part in the assessment program is not mandatory, but the developers took such great care in explaining to the managers how this program benefits them that everyone has willingly participated. "Once they saw that we had no tricks up our sleeve, the word-of-mouth on the program readily got them in the door."

Doubled Fun

Schoel sees that the bank is ahead in two ways from the data provided by the assessment studies. First, *the senior managers gain insight into the quality of their staff in an objective manner.* Using that, they are better positioned to pull together an organization chart that delineates the depth of talent in their areas, as well as the imbalances or potential holes. This data not only helps managers see problem areas, but also enables them to better select and place the right people in the right positions.

Second, *the human resources department is able to determine with far more accuracy the departments of the bank or a group of individuals that require more in-depth training.* For instance, if they find that most everyone in the credit area is rating low on communication skills, they can add more emphasis on that in earlier programs. Thus, the data serves as both needs analysis and prior program evaluation. The data also provides needed ammunition to request resources to develop new or different programs.

School gives most of the credit to SouthTrust's President, Julian Banton, for making this program happen. Although the idea had been on the table for a while, he moved it to the forefront in terms of priorities. He also made sure that the senior-level people understood what the bank was trying to achieve and that they would support the efforts. Comments School,

> Most important, though, is the mutual benefit we hope to achieve from the managers themselves. This program is sending a very strong message that we are clearly interested in them and their future at this bank. We provide them with the skills to be a superior quality manager—from them we hope to receive loyalty and commitment.

School feels that the senior managers have come to appreciate what they are slowly putting into place—a systematic approach to dealing with long-term issues. Eventually, it will lead to more full-blown succession planning. But rather than hitting them with a complex system for which they would have no real appreciation of its value, the paced introduction via the Professional Development Program allows them to see for themselves the impact it can have on their being able to consistently maintain a cadre of high-quality managers under them.

Racheting Up the Ladder

For a bank such as SouthTrust, which has already taken the basic steps in succession planning by identifying the organizational gaps and individual weaknesses, the next move is to create a more complex level of data expansion and integration. To develop a minimum solid basic information base, the bank would require responses to the following questions:

- What is the current inventory of individuals in key positions?
- What are the likely losses through retirements, transfers, or resignations?
- What is the future demand for individuals (expressed in numbers or percentage increases) based on the strategic plans?
- What are the imbalances between needs and supply?
- How many and who are currently available to be placed in the key positions without further development required?
- How many and who require further development to be superior candidates for the position?
- What attributes need to be developed?
- How long will it take to accomplish?
- How many need to be hired from the outside, and how much internal development will be required of the hirees?

Much of the information to develop this data base can be extracted from the annual performance appraisals. It should then be retained in a computerized system (several software packages are available in the market), which can utilize the data to analyze in various formats.

How Norwest Does It

"Your employees are your leading indicators; the business you do lags behind them," noted Richard Kovacevich, President and COO of Norwest Corporation. Headquartered in Minneapolis, it has had a fully implemented succession program for several years.

Holly Kurtz, one of the people responsible at Norwest Corporation for their succession planning system, comments:

We devised our own computer system to manage the succession planning data. But we're implementors, not utilizers of the data—that is, what emerges is not for the sake of the human resources department, but for the furtherance of the bank's business. Basically, it's line driven—what the managers feel they need and will use is what HRD tries to provide.

We call the program Development Planning—at this point it essentially addresses all exempts. The employee and the manager meet sometime during the first quarter of the year to discuss formally what often is done on an informal basis—the employee's future potential. HR provides an analysis tool, a development planning form, which covers the issues (1) what the employee wants, (2) what we want, (3) what should be watched for, and (4) what needs to be developed.

The succession planning process is done at a distinctly different time from the performance appraisal, mainly because performance appraisal results are so closely allied to compensation. We've found that the managers are more comfortable and more enthusiastic about doing development planning than they are about appraisals—it's more positive and upbeat, and there are no critical issues, such as pay increases, depending on its outcome.

In April, the HR area compiles the data and then makes it available to the senior management as well as the divisional managers. Review committees discuss the data. At the senior management level, those with the highest potential, as well as women and minorities, are addressed. Within divisional areas, the managers themselves decide how broad their review should be—in some areas, it will include all exempts; in others, only the higher-ranking officials.

From their decisions, we receive a listing of the developmental training needs, which we feed into the training programming process. Attending the recommended courses is not mandatory for an employee, but we usually find that they are adequately motivated to do so on their own.

We encourage the review committees to go as deep as possible; however, their review decision is one that fits their needs. We don't attempt to monitor the usage—our role is to guide the process and make sure the data upon which they make decisions is as meaningful as possible.

In any case, we don't have a real need for acting as policemen. The managers at Norwest have accepted this procedure the same way they've accepted the budgeting process—they know it's just part of running a business.

The keystone of the Norwest succession plan is its integration into the managers' "business consciousness"—they are aware that the bank does not require them to do more planning, but, if they don't, it will be the managers' own departments that will be impacted. They have come to realize that without this planning they will not be able to identify the people best suited, by virtue of their training, preference, and general abilities, to be "relationship managers" or "sales managers" or "department managers"—positions that have substantially different sets of competency requirements. The managers have become aware of the importance of focusing on the bank's anticipated need level for these positions so that the right people can be developed early enough to comfortably fill those positions when the time comes.

The development planning is also separated from the performance appraisal process. The performance appraisal process addresses how well the employee is performing now, inevitably leading to a discussion of the shortcomings. It is usually emotionally fraught by the implications on the employee's compensation or bonus. (See Figure 3–1 showing the basic succession planning system as described by Norwest.)

For many managers, performance appraisals are distasteful events (not much of a thrill for the employees either). It's replete with comments such as, "Well, this aspect is very good, but over here you're really not up to par . . . we had expected that by now . . . but you don't seem to be able to . . . therefore, we suggest that . . . and if we don't see change. . . ." One employee commented that he always envisioned his boss wearing a hood and carrying an axe during his performance reviews.

By contrast, development planning is a welcome experience, full of positive comments. "This is what we have; this is what you might be able to do; this is what you need to get

FIGURE 3–1
Basic Succession Planning System

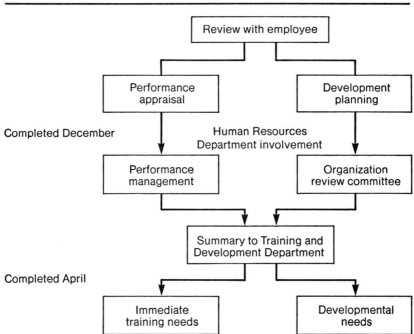

there—how does it mesh with your own self-evaluations and aspirations?" The lack of "must do's," implied disappointments, and potential emotional conflict keep the sessions mutually rewarding. (See Chapter 5 on Career Development.)

Take This Job and Shove It
Development planning also can play an important role in another key aspect of employee relations—the problem of the disenchanted worker. The leveling of the corporate hierarchy has caused many employees to realize that their future will fall way short of their expectations. They fall into a group known as the *passively plateaued*.[2] Unlike their happily plateaued cousins, the lack of future potential renders them

dispirited and disenfranchised. They see their current position as routine and funless and they are not even motivated enough to seek employment elsewhere, on the expectation that the "story" at another bank will be the same. What previously had been a sense of security and comfort for them has turned into a sense of boredom and pessimism.

They also are burdened with the notion that workers past 40 are set for life in their current position, and cannot foresee the possibility of switching to another career position after that age. This is part of a "macho" baggage image stemming from:

- If you haven't got it by now, you never will.
- It's an embarrassment to have to be learning how to do a job at this age.
- Fate has cast the die of life; you must accept it even if it doesn't work out.
- You're a loser if you plateau or return to a lesser function in your career; winners keep moving up and ahead.

Of course, these platitudes are the ones the society has created—and we've all bought into them over time. The question is how to reverse the attitudes.

Change is anathema to many people, brought about mainly by fear of the consequences. The problem is compounded when change is virtually unknown in a corporation environment and then comes swiftly in. These who have been operating in the same fashion for 20 or 30 years without any negative comments regarding their previous behavior are now suddenly told that their whole way of working is invalid. They must "dig in" or "ship out."

The implication can be devastating. The individual is being told that his or her current job approach and expectations, although highly regarded before, are now wrong. The whole system of work values has been completely negated. Therefore, what the individual thought was a good achievement in the past is actually now deemed to be of little value. And the bank keeps stating that if the individual doesn't change and continues operating in the same fashion, the future for that individual is doubtful.

It's not just that the individual is not "creative" enough to anticipate change. Another more basic emotion is involved. In changing, the individual must throw off the mantle of self-esteem and pride in work done that was built up over the previous years—a form of eating humble pie. It's a hard blow to any ego. Not surprisingly, resistance to change is high. The bank confirms its opinion—they're not just plateaued, they're deadwood.

Tom Kraack, who runs the Technical Institute University at Norwest, points out that the familiar seniority system only breeds mediocre workers. "Of course, workers eventually plateau. They see low reward for improving and a limited future, particularly if they are stuck behind a fairly entrenched senior person. It's our job to try to break that hold—and training is our best tool to do it."

Stamp Out Planned Obsolescence
The same individual's dream may change at different stages of his or her life. The person who envisioned being bank president at 30 may long have realized that the demands of such a position, indeed any executive position, are far more than that person's idea of a good lifestyle have grown. Or that person may realize that he or she prefers selling, not managing sales. For those that enjoy but have become bored in their current position, quite often the change of environment, projects and/or jobs is just as challenging and appealing to these employees as upward movement. These are people who have realized that achieving the feeling of success doesn't always have to come from the title, the private dining room, and the limousine.

The mismatch between desires and "normal" career paths generally becomes more evident as the employee moves into their "thirtysomething" years. However, by then, the cultural stigma attached to opting out of the ladder climb is well established. Thus, by the time the individual hits forty-something and is aware that the dream is neither achievable or wanted, the stigma of plateau or downward movement is even more acutely felt.

Plateaued and Productive

Not all plateaued people are unproductive or miserable. In fact, many may be quite productively plateaued. Although the job they are performing is not likely to change, they are happy in their position, continuing to find it challenging and emotionally rewarding. Boredom is staved off by the continuous introduction of new procedures, technology, problem identification and problem solving (either alone or in committee), high interaction levels with others, and recognition from the organization of the employee's efforts.

It's an Awful Job—I Just Love It

"Do you want to work in FX operations," one long-time manager at a money center bank asked of a group of new recruits in a training program.

It's very stressful work—every day we have to process hundreds of items worth billions of dollars with minimal errors under the most confusing circumstances. The traders make mistakes; confirmations are misleading; reconciliations statements are incorrect. Since we deal worldwide, I get calls at home at two in the morning—my wife is on a first-name basis with the Tokyo manager. And we never eat—it's three o'clock now and my lunch will be those cookies in the back of the room.

Sounds terrible, but believe it or not, I love working there. We're talking about a world-class operation. Which other department in the bank brings together so many elements? We talk to people all over the world. We interface with practically every other department in the bank. We're impacted by everything that happens in the bank and everything that happens in the world.

We're always trying to make the operation better. And it's worked. Two years ago we had a one-inch thick 'exception' report. Now we are down to one page. We did it by making some conscious decisions to achieve error reduction: we set up a standing instruction system, an automatic confirmation system, and an error-reduction reward system.

We also sat down with the traders and agreed to listen to each other, rather than being constantly at odds. We explained our problems; they told us what they're trying to achieve. Friction is now at an all-time low; in fact, they now rely on us for verification of their trading positions rather than screaming at us when there's a discrepancy.

The operation is smoother than ever, but we're still working on ways to set up new systems to further minimize errors and employee effort. You know, we even have corporate customers calling *us* to help them solve their problems with their dealings *at other banks*. And we do it—'cause every problem we solve is a feather in our cap.

This manager's position offers him the best aspects of what researchers have determined to be the elements of the happily plateaued worker:

- A job that's familiar but valued by peers and others.
- A desire to do the job more effectively.
- Routine work interspersed with a niche or pet projects.
- Recognition from others—often from outside the organization.
- A willingness to take risks.
- Open networks within the organization.

Although, clearly, the individual's own personality profile plays a great part in his or her approach to the job, the organization must contribute to stimulating the best of it. It must encourage and reward

- Taking the initiative.
- Risk-taking—even if the project doesn't pan out as planned.
- Having small achievements as well as the large ones.
- Participating in internal and external networks and work groups.
- Making contributions outside the organization.

How does the bank make it known that it will reward those who continue to strive for excellence: (1) by communicating it in the performance appraisals and management feedback and (2) by providing the knowledge base and skills to *achieve* beyond the narrow limits of the job description. Understanding the elements necessary for project management, team work, effective networks, and productive meetings does not necessarily come intuitively. It requires skills development.

The Sideways Maneuver

One Midwest bank has taken the stance of encouraging horizontal moves rather than vertical ones. Thus, someone in the money transfer department might switch to auditing, and vice versa. They have also structured dual technical management ladders. New technical and executive positions are equal in pay and rank to management jobs. For example, the bank has created senior lending positions and positions for accounting and systems specialists that are equivalent to senior managerial posts in those departments.[3]

We're so used to rewarding promotions that we as a society rarely focus on lateral assignment changes as a preferred change. Whoever hears the line, "I'm home, Honey. Congratulate me—I've just made a lateral move from cash management into money transfer."

The stigma of lateral change is still very strong: it reads as being "put out to pasture." In reality, the new opportunity can offer the excitement that comes with change, a new learning environment, mastering new skills, and general self-development. But any bank seeking to encourage lateral moves must first minimize the stigma.

To do so, banks should consider doing several things:

- Formalized multidirectional career opportunities should be established and made known at the recruitment stage that the bank encourages participation.
- The bank should have an active posting system that allows employees to determine what is available within the bank and precisely what job experience and education or training requirements are necessary to qualify.

- The bank should maintain or support an assessment center or assessment tools where individuals can determine their aptitudes and potentials for certain positions, as well as determine which areas need strength.
- Seniority or superior performance might be rewarded by encouraging part-time "research" or "teaching" positions within the bank.

Beyond the Peter Principle

Succession planning may at last put the right person in the right job at the right time. But as organizations change, so do the old career patterns. Banks today are reducing managerial positions, and more managers are finding themselves plateaued. Whether they grow bored and demoralized or continue to find interest and challenge in their work depends in a large part on the bank's commitment to skills development as well as to finding new ways to reward performance.

REFERENCES

1. Cascio, Wayne F. *Managing Human Resources.* 2nd Edition. New York: McGraw-Hill, 1989.
2. Kaye, Beverly. "Are Plateaued Performers Productive?" *Personnel Journal*, August 1989.
3. Cascio, Wayne F. *Managing Human Resources.*

ADDITIONAL READINGS

Cohen, Stephen L. "Information, Please." *Training & Development Journal*, July 1989.

Galagan, Patricia A. "Ronald E. Compton: Underwriting Business with Training." *Training & Development Journal*, October 1989.

Swanson, Richard A. and Deane Gradous, Editors. *Human Resources and Organizational Change: Theory-to-Practice Monograph*. Alexandria, Va.: ASTD, 1987.

CHAPTER 4

EMPOWER TO THE PEOPLE: THE SPREADING OF RESPONSIBILITY

"People don't come to work to do a bad job."
—*John J. Connolly, President of Constellation Bancorp.*

"Don't talk in terms of 'training' and 'education'—or even 'learning.' Talk in terms of work/personal/professional effectiveness. Tell them which of *their* needs you're trying to meet—and why."—*Tom Caperton, Director of Employee Development, United Carolina Bank, Whiteville, North Carolina.*

"Our first task was to give them confidence," commented John Connolly, who in 1983 took over the position of President of Constellation Bancorp, parent of the National State Bank, a bank with assets of $2 billion in Elizabeth, New Jersey. He was referring to the attitude of the employees he encountered as he toured the bank during his initial year there.

> I almost couldn't believe the level of ignorance. Nobody knew anything—not about the current state of banking, not about the goals of the bank, or even the roles they were expected to perform. They had no opinions at all. If I asked them if things could be improved, they said yes. If I asked how to do it, they said, "I don't know."

Connolly was walking into a situation that had been cast in concrete by the past management. The bank had been paternalistic in nature: all ideas emanated from the top. In the past, employees were never rewarded for making suggestions. If anything, offering up an idea was analogous to criticizing the current management. The result, as Connelly saw it, was a near-stagnant organization.

However, Connolly was not interested in laying blame for the state of affairs: his focus was on how to fix it. "First, we had to deal with their fear: fear of making suggestions, fear of taking responsibility. I presumed that once we could overcome that, then we could concentrate on developing the managerial and competency skills. I estimated that the change in the thought process would occur within six months or so; in reality, it took much longer."

PREPARING TO TRAIN

Connolly first started by introducing the basics of a planning process to about 150 officers and then asking those at the managerial level to contribute to the determination of their areas' strategic plan. Connolly knew that unless they set their own goals, they would not be in a position to make them work. But despite all the exhortations on Connolly's part, nothing happened. No ideas came forth. In essence, they were waiting for Connolly to provide them with the answers. They were just so used to being told what to do that they could not respond in any other fashion.

> I suppose we could have simply been more hard-assed—kicking out all those that couldn't adjust. But we decided to take another route. We called in a consulting group who worked with developing the managers' strategic planning skills without our being present. Removing ourselves from the scene made a substantial difference: the visible link to the past was absent, and they began to open up. They had a place they could safely unload their concerns and then start anew.
>
> After the goal-setting period was finished, we set about reaffirming that they, not just senior management, were now in charge of the bank's future. Meetings with small groups of managers were held, during which I told them that "it's not up to me; it's up to you." As logical as this seems, they were never made to think in these terms before. I emphasized that I believed that they *could* do what was necessary, but that

they had to develop their own conviction. Without that, they could never convey to their subordinates the importance of the mission. It would be doomed to failure.

But not everyone could subscribe to the new concepts. I had all kinds of emotions expressed, even tears. We let them dump their bucket, but then we said, "Try it first. Don't drop out until you've given it your best shot." In some cases, it worked; in others, it didn't, either because they couldn't overcome their own lack of conviction or because they simply wouldn't try. Eventually, the "couldn'ts" and "wouldn'ts" left the bank.

Those that did stay began to appreciate what was necessary to do the job right. First, the bank gave them the management-training skills so that they could understand how to motivate their subordinates to do the job correctly. Their most powerful tool was the establishment of job standards and the appropriate use of the performance appraisal instrument. Connolly began to hear a new response from the employees: "We want to do it, but we don't really know how. We need to be trained properly." At that point the bank knew that the training they would offer would work.

Everyone Should Be Allowed to Succeed

According to Connolly, losing the uninspired managers and employees was necessary, but painful.

> The people that work in an organization are not throwaways—something you can trash the minute they don't perform to your standards. Even ignoring the social implications, which I wouldn't, it is not realistic to presume that they could be replaced with a better employee, given today's job market. Besides, our role as managers is to give employees the motivation to want to do their job and the skills by which to do it. If we don't achieve that, we're not performing in our roles.

The whole process took much longer than Connolly anticipated. In the case of the branch system personnel, who had the most ingrained attitudes, it took four years, with a 100% turnover of branch managers (many for the usual reasons of attrition). However, during that time, the organization has grown threefold, from $600 million to $2 billion in assets with an even greater percentage increase in income.

FROM CLUB TO ACADEMY

What Connolly did, and what other banks are in the throes of doing, was to switch the whole organizational attitude and form. Jeffrey Sonnenfeld, Director of Emory University's Center for Leadership and Career Change, has researched types of corporate culture and the career paths that are implied in each. Basically, he has come up with four different types of structure, the "club," the "baseball team," the "academy," and the "fortress."

Club atmospheres encourage people to fit in, a situation that rewards employees with slow corporate escalation and tenure. Clubs groom managers as generalists, with initiation beginning at an entry-level job, where most of the training is concentrated. "Don't rock the boat, and it won't rock you" is the unwritten motto on the clubhouse wall. Change is not an issue; in fact, it is anathema.

Baseball teams are at the opposite end of the scale. People are hired strictly for the ability to produce and are rewarded accordingly. They are rarely trained; they come in knowing their job and exit quickly if they don't live up to their company's expectations, or vice versa. Investment banks are classic examples of this category.

Fortresses are organizations under siege, either by other organizations or by the threat of failure. Their mentality is centered around change, but its focus is short term, one of getting through the immediate crises.

After that, their attitude might shift to one of long term—into that of the *academy*—where constant small shifts in organization structure and mission are part of the strategy. Accordingly, the individual is encouraged to embrace change and to orient oneself to assure that it occurs. Managers are rewarded for providing the individual with the guidance and encouragement to meet that challenge. But achieving the goal is the domain of the employee.

Banks have been struggling to get out of the shell of the club atmosphere, which they are finding to be completely inappropriate in an era that demands change. Some found themselves as fortresses, where long-term development was put on hold until assured survival was apparent. Others have become baseball teams, where the greatest reward comes to the biggest producers. More commonly, though, is the attempt of the clubs, such as National State, to restructure themselves into an academy.

Deciding on the organizational structure is easy; changing the structure is less simple. Managers are in essence asking people to move from organizational reliance to self-reliance. Not surprisingly, the inability to buy into a process that completely reverses their former roles has taken quite a toll on the old-time club members.

A manager at one of the money center banks saw many of these changes slowly reflected, particularly in retail banking in the 70s and more recently in the wholesale bank side. He pointed to many of the recent early retirements that have been endemic in the industry. "You basically have that 20% that thinks that the idea is great, 20% who can't accept it at all, and the remaining 60% that says, 'I know where we want to be, but you have to help me get there.' For them, you must provide the safety net."

"Owning" the Business

To help drive home the point of change, some banks are describing their employee communications in terms of "ownership." The allusion is easy to understand. What you own, you must be responsible for. It's up to you to reach out to be able to fulfill that responsibility. If your children are sick, you cannot wait for the doctor to call you. If your sales are down, you cannot wait for the customer to come to you.

For instance, at Seafirst Bank in Seattle, branch managers are taught to think in terms of having a franchise rather than of merely managing a department. Descriptions in brochures describing training courses for the various levels clearly illustrate their concept. The following verbiage describes the expected levels of achievement for an individual starting as a personal banker at a branch:

Personal Banker Tier I: You are skilled to serve the basic customer needs regarding consumer products.

Personal Banker Tier II: You will be "relationship trained" and will anticipate and handle all consumer- and small-business customer needs. You become an "owner" of a portfolio.

Personal Banker Tier III: You will have the best sales skills, the best credit skills. You "own" a portfolio of customers, and you are a potential franchise "owner."

Branch Manager Tier III: You "own" a franchise. You will have sales-management skills, people-management skills, advanced-marketing skills, and the responsibility for the success of the franchise.

The message to the reader is clear. If you reach the level of branch manager, *you* are given the charge of running your own business: *your* efforts will determine its success or its failure; *your* decisions will impact the future of the organization. Even at lesser levels, the implications of empowerment are clear.

Seafirst doesn't stop at verbiage: the training supports the concept wholeheartedly. In fact, at the Branch Manager level, one of the core-required courses offered is "How to Manage a Franchise" cosponsored with the University of Washington Executive Program.

The Banking Franchise

Luke Helms, the bank's President, did a survey of its customer base and determined that Seafirst at that time had 60% of the households and 25% of all retail business handled in the Seattle area. While most banks would have been content with those statistics, Seafirst went further with its survey and discovered that its customers were becoming older, smarter, richer, and more interested in making their own choices.

Helms felt that in order to continue its success, the bank would need retail staff that could go beyond basic sales and service—staff that could listen to and understand the local customers and cater specifically to their needs. "Looking around the banking industry, I did not find a role model," noted Helms. "But when I looked outside banking, I was bowled over. McDonald's, Ford, and Coca-Cola handled its retail customers—through local franchisers—and they have had tremendous success. McDonald's tells their people that they can do anything they want, as long as it meets basic standards. And those people will get compensated for their efforts."

Helms took the concept to heart and worked with the University of Washington to help revamp the training program, ultimately establishing the Seafirst College.

> It was a real gamble on our part—telling employees that it's their show as much as ours and that they were accountable for its success. Would they embrace it or reject it? The new retail training program probably cost six times as much as the old one, so we were putting our money where our mouth was. And the commitment was beyond money. We, meaning Dick Cooley (the Chairman) and I, were also willing to go out and personally do some of the training. We *want* those people to succeed—and we'll do what we can to help make it happen.
>
> By now we've put at least 2,000 employees through some kind of training. We decided to judge our success on the basis of how many of them would latch on to our vision. Just now, about two years after the program's been fully in swing, I'd say roughly that about 25% of the employees have not bought in, another 50% love it, and the remaining 25% are still fence-sitters. So we're still waiting for all of the jury to come in.
>
> Success in terms of the bottom line? Oh, that's easy. We're opening at least twice as many accounts as two years ago. Before, we had 25% of the business; now, it's 30%. Turnover is the lowest ever, and some of our branch managers make more money through the new incentive plan than they ever expected under the old system.
>
> The program as it stands does exactly what we want it

to—it helps people feel good enough about themselves to want to do more. Once we took away the barriers to achievement, the barriers to advancement, they pushed right through. But we're still learning and fine-tuning the program. We learned that every dollar of commitment, every hour of effort has paid off handsomely—and we're not going to let it slide.

He Who's Got the Power

It stands to reason, that if power is transferred to one group—the worker group—that it will be diminished in another group—the managerial group. One consulting firm recently defined the need for power as a concern for recognition and status, control of situations, and the ability to arouse strong positive or negative emotions in others.[1] Those who aspire to the managerial positions share these needs to some degree, and, for some, it is all consuming. Accordingly, requiring managers to give up power once it has been attained is a difficult task.

The point of empowerment is to spread the decision making around adequately so that the bank's response time to the customer is competitive. Managers who will greedily hang onto power at headquarters or who must have every detail pass across their desk are going to be too slow at decision making either to satisfy the customer or to respond to market forces.

As Connolly from National State noted, changing a power structure is a very difficult task. Both the power-loser and the power-gainer have difficulty adjusting to the new situation. "You are now in charge" is as disturbing a notion to some people as "you are no longer in charge" is to others. Banks that have gone through the changeover, without exception, report that the effort yielded more turnover than that anticipated from both manager and employee.

Despite all the headlines and publicity, people still wend their way to banking because it represents security. Security to the typical bank employee means many things: not likely to be laid off being the foremost. Those attracted to banking for security are naturally those types who shun risk-taking. They don't want to have to go out on a limb.

Just as at National State, when Seafirst implemented the new concept, not everyone could comfortably ascribe to the idea of having to take control. The old ideas of a bank being an institution where a good attendance record guaranteed security were being laid to rest. The message to the employee is clear: "You either reach for the brass ring, or we will take away the carnival ride."

UP THE HIERARCHY OF NEEDS

At its most basic stages, everyone is seeking *physical comfort* and a *sense of security*. This has been well researched and documented in Maslow's famous needs hierarchy. As we move into emotional levels of need, people seek a sense of *belonging, peer approval*, and *self-esteem*. One consultant, John Morrison, summarized it in more familiar terms: the rewards for each moment of existence are the "warm fuzzies" that accompany a particular activity.[2] He notes that one remembers only those events that were accompanied by a personal emotion of some kind, whether it be a successful presentation that everyone applauded or a disastrous meeting with a fellow worker.

Banks—all employers in general—tend to ignore these basic human needs when they present a new organizational order. Much of the unwanted turnover or attitudinal hostility resulting from organizational changes can often be traced back to the needs hierarchy.

- The *security* seekers suddenly find themselves exposed to losing their jobs if they don't perform.
- Those seeking *belonging* are told that they must act on their own.
- *Peer approval* is especially eroded for those who previously had power and now are disenfranchised.

- *Self-esteem* is threatened if performance quotas are not met. And those have been happily working all along, only to be told that their work style is no longer appropriate, suddenly feel as if their whole contribution has been invalidated.

Those who are at higher levels in the needs hierarchy cannot readily understand the emotional distraction of those who are in lower ones. People for whom security is not an issue, or whose sense of self-esteem has long been established, cannot imagine the anguish of those who must face the loss of it.

Further, as a group, we naturally presume that changes for the good of the organization will automatically be lauded by all employees, no matter how they will be personally affected. And we are even more surprised when an apparent promotion in an individual's work situation causes a negative reaction or resentment.

After all, many joined the bank because of the club culture, where everyone fits, and commitment to doing things for the good of the group is of paramount concern. With empowerment, the organization appears to be moving towards being a baseball team, with its heavy emphasis on individual achievement.

Look Before You Leap

We don't mean to suggest that a bank should scrap a planned organizational change because it rocks personal or emotional boats. But for the transition to be the smoothest, all the subtleties should be taken into account.

It's not just a matter of asking people to shift from a certain comfort category to another. The true concern being addressed is the fear of failure (or the appearance of failure, in the case of the managers). The bank is asking its employees to do something more than they initially envisioned and is perhaps beyond their ken.

Roger Raber, EVP, at the National Council of Savings

Institutions in Washington, D.C., summarized the role of the worker in an empowered situation. An employee must be able to:

- Define the need or problem.
- Quickly assimilate the relevant data.
- Conceptualize and reorganize the information.
- Make deductive and intuitive leaps with information.
- Ask hard questions about information.
- Discuss findings with colleagues.
- Work collaboratively to find solutions.
- Then, convince others.

It is a tall order—especially in organizations which are structured so that the employee essentially only has to carry out orders. "Just tell me what to do" is to be supplanted with "I'll figure it out myself." The obvious implication is that we want followers to turn into doers. The issue is very complex. An individual's fear of failure may indeed be warranted if being a self-starter is not in his or her natural make-up.

At Seafirst Bank, the fear of failure is being smoothed over with the establishment of the Seafirst College, whose goal is to provide a basis of support—both knowledge-wise and emotionally. Essentially, Seafirst is making a pact with the employee: We'll teach you what you need to know; you go out to do it. Wherever you (or your manager) feel there is a knowledge or skills shortfall, we'll provide you with necessary training. We will not leave you to sink or swim: our resources are always there to provide you with the necessary know-how to meet our mutual goals.

The Service Empowerment

We tend to equate empowerment with platform relationship development, but that would be underestimating its value. The complete spectrum of all interpersonal activities benefit from empowerment—from customer sales to interdepartmental service. Service is, after all, a form of commitment of performance to another, which the performing individual must take responsibility to accomplish.

The apathy that seems to distinguish many employees

in service organizations is in part a reflection of the institution's attitude as well as the individual's. Most often, this apathy can be traced back to limited directives on the institution's part as to what level of service is really expected. It then follows that even less is done to encourage the employee to achieve that level.

"The customer comes first!" as a motto on every wall is an excellent start, but wholly inadequate to truly inspire employees. The empowered employee is one who *appreciates* the goal, *knows* how to achieve it, and is continuously *urged* to do so. If you take away one of the elements, quality service will not occur.

Making the Point at Sovran

The operations group at Sovran Financial Corporation is an example of a division that is committed to quality service to its customers, both internal and external. They revised their mission statement to emphasize the service orientation. "But we realize that having a commitment to service is one thing; having everyone within the organization understand and apply that commitment is quite another," noted Robert Hamilton, in his recent position as head of operations training.

Sovran took several steps to translate that commitment into action. First, they defined the goal: commitment to service should permeate the entire organization, not just the areas that interact directly with outside customers. They reiterated the service philosophy that states that every person an employee deals with professionally is, in effect, that employee's customer, even between one bank office department and another.

With those goals defined, they then developed and expanded three training programs. The first program was designed to communicate the message; the second was to teach people how to apply it; and the third was to aid managers in refining its application in order to build stronger team units.

Within two weeks of being hired, a new employee to the department (no matter how long in the bank) must attend an introductory program they developed internally called *Quest*, which addresses three questions: What is the direction of the banking industry and how does Sovran fit in? What is the structure and mission of the operations group? What does the concept of service quality really mean? In addition, Sovran trains individuals in the basics of good communication style and interdepartmental access so that all attendees have the knowledge needed to take the first steps in solving a customer's service problem immediately upon starting their jobs.

> To us, that program is the most critical training we do. Everyone knows what we are about. There's no mistaking our missions and goals—and how the employee fits in. In fact, one new hire, who had worked at another bank for seven years as a proof operator, told me that she learned more about Sovran and what the bank was trying to achieve than she had during all those years at her other bank. Now, I ask you, At which bank do you think she will be the more enthusiastic worker?

Learning How to Service
After the Quest program, employees are involved in a two-day program, Quality Service Skills Training. Attendees learn how to listen, convert the information into action, and how to convey to their customers the sense that their problems are important. All employees from retail banking support staff to security guards are to attend. This reinforces the notion that each employee is another's customer, deserving as much attention as outside customers receive.

The last part of the program, Interpersonal Communication, is primarily for managers and supervisors. It draws heavily on the Herrmann Brain Dominance Indicator and the Myers-Briggs Type Indicator. The program makes managers more understanding of others' personality types and therefore more tolerant and willing to adopt to the communication style that best suits the employees' needs. The ability to build stronger, more effective teams is one of the applications, emphasized in class.

Sovran is not relying only on telling employees that they should "provide service," but also translating that appreciation into something that the employees can act on. That bridging process is what distinguishes their program from that of other banks which never go the extra step—but rather expect employees to figure it out for themselves.

Money and Empowerment

Actually demonstrating to the employees that they had the power to change the organization procedures was the element that caused an immediate improvement in employee attitude at one California bank. It sent 450 service managers from platform and back-office departments through a program called Branch Production Management. Each attendee had to complete a work project utilizing the skills learned during the program. The content of the projects, which addressed work-flow procedures, management processes, or production efficiency, was determined by each attendee during the last day of class. To be accepted by the line review panel, comprised mainly of district managers, the project's recommendations must have the potential for saving time, effort, and money within the service area reported on.

To assure continuous application of the skills learned, the production management responsibility has been added to job descriptions, as well as being part of the performance review. Further incentives include awards for outstanding project recommendations.

Employees began to realize that they themselves actually have the power to improve the work flow and the quality of their bank. Their ideas and actions can create a positive change. The implementation of their ideas has already saved the bank hundreds of thousands of dollars—far more than was expected during the initial stages of the program. The best effect, though, is that employees no longer grouse about problems, but use the skills learned to make recommendations for changes in the system.

Knowledge *Isn't* Power

"Knowledge is power" is the old chestnut and perhaps the most misunderstood comment of our times. In fact, knowledge is just that, knowledge. It only becomes power when it is *correctly* applied to a situation.

Powerful people already intuitively understand that. The great masses don't (or they too would be powerful). What therefore is missing in their learning is how to bridge the gap between knowledge and action.

More to the point, as trainers and managers, we often make the mistake of presuming that a knowledge-based course will impact behavior. It probably won't. Educating the platform staff about the bank's roster of retail products will not mean that they sell more or even make the connection between the existing products and an announced need by the customer.

If the behavior sought is that the platform person should (1) inquire about the customer's financial status, (2) discuss the retail products that can fill a need, (3) suggest consideration of the product, and (4) follow up to determine the customer's interest, then those sets of behaviors must be specifically taught.

Learning by Doing

Behavioral learning is accomplished by doing. As obvious as it sounds, studies show that this concept is not something that everyone applies. We automatically revert to the learning patterns we were subjected to during our kindergarten through college experience, in which the teacher talked and the participant took notes.

Unfortunately, semantics is a problem. When we speak of training, we all throw education and development into the pile. For better clarity, in the rest of the chapter, we will use the following definitions (the rest of the book will generally revert to the word *training*, despite its shortcomings). *Education* is knowledge-based learning accomplished by mental study and memory retention. *Training* is the learning of specific tasks accomplished by comprehending and performing an activity that then becomes a pattern of behavior. *Development* is learning accomplished through insight and deduction, which then allows the learner to be more successful at complex, unspecified tasks.

Knowing versus Doing

The semantic confusion between education, training, and development occurs continuously, even among trainers. I recently consulted on a project at a large bank regarding training branch managers on credit issues.

As a result of having the branch managers more active in calling outside of the branch on small-business customers, they were more frequently asked about commercial banking needs. The branch managers were well drilled in retail products, but unfortunately completely unknowing in commercial banking. Accordingly, many responses were off-putting, or worse, erroneous.

The training area then devised a training program consisting of a lecture and discussion of the various types of commercial lending products that the bank made available, how they were priced, and so forth. The presentation, which would take a day, was generally hailed as an inexpensive yet superior solution to the problem. The program would allow the branch managers to knowledgeably discuss the commercial products available at the bank. In short, it was a course in credit literacy.

Unfortunately, one question was entirely sidestepped: precisely what were the branch managers expected to *do*? How were they expected to behave? If a customer says, "I need some more money for my business," was the branch manager then expected to respond by saying, "Well, we have working capital lines of credit, machine loans and leases, and accounts receivable financing. Which do you like? You think accounts receivable financing might be appropriate? OK. I will tell them that in the community lending area, and they'll be getting back to you."

Or was the branch manager expected to say, "Tell me something about your business. And we would like to see some financials. Ah, it seems that from what you said about your current financial situation and the status of the market situation, your needs are short term and seasonal. My first thought is that your best bet is a working capital line. What is available for collateral? Very interesting. I will relay your request for a line of credit for financing new inventory, along with our discussions about collateral and your financial statements to our community banking lending group. I can make no promises at this point, but it seems we have a good starting point. Either I or they will get back to you within the next few days with either a request for more data or a preliminary response."

The difference between the first and second scenarios involved considerably more complex issues than immediately apparent. First, the branch manager must not only know when a particular type of product is applicable, but also be aware of which circumstances will be bankable and which will not. With that, the branch manager can actually screen a customer, rather than send the troops on a goose chase. Also, the branch manager can ask intelligent questions, rather than being merely a relay point.

If screening and questioning are skills that the branch manager should employ, then merely being "credit literate" is inadequate. The training has to encompass enough role plays to allow the manager to act comfortably in a similar one. It simply cannot be done through a lecture format. The training needed is to go through all the basics of credit analysis as well as case situations to teach the necessary foundation and skills.

What's in It for Anyone

We are all prone to underplay the importance of precisely defining training outcomes. Partly because so many of us have been able to make the jump from "education" to "action," we assume that others can do so as well. We may learn the basics of credit (types of facilities, ratio analysis, and such) by rote, and eventually learn to apply it through on-the-job training.

Why should we assume others can or will do the same—

particularly if the training does not relate to a primary aspect of their job. In the case of the branch managers (see sidebar), is there a reward factor for making the effort to make the jump between learned knowledge and behavior? If the answer is no (other than some self-satisfaction), the inducement is even further diminished.

Banking has many parallel situations. I've attended training sessions for cash management products, which consisted of a cash management expert doing a run-down on the features of the products, using highly technical verbiage. The account officers sat there with glazed-over eyes, bored by the learning process, irrelevant to them since they have little inducement to use the information.

My Eyes Will Glaze Over, Unless . . .

The competitive atmosphere of banking today does not allow us the luxury of doing training that is only marginally effective. If we want to have people "grab the training and run" we need to meet certain basic criteria. The training must provide the learner with the precise skills necessary to perform the task, and be designed in a fashion that will induce the participant to want to learn.

Too much of our "training" still comes under the rubric of "education": it simply doesn't meet the criteria. That people *should* learn something doesn't mean they *will*. We are all tempted to be petulant with someone who sat in a classroom for seven hours and still can't do what was taught. "What were you doing? Sleeping?" However, the reason for the failure to learn is not entirely theirs. Trainers point out that adult learning is different from childhood learning. Adults learn when certain elements exist.[3]

- A need-to-know or reason for learning must be apparent. As a result, overview courses tend to bomb.
- Learning is not "it's own reward." Something else must be a motivator—such as the ability to perform better on the job.
- The information learned needs to be integrated as soon as possible.

- Adults prefer specific, straightforward, how-to courses that focus heavily on the applications of the learning to the problem.
- Adults need to feel confident that they will succeed in any behavioral change; otherwise, they will not risk trying it on the job where they can lose their self-esteem.
- Adults care about their losing their self-esteem in a classroom situation as much as they do in a job setting.

Comparing that rundown of needs to our own undergraduate educational experiences, it explains why most of us could barely stay awake in Chem I and forgot everything immediately after the final test was finished. For the same reasons, I also have forgotten everything I learned in the cash management systems lecture.

Competency-Based Training

Teaching employees "what they need to know exactly when they need to know it" falls under the general training rubric of competency-based training. It suggests that the employee's job is analyzed to determine the precise knowledge- and skill-based competencies that the job requires. A program is then designed to allow the employee to gain mastery of those competencies *prior* to having to function on the job.

It sounds simple—it *is* simple—but it's, well, tedious and time consuming. So the simple fact is that it is the most often overlooked part of training development.

"I want to do a job analysis," noted one outside consultant, "but most training directors don't want to be bothered. They just ask what programs we have, and, if the outline looks good, we just do it."

Exactly the Training We Needed

"I could have simply used an already prepackaged product," commented Liz Freeman, then a member of the training staff at National Westminster Bank USA. She was referring to the request from senior management to create a program for training negotiation skills to the bank's officer calling staff, "but I sensed that what was on the market would not fully meet our needs. In fact, at that time, I wasn't even sure what our needs were."

In the process of determining those needs, she discovered that management's own perceptions of good negotiation qualities were less than consistent. "They said a good negotiator needed sales, credit, and organizational skills, but nothing they said really translated well into a three-day program. So I knew my first job was to gain agreement on the definition of what a successful negotiator really is."

One thing that management did agree on was that good negotiators consistently met the expectations of the bank and the customer. "Thus, I knew to develop qualities that contributed as much towards a 'win/win' negotiation as towards consistency."

Freeman began by obtaining from management a list of individuals within the bank whom they considered to be either consistently successful or less consistently successful negotiators. After amassing 30 names of each type, she then tape-interviewed each person (on a "blind" basis) about their negotiation "war stories" and about their own perceived strengths and weaknesses.

At the end of the interview period, Freeman and her staff carefully reviewed each tape, noting the qualities and skills indicated and the ultimate outcome of the negotiation experiences. From that, she drew what appeared to be "winning" behaviors and practices and compared that to the original successful and unsuccessful listing.

> We began to see certain behavioral traits and qualities that stood out—ones that could not have been readily anticipated, much less articulated before the analysis. They seemed so logical, so "common sense," they were just ignored. Since some of the elements are unique to our bank, we then ran focus sessions with senior management to see how we could translate behavioral modes into tactical

moves that everyone could readily grasp and utilize. After that we surveyed internal people, managers, and customers for feedback on the selected attendees prior to the program.

The findings were ultimately translated into a three-day off-site program. "We consider our training successful if at any point we can stop the clock during the role-plays, and the participant can precisely identify where he or she is and where the negotiation will ultimately lead. Also, we had them identify tactics and develop a plan to apply their learned skills back to the job."

Follow-up includes doing a second survey within the year. "I already know the effort was worth it: it taught me to never begin training until you know the exact problem. Doing it any other way is nothing but a quick fix and a guarantee you'll be fixing the problem again six months later."

In skipping the analysis part, those training directors think they are getting off cheaply—at no additional cost and with a program delivered now, not later with several costly changes. The line managers rarely know better; they see their people getting the "necessary" training right away, so they are content.

As a result, a lot of education is passed off as training—programs in which the individual learns *about* a topic, but not how to apply it, much less master the related skills adequately to feel comfortable on the job. Just because the program covers, say, everything you ever wanted to know about residential mortgage financing, it doesn't mean that the employee will learn how to actually *do a deal*—no more than reading a dozen books about negotiation skills will ever transform the average person into Donald Trump.

The empowerment of an employee will only occur when the employee feels comfortable taking the responsibility for his or her actions. Any sense of impending failure will cause the individual to immediately retreat to the comfort zone of "don't ask me; I'm not responsible." Training programs should simply tell employees precisely what they need to know, show them to apply it, and make sure that they are comfortable doing it.

Line managers and training directors who think that they are saving a dime in not doing the necessary up-front analysis may end of ultimately wasting a dollar.

Of Course, Education Is Important!
Don't misunderstand me. I'm not suggesting and would never suggest that we dispense with education or an academic learning style (although a good case is made for it in *Educating America* by Jack Bowsher, former Head of Education and Training at IBM.)[4] Education is the foundation on which we live. In banking, the education process provides a critical framework on which to hang the training hat. Financial services is not an industry that is "intuitively obvious," as, say, the fast-food industry is. People entering the bank cannot readily figure out its organization, the regulatory parameters, the market structure, the role of various types of institutions. In fact, they can figure out almost nothing about how it functions. All *that* has to be learned—and arguably is learned best in an academic learning approach.

Absolutely, all employees must begin with a solid base of knowledge (see curricula designs at the end of the book). Principles of banking, accounting basics, overview of the financial markets, and a series of other courses are all deemed critical and should be taught with a special vigor to make sure the proper foundations are laid. But *education should not be substituted for training*. Education is the start of the road—not the end.

Indeed, education need not be limited to industry-related information. All of us readily send ourselves and our children to colleges to learn in depth about topics that will *not* be directly applicable to our day-to-day functioning—because we are instinctively aware of the value of learning about various disciplines in broadening our ability to think. So, too, *training should not be substituted for education*. If a bank wants its employees to be a body of thinkers as well as doers, it must encourage and support advanced education independent of training.

Nor should advanced education only be a privilege of those at the highest level. It can be integrated into lower levels in an informal and less expensive manner. The operations areas are typically the ones to receive the least attention, education-wise, yet are required to offer at least as much creativity in developing job systems as other areas are in theirs. John Sponksi, Corporate Executive Officer at Sovran Financial Corporation, is one who is not willing to relegate the operations employees under his command to only competency-related training. He noted:

> We are constantly attempting to orient and reorient people to their job position. As managers we often have learned many superior concepts during our lifetime, but over time we lose the perspective and tend to deviate from the learned idea. Continuous education aids substantially in keeping the focus.
>
> Our managers have a training and education program that must be accomplished within a three-year period. But we leave it up to the individuals to design their own learning program. If they wish to take a course in great books, we will accept that. In fact, we welcome anything that promotes and stimulates thinking.

Having Fun at Norwest

The ideal situation occurs when the employees themselves see the need for more learning and reach out to embrace when it becomes available. It will most often occur during a time of change, when the organizational and cultural structure is unfrozen, causing a realignment of needs and expectations. Norwest Corporation in Minneapolis is a case in point.

"Norwest was having a rather rough time," noted Ken Murray, Executive Vice President in the Community Banking area, speaking of the early 80s. It was during that time Norwest had experienced extensive loan losses as well as a disastrous fire that gutted its headquarters business. "It was apparent to everyone that we needed to change and a new awareness that the process of change would always be with us."

Norwest University was created when it became evident that the employees wanted something to help them deal with change. Added Murray:

> It was founded around a table. You see, in 1986, we set about completely restructuring the community bank. Every job title and function was revised, with perhaps the sole exception of teller.
>
> Now that is a tall order for most employees—finding out that they are not going to be doing the same thing as they had anticipated. Not that the new jobs were so radically different; it's just the process of change that's so very daunting.

Process Not Project

Norwest wanted to give them the tools and confidence that they needed to embrace their new functions. They also wanted to convey the idea that doing their jobs better is not something that should be undertaken as a project that ends in six months, but rather an ongoing process. So they decided to use the concept of a university, which implies continuous learning, rather than a one-shot deal.

They introduced it through "jump starting." It was kicked off with great fanfare, culminating in having the managing officers (primarily the subsidiary bank presidents) at a three-day conference. Norwest included a lot of hoopla, dinners, and entertainment—something that they have discovered to be very successful in building up interest and breaking down resistance.

The Bank Like It Never Was

"It was more than rah-rah," noted Murray.

> Specifically, they were there for a workshop on Financial Modeling, which deals with setting and attaining goals. They would now be responsible for doing this—something that had always been handed to them from on high before. Just telling them to start doing something on such-and-such date would not have been enough. We initially had to "sell the vision" one-on-one. We knew that they could do it themselves, but *they* had to feel the same way. The workshop provided them with the tools to accomplish it as well as the confidence to attack it.

Of course, most everyone would have preferred it "the old way," where we just tell them what to do. As one of the older bankers commented about the others, "They remember the bank like it never was and wish it were that way again." Fortunately, though, memories are short. Once they became comfortable with the new ways—with the help of the training—they began to buy into the process.

In the end it was a "howling" success. Norwest achieved its primary end: have the managing officers pick up the reins that Norwest management was passing them and have them be so impressed by the Norwest University concept that they would "sell" it back at the offices. But to the bank's great amazement, the success was even more spectacular in terms of the financial goals that they had set for themselves.

"They just blew right past them," Murray noted with great pride.

They learned more than we had anticipated—that they could make their own decisions about the future and they could impact the outcome. It motivated them to do more, and, just as important to us, to have their subordinates become enthused in the process. Otherwise, Norwest U would have not truly succeeded in helping people find the tools to deal with the changes they were going through—and undoubtedly will be going though as banking continues to evolve. It would have been just another training center.

No More "Profit by Accident"
"It was the management by objectives, combined with performance-appraisal system that changed the behavior of the employees," noted Arthur Campbell, EVP in the Community Banking Division of the National State Bank mentioned at the beginning of this chapter.

Before that, we had "profit by accident." Our branch system was about to take a full frontal attack in the light of deregulation, yet that had no plan of how to survive it. We helped them determine their goals and then gave them the measurement systems to analyze it.

In particular, the performance appraisals gave them the ability to see what they could achieve if they tried and what needed to be done if they fell short. It provides them with a sense of being in charge.

It tells us what we need to do to help them. But rather than just pulling together a program that addressed a particular shortcoming, we fully dissected each set of tasks that formed the whole cloth of the job. Then, based on that, we designed our training to match the function.

We then had a combination of the employee-manager perceiving the need for the training and the training being made specifically relevant to their job. We thus were able to avoid training for training's sake. The impact has been extremely gratifying

Such competency analysis is becoming more common in determining training issues. "We reward managers for breeding new managers within their area. We discourage territorial disputes."

SWITCH RATHER THAN FIGHT

In an era of change, banks need take-charge workers. Fear of failure prevents some people from making that switch from followers to doers, and they would often rather fight the system than accept the challenge. Even highly motivated employees need education and training in order to be able to comfortably make the changeover. Clear job descriptions are a vital part of effective training. Competency-based training must teach employees the precise skills needed to perform the required task and must be designed to make the participant want to learn.

Arthur Campbell may have given the best summary of the situation: "Management's role is to give people a reason to come to work every day. It is up to us to create the environment in which employees can succeed. If the plan is reasonable, and we provide them with the right tools, bottom-line success is bound to follow."

REFERENCES

1. Korsvik, William J., and Hervey A. Jaris. *The New Frontier in Bank Strategy*. Homewood, Ill.: Dow Jones-Irwin, 1990.
2. Ibid.
3. Zemke, Ron and Susan. "30 Things We Know for Sure about Adult Learning." *Training*, July 1988.
4. Bowsher, Jack. *Educating America*. New York: John Wiley & Sons, 1989.

CHAPTER 5

CAREER DEVELOPMENT— DESIGNING A YELLOW BRICK ROAD

"If today's managements think that the labor surplus they grew up with will continue, they're in for a shock."
—*Clifford Ehrlick, Senior Vice President, Marriott.*

"Tomorrow's illiterate will not be the man who can't read; he will be the man who has not learned how to learn."
—*Herbert Geruoy, consultant.*

If the baby-boom population is causing a glut in the available middle-level managerial candidates, a contrary demographic phenomenon will impact the new hires and the lower-grade positions—the baby bust.

In 1985, the first of the baby busters began to enter the employment market after college graduation. Since the low-level-of-births period lasted for 16 years, ending in 1980 when the so-called echo boom began, the 90s will definitely bring years of declining workforce. We should expect 25% fewer people available during the next decade in the 15-to-25-year-old category, comparing the peak of the boom to the trough of the bust.[1] And when we combine that problem with a low unemployment scenario, the previously simple task of finding qualified workers doubles in complexity.

NO PROBLEM—WE'LL JUST LOOK LONGER AND HARDER

It's easy to be indifferent about demographic data. Up till now, it's been all talk—with little evident effect outside of urban areas. Besides, superior selection and assessment tools abound at many banks, enabling them to weed out less qualified candidates prior to hire. In any case, most banks are not looking for a "highly skilled laborer" or someone with unique abilities for the majority of positions they need to fill. Instead, they merely require someone adequately educated, socially mature, reasonably capable of turning a problem into action, and who has the time and energy to devote to the job.

Sounds Simple, Doesn't It

In order to be able to select people with those characteristics the workforce must be relatively homogeneous. But it isn't. Not only is there shrinkage, but the mix is changing as well. In addition, the population is being drawn apart by various forces that will have a wide impact either on their ability to master the job or to fully devote their time or energy to it. Note the estimated statistics about the population as of 1990:[2]

- 23 million cannot read at the 4th-grade level.
- 90% of the workforce is from dual-income families.
- There are more second marriages than first.
- There are more single-parent households than dual ones.
- 1 out of 16 is on drugs or alcohol.
- 25% of people over 40 provide care for their parents.

The impact these demographic changes will have on the organization cannot be overstated. The workforce will be less flexible, more burdened with responsibility, and more likely to be absent or quit rather than fit their lifestyle to their job. And the situation is not likely to reverse even after the baby-bust period pushes through and new resurgence in the entering workforce begins. Note these even more startling statistics.

Of the four million children entering the first grade in 1988:

- 1 in 2 has a mother in the workforce.
- 1 in 3 is a latchkey child.

- 1 in 4 lives in poverty.
- 1 in 5 is at risk of becoming a teenage parent.
- 1 in 7 will not complete high school.

No wonder personnel managers who have the task of recruiting the teller positions, traditionally the most difficult to fill, have been screaming. The averages now show that only 1 out of 25 applicants in big-city situations meet minimum standards, and stories of 1 out of 50 plus are becoming more commonplace. The banks from the suburbs and smaller cities report a better ratio of acceptable candidates, but find far fewer candidates. Some banks have even resorted to busing people in from nearby urban areas.

Simple to Say; Hard to Do

Banks determined to deal with the situation realize that their best defense against an overly diverse workforce is to be able to

- Obtain the best.
- Retain the best.

Hardly a new prescription for human resources management, you say. Our bank has been following that dictate for years. But has it? Has there truly been a push to reduce the bank's voluntary turnover among the better performers, or has it only been a platitude of the bank's—more a slogan on the wall than a concerted effort?

Turnover has always been a plaguing problem, but most non-HR professionals tend to think in terms of the *bother* of losing employees—time and productivity lost—rather than in terms of a hard dollars-and-cents cost. However, a bottom-line figure can be calculated (albeit imprecise), and in doing so, give a much clearer picture of the impact of employee loss. In determining the marginal costs of each "turnover," the following data should be taken into account:

Cost of a New Hire:
Communication of job availability.
Time involved in interview process.

Testing time and materials cost.
Time in staff decision meeting.
Travel and moving expense.
Preemployment dissemination of information.
In-house medical examinations.
Informational literature.
Orientation programs.
Formal training programs.
Time involved in on-the-job training.

Plus the cost of a separation of the old employee:

Interviewer's time.
Employee's time.
Administration costs.
Separation pay (if any).
Unemployment tax (if any).

In general, the cost of replacing an exiting employee is estimated in the range of $5,000 to $10,000. If 100 people a year leave, the cost can easily run $500,000 to $1,000,000. *And these costs presume that the entering individual will be as productive as the exiting one.* In the 90s, with the dual situation of cost-consciousness and declining resources, passive approaches to human resources management will no longer fly.

Retaining: Not by "Bread" Alone

Salary is and has been the most traditional way to attract and retain employees. Pay them more than the competition, and they will more readily join the bank and stay with you— if for no other reason than that they cannot match their compensation elsewhere. However, such a practice eventually turns into a greater fool's game: it only serves to force up pay scales of the neighboring banks. In times of deteriorating margins, this is the least cost-effective approach to solving a turnover problem. (Paying selectively for performance is another, better-considered option and is dealt with separately in the chapter on Motivational Techniques.)

In any case, most people want more from their jobs than

money. If we talk in terms of Maslow's needs hierarchy, once the basic psychological and security needs are met, the individual starts reaching out for peer approval, self-esteem, and ultimately self-actualization. In short, people need to feel a sense of accomplishment and respect. Pay is one form that companies use to provide respect, but since it is so institutionalized, it does not translate to *real* respect, but rather an obligation on the part of the employer.

The Hay Group, a well-known human resource management consulting organization, recently completed a study regarding new employee attitudes towards work. Their findings indicated that there is a growing lack of commitment in the U.S. workforce based on employees' beliefs that their work is not being properly rewarded.

Some of the statistics gathered in a national poll of over 2,000 companies are startling. Only about half of the middle managers and a third of the professional staff feel their pay is linked to their performance, and fewer than 4 in 10 managers and 25% of the professional staff think they have a chance to advance within the organization. Only 1 in 4 employees believes the company is doing a good job of retaining high-quality employees, and only half of middle managers and even fewer of the other employees say the company treats them with respect.

The Hay Group's conclusion is that companies wishing to gain and retain the best employees will have to take definitive actions to do so and not rely on chance to bring them in and inertia to keep them there.

R-e-s-p-e-c-t

Real respect is something else—although much more difficult to quantify. As in the 60s song of the same name, it can be spelled more easily than it can be defined. According to the data presented in an article in *Fortune* magazine[3] in 1983, 40% of the hourly employees felt they were being treated with respect and consideration. By 1988, that number declined to 30%. Although hourly workers are traditionally the most disaffected group, the drop in the sense of respect is also apparent in professional workers—from 50% to 42%, and most surprising in managers—from 63% to 54%.

Generally, experts agree that respect encompasses a better level of management sincerity about the well-being of the employees, a good system of communication between managers and employees, and increased recognition of the employees' contributions, needs, and potential. Do banks stand out from the rest of industrial United States in the degree that they offer these elements of respect? Not according to Bank Administration Institute studies.

BAI, through its substantial data collected over many years from employee-attitude surveys conducted at banks of all sizes, finds that

1. Approximately 57% of the employees believe "that top management has a sincere interest in employee satisfaction."
2. Only about 50% of the employees are "satisfied with information from management about the bank." Even fewer, about 40%, feel that "communications on the reasons for changes in bank policy are thorough."
3. Only 43% felt "satisfied" with their "opportunity to get a better job in the bank." Just half of the employees believed that "the most qualified people are selected for promotion." Approximately 43% indicated that they were not "given a real opportunity to improve (their) skills in the bank." The same number did not feel they were given adequate "information available on bank job opportunities."

Reality or Rationalization?

Despite the value of employee-attitude surveys, frequently managers discount the data by rationalizing that the degree of employee satisfaction is generally irrelevant, because, to their mind, job satisfaction will vary substantially depending on external factors. For instance, during the recession in the early 80s, the degree of "happiness" on the job was high, because individuals were "happy" just to have jobs. During periods of full employment and boom, detractors point out, employees are less worried about expressing their "sensitivity" to issues of trust and respect. In short, detractors argue, people don't know when they are well off and when they are not—so why feed into their mistaken perceptions.

Possibly true. But since people make decisions based on their perceptions rather than on reality, managers must still meet the employees' perception of their needs. Otherwise, the employee is either producing below optimal levels, or worse, has quit—both to the detriment of the bank.

Thus, it is to the bank's advantage to always be creating the conditions that foster opportunities for self-expressions, self-assertion, self-respect, and self-advancement, which are also consistent with high productivity and job loyalty. If it doesn't, the bank will be subject to the vagaries of the external world, not the least of which will be the changing configuration of the workforce.

Obtaining the Best

If an individual's sense of self-respect and sense of achievement are compelling needs, then appealing to that makes logical sense as a method for attracting and retaining employees. Individuals would reasonably want:

1. Opportunity to determine their aptitude and capability.
2. Opportunity to develop into a superior or "world-class" professional.
3. Opportunities for advancement.
4. Opportunity to determine future course of career (whether it be advancement or lateral move).
5. Opportunity to contribute outside the immediate parameters of the job.

In short, the employee wants to know: What is my potential? Where can I go with it? Who will make the decision? What else can I offer? The sum of the responses constitutes the development of a career path.

The Well-Respected Teller

National Westminster Bancorp, located in New York, has had excellent success in reducing its teller turnover rates in a area of the country where annual turnover can run at over 70%. "We treated the problem systematically, not just superficially," noted Edward F. McDougal, Jr., Executive Vice President and head of Human Resources. The bank addressed every aspect of a teller's experience with the bank—recruitment, selection, training, development opportunities, and even auditing procedures.

The bank created "teller action teams," which came up with several ideas to address the problem. "Our first line of attack was in recruiting. We deal directly with high schools, taking in summer interns and generally making ourselves known. We even invite the school's faculty to our managerial training to develop better relationships," noted McDougal.

They also improved their selection techniques to test more carefully for the characteristics they considered critical. For instance, they used to rely on skills testing alone, but have since minimized testing on addition and division, which is now done by calculators, replacing them with other tests such as visual number-and letter-matching. In addition, increased emphasis is placed on testing for personal values and attitudes, which weeds out those who have a hard time fitting into the organization.

Most important is the bank's own attitude towards their tellers. They give more than lip service to the notion that the teller is the most important person to the bank's image. McDougal continued, "We can't make being a teller a dead-end position while expecting tellers to really go all out for us. If you say that the teller is the most important position in the bank—then you must follow up on your philosophy."

The bank does that in several ways. One is through thorough training: each teller has one week of classroom training followed by two weeks of simulation before being considered "window ready." In addition, a trained on-the-job mentor is assigned to each teller after he or she has returned from the formal training. Tellers also have full access to the bank's career development opportunities that arise as part of the performance-appraisal function—they can move into sales, operations, or possibly the branch-management development program.

The thrust of the program is recognition. The bank even has "teller recognition days" in which the branches do something special for the tellers. They usually hold dinners and cocktail parties. One branch manager even cooked dinner for all of them. Once the bank posed the question, Why should anyone who is not respected for their contribution stay in their jobs? they were halfway to finding a solution.

Career Development—Level One

For all of you saying, "Oh, that! Sure, we do career development," let's make certain that we both have the same level of definitions of the term.

Level I career-development system is most commonly related to a specific or "normal" progress. For instance, a new hire would expect to hear, "First, you'll be a teller; then two years later, a customer service representative (CSR); and then in two years, an assistant branch manager. However, we should tell you that like the 'merit raise,' it is automatically offered if you meet a minimum acceptable standard. And your opportunities for advancement are frankly rather limited outside the specific area of hire. We hire you for this area, and we want to keep you here."

The training offered will support the career-development structure. The training can be formal or informal, but nonetheless intent upon having retail banking personnel focused on their future potential within the area as well as on their current capacity. A typical career-development program is at BayBanks (in Massachusetts), which began by designing a Model Branch Program in 1981.

They started with five levels: CSR, Sales and Service Representative I, Sales and Service Representative II, Product Specialist, and Customer Service Manager. BayBanks has since expanded the CSR level by an additional two, Lead

CSR and In-Branch Trainers, who do the on-the-job teller training after the tellers have completed classroom training. The job requirements were expanded in order to have certain individuals focusing on special branch needs. It also served to provide the CSRs with more diversity in their function.

At BayBanks, everyone on the platform is exposed to the broad and the narrow aspects of their job. At each major level, the employees must fulfill certain training requirements that lead to certification. Being certified at one level allows them to progress to the next level. Product knowledge, sales skills, and service training are offered at all levels.

In addition to the standard programs, lead CSRs receive additional training (in the form of a self-study written workbook), which covers the functioning of the operations department. BayBanks also offers additional training in communication skills at the expanded CSR levels and the managerial levels because they have more personal interaction with others, particularly in team building and coaching.

Career Development—Level Two

A more sophisticated career-development system provides a much greater range of possibilities within the organization. A *level II career-development system* encourages movement, both lateral and upward, both in and outside of the job family. Assessment tools are made available to help employees determine their aptitude for other areas. An employee can move out of a job classification altogether into another one without penalty for leaving the other position. The bank also maintains a "job-posting system," which specifies the bank's job opportunities and the requirements, thereby allowing those with the right background to be able to apply directly for a position without the supervisors' or managers' permission.

Back to School
Seafirst Bank in Seattle has created a career development system that provides an array of options at nearly all levels

of employment. The cornerstone of the system is the Seafirst College, which was formed in 1987 with assistance from the University of Washington, to help employees go through the transition from a bank under stress from a recent reorganization to a more dynamic sales-oriented institution. Its immediate function was to provide training for the retail platform staff (see chapter on empowerment for more details), but is being slowly expanded to commercial and corporate training.

"The college concept helped forge a sense of urgency about messages we wanted to deliver to our employees," noted Luke Helms, President of Seafirst. First, Seafirst wanted to impress upon them that they had a different type organization that required more responsive individuals as employees. The college would be there to help them gain the skills necessary to fit the new mold.

But, as important as developing skills for their current position is the emphasis placed on career development. The second message delivered by the bank is that employees who perform well will be provided with opportunities to advance along a career path *they help design*. Career opportunities are in and of themselves the reward for good performance.

To get the employees to start thinking in terms of their future, the bank provided the employees with smart-looking literature (Helms was involved in the design concepts) about Seafirst College, which introduces them to

- The course work required for different positions.
- Possible career pathing alternatives (see Figure 5–1).
- A career plan form jointly filled out by the employee and the employee's manager, noting short- and long-term career goals and the type of training the employee will need to achieve these goals.
- A training plan that supports the intended career goals.

The impact cannot be underestimated. Through a review of the literature, employees can easily envision future employment at a higher level in their own department or in a completely different area of the bank. It's far more than vague promises that "if you do well, you'll get ahead."

FIGURE 5–1 Sample Career Paths for Personal and Business Bankers at Seafirst Bank

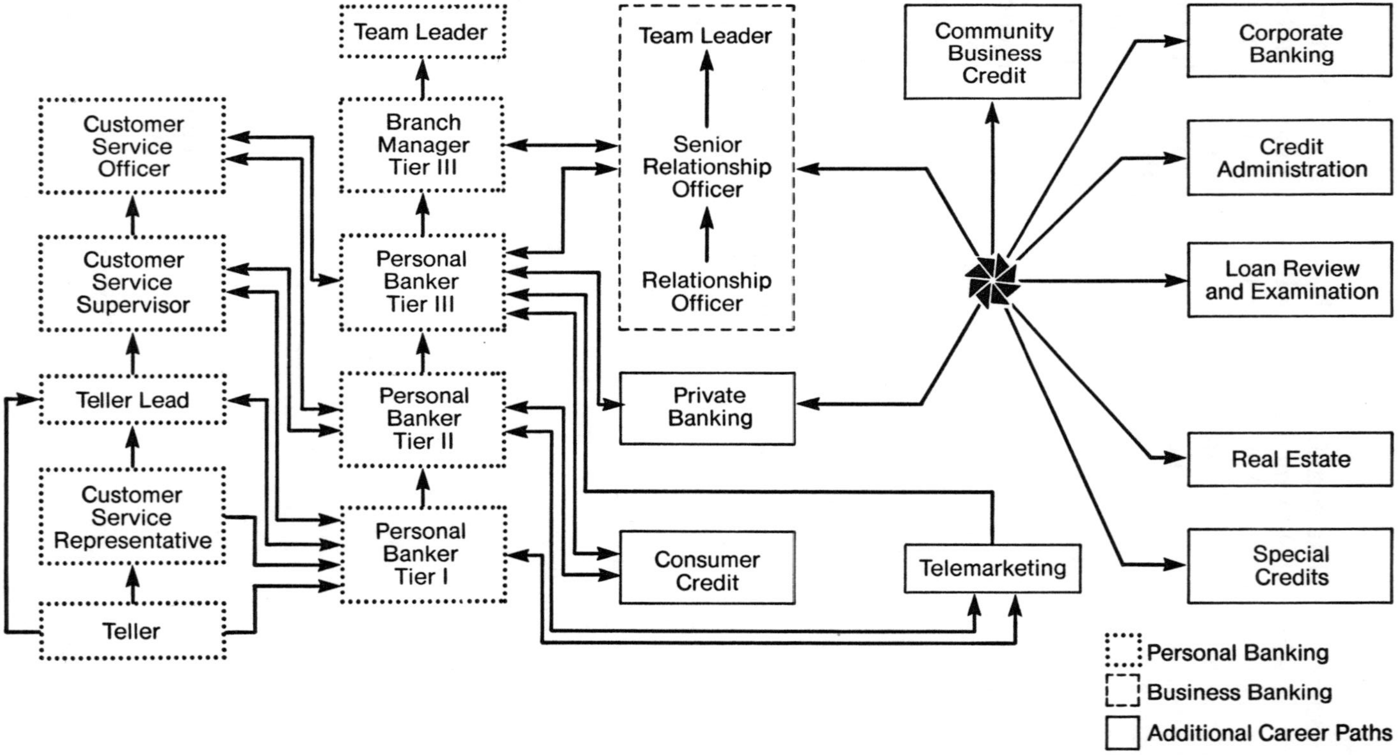

Source: Seafirst Bank

Added Helms,

> We respect the employees. But there is nothing automatic. They have to earn the respect. Just because they want in, they don't get in. I personally review every candidate for the college. They are even videotaped so that I can see their personal behavioral style. We deliberately make it competitive so that they can stretch themselves and reach for their personal best. Otherwise, the college is just another training medium.

Career Development Is a Partnership

Seeing a picture in a brochure is one thing, but it takes three groups working jointly to effectively create a solid career-development system:

- *The managers*, who can provide objective insight into the individual's career potential.
- *The human resources area*, which can give direction and the training necessary to effect the change.
- *The employees themselves*, who must take charge of their own development efforts.

The last group is the most important. In most all banks which offer career development opportunities, it is a self-directed function. The responsibility lies on the shoulder of the individual to pursue opportunity. If initiative is not taken by the employees themselves, nothing else will occur. For instance, Seafirst requires the employee to fill out their career-plan form and submit it to the manager. The manager does not require it from the employee.

As one human resources manager noted,

> We're willing to lead the horses to the water—but that's all that we intend to do. If they want to drink, fine. If not, also fine. But we will not define an upward and outward path for them. We tried that, and it led to too many problems. Sometimes they really didn't want to move. Other times, we couldn't make good on our own recommendations. Besides, we want to promote those who are self-starters, not the ones you have to lead around.

To bring the message home to the employee, many banks run training programs on how to optimize career-development opportunities. Most emphasize that the responsibility for career improvement lies with the individual. Most courses outline a strategy for designing a reasonable development course, for building up the appropriate credentials, and for identifying options vis-à-vis current and future managers. The individual generally gains a better sense of self: both in terms of current and potential capacity and the ability to chart one's own course.

The Role of the Manager: Don't Give Me the Rejects
Without the enthusiastic support of the managers and supervisors, the developmental concept would soon fall apart. Their role is pivotal—they've got to be willing to:

- Provide objective input as to the employee's potential capabilities.
- Review the developmental data with the employee at the appropriate time.
- Take steps to insure employee transfers when openings occur.
- Encourage employees to use any assessment tools and/or counseling centers.

Actually, many managers intensely dislike the concept. "I know what will happen," commented one operations department manager when the idea was suggested. "It's a guaranteed event. I will lose all my good people, and then, to fill the empty slots, I get everyone else's rejects." As in all generalizations, there is a germ of truth: advanced career development and job posting do leave less exciting departments exposed to attrition (although it's worth the manager's time to determine what can be improved to make the department more exciting).

Not only is a department manager's probability of losing good employees increased, but maintaining a developmental system requires additional managerial enthusiasm and effort. Much relies on the supervisor's or manager's willingness to become part of the process. Uncooperative managers are not just expressing a lack of desire to do the necessary evaluation work (although who needs more work?); they are also concerned about the immediate impact on their department. "Heads, you win; tails, I lose" is real fear. Who can blame them for this attitude? Managers are not generally recognized or rewarded for their long-term development efforts, yet they are penalized when productivity falls due to personnel rearrangements.

Some Ways to Motivate Managers to Participate

Managers will participate in employee-development programs if they are designed with the managers' needs in mind. Some tips to do that are:

• *Make it easy for them.* If you want to foster an atmosphere that stimulates employee development, you have to make it easy for the managers. The forms and systems maintenance should be minimal and easy to do, not burdensome for the manager. "The last thing you want to do," commented McDougal, "is create a system that is really a monument to Human Resources. It's a formula for failure."

• *Reward supervisors and managers for their developmental efforts.* At minimum, the efforts should be commented on in the supervisors' performance appraisal. More effective would be an award or commendation based on a simple tracking system—for instance, for the number of employees who were able to transfer into a position at least one job grade higher.

• *Show supervisors and managers how the efforts can directly benefit their own department's productivity.* Most managers can see productivity decline when someone *leaves.* What is less evident is the overall lower productivity resulting from low employee morale. The manager *perceives* a career-development program will only generate more turnover. In fact, it can lead to *greater productivity, despite the turnover.*

• *Use the stick as well as the carrot. Provide the employees with the power to assess their managers.* The assessment of the management can be done through commentary on the performance appraisal forms and through anonymous surveys of the employees. Also, maintain an "open door" personnel practice, which provides employees with the right to speak to their managers' superior, if they feel unsatisfied with the efforts of their own manager.

• *Give the employees the right to leave the department after a certain period of time, if they so choose.* Employees can then vote with their feet if they feel stymied or otherwise frustrated with their attempts at career advancement. The manager is then forced to deal with the reasons for the level of turnover and come to grips with a need to improve employee relationships.

If all managers are willing to support career development, then a viable data management system can be created. The managers with weak candidates will not be solely interested in pushing them out; those with strong candidates will not thwart growth. That's because they will realize that doing so amounts to a zero sum game: only the low-performance people will be moved out, leaving the high performers without any access to advancement. Therefore, no one will win, and eventually the game will be stopped. But if those who are better suited to other positions are allowed to pursue their potential in another department, then the receiving department wins, and the department that gave up the employee has as much expectation that they will be able to get a candidate who wants to work there. Without a strong participative effort from managers, the whole effort is wasted from the start.

Career Development Is Not Performance Management

It's easy to confuse *performance* management with *development* management. Supervisors and managers often believe that because they've given their employees a performance appraisal (which usually leads to the discussion of next year's goals) that they've addressed "where do we go from here." Not true. Performance appraisals are aimed at discussing strengths and shortfalls in current performance. They are "here and now." They rarely lead to focusing on the future.

Besides, many managers have typically been reluctant to expand on what is already an uncomfortable experience (well, who can blame them?). They feel that they are in "deep water" in trying to evaluate and relay information regarding the vagaries of their subordinates' work habits and capabilities. Indeed, they often don't believe it's really their responsibility. Many managers complain of having to "waste a day" going to "those human resources" training sessions on topics such as Doing Effective Performance Appraisals to learn how to do "human resources work." After all, what do those programs have to do with their main job—managing the work flow? (See Chapter 2 on management for further comment.)

The Role of the Line Manager

It's easiest to point to the human resources department as responsible for gathering and collecting data about employees. It did make the most sense when the necessary data was limited to grade, age, years in department, education, and so forth.

Black and white isn't enough anymore. But in order to add the gray tones, management must be willing to take up the slack—either in the form of additional testing facilities or in the form of additional attention paid by line managers and supervisors, and preferably both.

What managers can provide in terms of input can often be directly lifted from a performance-appraisal form, such as:

1. Employee's observed performance relative to the various job requirements (e.g., good interpersonal skills, poor analytical skills).
2. The perceived shortfall in the employee's potential that can be corrected (e.g., poor writing skills).
3. The perceived shortfall in the employee's performance that probably cannot be corrected (e.g., illogical deductions on a credit analysis).
4. Employee's work habits and attitudes.

Equally informative, and definitely more objective data can be drawn from assessment testing done by those not directly working with the employee. Such data could also serve to support the bank's position on grievances raised by employees who feel that they are being unfairly treated.

Four Steps to Partnership

New York Telephone has recently introduced a four-step process designed to develop its employees. Its basic philosophy is that career development is a partnership between the manager and the individual and that the process must be moved forward by both parties: neither party is solely responsible for the career movement of the employee.

The first step is the annual development review, in which the manager and the subordinate jointly discuss the development plan. Among the available reference materials is a Job Outlook, which summarizes the opportunities for lateral movement likely to occur within the next 12 months.

NY Tel is aware that managers tend to block their subordinates' moving out of their departments (for all the reasons discussed above). To prevent that from occurring, the company established a "Releasability Policy," which states that any management employee who has worked in the same salary grade for three years is releasable to a lateral assignment, despite the supervisor's protestations.

Step two is on-the-job development, which is determined by the activities agreed to in the development plan. Step three is managerial accountability, which addresses the role of the managers and how they will be held accountable for the development of the subordinate. Both the manager and the subordinate must complete a confidential form that asks questions regarding the manager's involvement in employee development.

The managers' supervisors are also apprised of the findings on an anonymous basis. That data is the basis for step four, in which both the managers and the subordinates are appraised formally for their efforts in career development—both as managers and as individuals.[4]

Using Assessment Tests

In our educational experience, we're so indoctrinated to the importance of the standard IQ test as the measure of intelligence that those who have not been exposed to other testing instruments will be surprised by the variety available. Best of all, these tests do not presume that an individual's IQ is the sole judge, or even any judge, of that individual's ability to perform well in a function. (If IQ were the sole factor for determining professional success, all the members of MENSA, who are required to have IQs of at least 140 to apply, would be millionaires, which is hardly the case.)

Different assessment instruments are available for testing different functional abilities. Some are even available that require no reading skills at all. Typical ones are mostly used in a pencil-and-pen format to test individuals in their ability to:

- Apply critical thinking.
- Solve problems.
- Understand and follow oral directions.
- Do accurate intellectual work.
- Understand quantitative relationships.

Other tests are related to the personality and temperament of an employee to determine whether he or she would be suited for a particular function: Not only do they characterize by general personality style, but some also seek such traits as assertiveness, emotional stability, shrewdness, self-sufficiency, imagination, neuroticism, and the like. Yet other tests seek out the individual's own perceived areas of vocational interests—in a "know-thyself-better" approach. Tests can even be devised to compare an individual's profile with a standard profile of the bank's own managers.

Without a doubt, any assessment and development system requires amassing and monitoring data. Turning the data into something that will benefit the organization, and not become a "monument to human resources," is the ultimate goal. Better management of current performance is the expected outcome of well-managed performance appraisals. Similarly, better use of employees' talents and capabilities, as well as a steady level of current productivity, is the expected outcome of well-managed development systems.

The Role of Human Resources

Human resources must provide the cement that binds the elements together. At the least, it should provide for current job posting and the maintenance of the development data. Since both are passive activities, the HR department must not automatically assume that these activities are being used correctly and are not being foiled by the less enlightened managers.

• *Current posting and position descriptions*: These provide all employees with the knowledge about other positions available within the bank. However, some banks require that the current manager be informed if the employee applies for another position; others don't. Fortunately, gone are the days when a visit to another department's manager, if discovered by the current manager before the transfer was finalized, would spell certain job termination, as this author has frequently witnessed. (A desire to work in another department should not be considered an act of treason.)

However, managers can still foil transfers by casual comments and desultory remarks to the potential managers. HR should check to see that every department is contributing its fair share of transferees through the posting system.

• *Maintenance of performance appraisal and development data:* Unfortunately, the data assembled by the manager is his or her observations about the employee—and naturally subjective in nature. The HR area may attempt only to generate relevant and objective data, but if the manager abhors the employee's personal style, chances are this abhorrence will cloud every other aspect. Of course, employees have an opportunity to respond to the commentary about them, which provides another source of input into the data bank.

However, we all know that a manager on the offensive will hold more weight than an employee on the defensive.

Seafirst has devised relatively simple forms, available in every Seafirst College catalog, which provide a maximum of data with a minimum of paperwork. See Figure 5–2 and Figure 5–3.

Does the System Need More? Ask the Employee

Even banks that believe they are doing a superior job in encouraging career development may find that their efforts still need improvement. Seafirst Bank had felt that it had made an excellent attempt at providing career opportunities until it read one of the employee general-opinion surveys. One of the areas they felt that the bank had fallen short was "in providing adequate opportunity for advancement."

Seafirst decided to dig deeper into the problem. It convened a focus group on career development. VPs, down to data clerks, were selected to attend, with Dick Cooley, the CEO, and Luke Helms, the President, occasionally visiting the proceedings. To sum, the group expressed the desire for:

- More career-focused training.
- Better communication regarding career development resources.
- More information about composition of various jobs and positions around the bank.
- Structured career guidance and counseling.
- More participative goal development.
- More tools for self-assessment.
- Innovative motivational systems.

"Even though we were proud of our activities to date, we realized we still weren't living up to expectations," noted Barbara Phillips, Manager of Corporate Training and Development. "But it seems that the more oppor-

FIGURE 5–2
Career Plan

Name _____   Date _____
    First   Last   Interoffice phone number _____
Current position _____   Interoffice mailing address _____

In the ✔ column, check skills or knowledge necessary to perform the job.
In the C,N column, designate your current level of expertise with the skill or knowledge.

C = Competent You are skilled in this area.
N = Needs development You need further development in this area.

	Current Position		Short-Term Career Goal(s) (1–2 years) A		B		Long-Term Career Goal(s) (5 years) A		B	
	✔	C,N	✔	C,N	✔	C,N	✔	C,N	✔	C,N
Sales/Referrals										
Communications										
Written										
Verbal										
Interviewing										
Presentation										
Interpersonal										
Marketing										
Product knowledge										
Liabilities										
Credit										
Investments										
Retirement										
Insurance										
People management										
Administration										
Time management										
Planning										
Franchise management										
Credit										
Consumer										
Community business										
Business banking										
Credit policy										
Credit submission										
Credit adm.										
Negotiations										
Problem loans										
Cash flow analysis										
Pricing/rate adm.										
Asset based lending										
Legal aspects										
Fin. state. analysis										
Spec. credit facilities										
Technical										
Teller										
Operations										
Electronic tools										
Accounting/Finance										
Other										

_____   _____   _____
Your signature   Manager's signature   Date

Source: Seafirst Bank.

FIGURE 5-3
Training Plan

Name _____ Date _____
First   Last
Current position _____ Social security # _____
Interoffice phone number _____ Interoffice mailing address _____

PAST TRAINING

Formal schooling/Degrees/Certificates/Licenses

Name of School	Area of Study	Location	Dates	Degree/Cert/License

Previous courses

Course Name	Offered by	Completion Date

Attach an additional sheet if necessary.

FUTURE TRAINING

A. Prerequisite courses identified in preceding levels

_____   _____
_____   _____
_____   _____
_____   _____

B. Required core courses needed for certification in present position

_____   _____
_____   _____
_____   _____
_____   _____

C. Elective courses

_____   _____
_____   _____
_____   _____
_____   _____

D. Core courses for future career development

_____   _____
_____   _____
_____   _____
_____   _____

Manager's approval _____
Team leader approval if necessary for waiver/test _____

Source: Seafirst Bank.

tunity we offer them, the more they want. In one way, it's gratifying because we want to develop workers who are proactive and thoughtful, and we're delighted to be able to support that in any fashion."

With regards to their immediate requests, Seafirst added several features to the career development system they already had in place. A major change was the addition of a Career Development Officer in Personnel. Seafirst also set up a section of the corporate library for data on jobs and self-study training materials and has added survey forms to elicit information on additional training materials the users would like to have.

But I Don't Know What They Don't Know

"But how do I know what people can or cannot do if they haven't done it yet?" This is a reasonable query by any manager. In other words, how can the manager judge the potential shortcomings of someone not yet in the position of manager or in a highly analytical position without having observed that person doing it? How can the employees themselves know what they are capable of doing? After all, the world is filled with "wannabes" ("wannabe an FX trader," "wannabe a head of a department," "wannabe a bank president").

Fair question. Some banks employ assessment testing, (discussed above) to determine the specific strengths and weaknesses of an individual in many functional areas. Typically, these assessments tests, which ask questions about the perceptions of job functions, are completed by a minimum of three individuals—the individual, the individual's superior, and at least one of the individual's peers. The data is then compiled and usually only given to a counselor or consultant, who then draws up a development curriculum appropriate for the intended career direction.

The questions cover such topics, or competencies, as technical proficiency, performance management, communication skills, decision making, interpersonal skills, or whatever else fits the criteria, ranked by relative importance. The assessment tool points out a person's specific competency profile, which in turn suggests where training is needed. If the individual and the counselor agree that the competency shortfall is unlikely to be solved by additional training (as in "let's face it, you'll never be an analytical whiz"), the counselor can then suggest other positions that better matched that employee's own profile.

Assess Thyself

Several banks offer to help individuals get a truer fix on their own needs through the use of an assessment center. American Savings started one several years ago, with an interest in helping the individual determine if he or she was well-suited for the position and what shortcomings needed to be overcome. The program is particularly aimed at managers, assistant branch managers, and supervisors. It most specifically looks at the individual's communication- and sales-awareness skills as well as technical abilities.

The assessments, which used to be done without grading, now are done on a pass or fail basis. Should an individual fail in any aspect, then the bank provides guidance on how to obtain training to overcome the shortcoming. The bank also provides career counseling.

Such assistance sends a powerful message—more than the one sent during a typical performance appraisal. It's one thing to say, "We would like you to write better, and we think you should do something about it." It's quite another to say that "you need to develop a particular skill more, and we suggest that you enroll in this seminar or class to do so. If you don't, your future in a particular position is uncertain." In short, if the bank truly values the skill, it will do something concrete about insuring that the individual acquires it—something beyond the usual palaver of the appraisal form.

Dealing with Diversity

Another great advantage of using assessment testing is that it eliminates a substantial amount of the biased thinking all humans are subject to. True, even without assessment testing, a good counterbalance for bias exists in the form of the EEOC statutes and formula. Unfortunately, neither objective testing nor regulations serve to reduce prejudice per se. They merely mitigate its effects.

Some banks, such as Bank of Boston, are taking more positive steps to actually change the attitudes of employees, mainly managers, with the intention of reducing bias. "EEO is a social issue," noted Rosa Hunter, Director of EEO and Affirmative Action. "However, diversity is a business issue. Banks, any organizations, which do not develop employees to their fullest potential are doing themselves a disservice."

Actually, noted Hunter, bias works in all directions, not just from the domestic-born, white, protestant, heterosexual males outward. (That's our own bias if we believe that.) Almost everyone is prejudiced about some social aspect, and many are not even aware of it. "The first step is to sensitize people to their own thinking. To do that, we developed a two-day seminar to which we bring a complete cross-section of our managers in order to bring out as many of these hidden biases as possible."

Training the Diverse Group

After making people aware of their attitudes, the program then shows managers how their attitudes are manifested in their day-to-day activities, either passively or actively. Passing over someone for a promotion is an obvious active subjective activity. The passive activities are more insidious. For instance, Hunter pointed out, subordinates learn their job not just through formal training, but through the bits and pieces of information that the manager passes down to them. Frequently, managers simply pass more information—feedback, pointers, ideas—to those they unconsciously favor.

Moreover, managers presume that everyone learns in the same fashion they do—through reading an article as an example. Those who don't learn in that fashion because they process information differently are at a disadvantage. The manager deems them to be less intelligent, even though they might, in fact, have a superiority in doing something if they were "taught" differently—for instance, through role play or simulation.

Thus, managers must learn to adjust their communication and coaching styles to adapt to the level at which the employees can best absorb them, rather than expecting the employees to be able to meet the managers' level. Hunter added,

> Those of us who had the benefit of going to a good school know that the element that distinguished it was the teachers' willingness to spend time explaining ideas in different ways until we all understood. Managers must do the same.
>
> Employees coming out of training programs need to have their manager help them reshape the information learned to fit the work situation. The manager, in turn, must respond to that need differently for different employees. Managers must also realize that employees will progress in different ways. The managers must be ready to reach out to all employees to help them along, not just the ones whom they are most comfortable with.

Managers should be taught how to give everyone the same level of access to information and to their own potential as employees. Otherwise, managers will automatically do what all humans do unless shown otherwise—flock together with birds of a feather.

Bank of Boston does more than talk about the value of the minority workforce: it goes out of its way to honor them. For instance, during February, which is Black History Month, the bank has a "multidimensional" program, which differs every week into the beginning of March. It includes an art show with art drawn not only by bank employees, but also by various other artistic groups; a music program, including gospel music, chorales, and bands; special foods representing different locales and cuisines; and panel discussions on political and social issues prevalent in Boston.

Preventing the Dispirited Worker

Not all prejudice is aimed at people who are "different." Older people also suffer from great misconceptions about their ability—one of the most prevalent being that they cannot be retrained. That perception is transferred consciously or subconsciously ("you can't teach an old dog new tricks") until the employees begin to believe it themselves.

Employees who have reached the top of their professional ladder are also subject to a particular bias (the problems of the plateaued worker is treated more generally in Chapter 3). Managers feel that they, like older workers, are "over the hill" of productivity and are beginning a long downward slide. They are not given as much access to information, either directly or through training, and, as in any self-fulfilling prophesy, *do* ultimately slide downward.[5]

Some employees, particularly the older or plateaued workers may not be motivated as much by money, but they are still tied to the need for security and self-respect. Managers should not devalue their worth by allowing the slide. Not only should they be shown the same treatment as others, but equal effort should be made to place them in positions that best meet their abilities, which may begin to shift over time. However, managers must also help by:

1. Helping the employees to perceive that lateral change can be as rewarding personally even if its dollar-salary increases are limited.
2. Encouraging changes in jobs. Retaining older but loyal, hardworking, and conscientious workers is to the benefit of all. The workers will be more content, and the bank will not always have to be in a recruiting and hiring modality.
3. Creating the cultural atmosphere that honors changes with the same dignity as any other positive move.
4. Preparing the employee so that he or she will be a success in the new function.
5. Establishing a game plan early enough so that the employee can mold his or her thinking around the expectation for changes, seize opportunities when they arise, and have adequate time for preparation.

Literacy Training—What Everyone Talks About

Unfortunately, banks are full of illiterate or innumerate people. They are more likely to be seen as dumb or lazy, but not undereducated, which is their true problem, as one bank trainer noted.

As bankers, we tend to think that the "system" will automatically weed them out. But in a recent ABA survey on basic skills, 80% of the respondents stated that at least 23% of employees holding at-risk positions (tellers, bookkeepers, CRSs, loan officers) experience some performance problems due to poor basic skills. They also determined that oral communication and written communication were the areas with the most prevalent deficiencies.

It's not that the workforce is less competent, but the job requirements have become more complex. The typist we hired 10 years ago comfortably got by with a grammar-school reading level. Now, a similarly qualified person must have a 12th to 14th year reading level just to get through the computer manual. "Dummying-down" reading material is a poor solution because it tends to oversimplify.

And even if we had the luxury of only hiring those who already had the necessary skills, what of those on the current staff? The proof operator who had adequate skills when first hired is now a supervisor and discovers that he or she cannot cope with the reading and written demands.

The Great Cover-Up

For the employees, the obvious solution to this dilemma is simply covering it up, hoping that their secret isn't discovered and that they don't lose their position. Those who slip through are so clever—they wouldn't have come as far as they did if they weren't—that very often a long time elapses until the true situation is revealed.

Tricks of the functionally illiterate include pretending to have lost a critical memo and asking for an oral summary, skipping out at a meeting just before being called to present data, or taking home forms or applications to fill out, where relatives and spouses can work on them. The popular notion is that they have a learning disability, but that's rarely the case. More commonly, they are people that simply slipped through the education cracks, perhaps because they had to leave school to work.

Their learning style requires information that can be directly applied. Even learning to read a newspaper can be too much of an abstraction. They want to learn what they can use today: how to tally a proof sheet or read today's list of account types and interest rates.

Some banks provide counseling to employees about which type of program might be most appropriate for them. Using outside adult education services is not deemed as "remedial" nor is that type of emphasis put on it. In fact, for the most part, the illiterate employees themselves select to attend the program as a result of information they heard from others. As a result, the motivation to stick with it is high.

The Aetna Solution

A Hartford company, Aetna Life and Casualty, does not have the logistical problem of a branch system, giving it more leeway to provide a wider range of programs in-house. Through its Aetna Institute for Corporate Education, it has established the Effective Business Skills School, so named to avoid negative connotations which might result from the use of such terms as "literacy" training. "Our emphasis is on the three 'Rs—reading, writing, and arithmetic—plus oral communication and computer literacy skills," noted Ira Mozille at the Institute. It's offered in traditional classroom (individual and small group) and self-paced formats. Nearly all of the material was developed in-house, so it relates directly to the improvement in productivity on the job. Since the program began in 1988, over 600 people have attended.

The school is basically used in three ways. First, employees may take daytime classes through supervisory referral, with the cost being charged back to the department. Secondly, the school is available after hours free of charge, avoiding the need for the supervisors to be aware of a problem. Thirdly, in coordination with community-based organizations, Aetna offers a train-and-hire program that allows for preliminary training for keyboard entry-level positions, with an enrichment training portion added just prior to hire.

The reason for the program goes beyond our immediate job needs—we are specifically looking towards the future. We obtain our employees from the local workforce, so it's to our benefit to create a superior workforce. We want these employees to be the best candidates for promotion into the higher-level jobs.

As we continue to develop the program, we will put more focus on the personal cultural aspects of work in general and our own company in particular. We are now realizing that it is not just lack of skills that has hampered people in the past, but the emotional elements that come with it. Hence, future training efforts will be designed to help the student help him or herself.

A common problem of all programs is the participants' fear of failure. Instead of taking risks and possibly bettering themselves and their situation, they play it safe. Another problem to be dealt with is the low self-esteem that accompanies the poorly educated. Aetna attempts to drive home the point that if they expend the effort to learn, they probably will be more successful, which in turn improves their sense of self-importance.

Lastly, Aetna tries to provide them with a greater appreciation of their own contribution to the organization. The lower levels tend to feel like "cogs on a wheel," which can easily be replaced by the next entrant. In fact, the opposite is true: we spent nearly $900,000 on basic-skills training last year because these people cannot be readily replaced. To us they are our future.

Aetna's Institute Is Great, but Let's Get Real

Most banks simply do not have the resources to deal with the problem to the extent that Aetna has. But some banks are taking action on a more practical level. In a broader context, National Westminster Bancorp in New York is focusing on the materials and job aids that can provide ongoing data and information so that the individual needn't rely on memory to be able to access information.

In particular, the bank had reconsidered much of the

computers and systems data that employees are expected to be facile with. "Imagine if you will," noted Joan Ustin, VP of Training and Development, "a letter-of-credit checker who may have English as a second language suddenly having to face a computer screen full of data written in abbreviations and techno-talk. To stave off that problem, we deliberately recruited someone from the systems area to work in training. His role is to design systems and systems training first-time users will feel comfortable with."

It's not just the "dummying-down" of materials; it is also a matter of providing information in a fashion that suits the user. Not everyone readily absorbs material written in full sentences and grouped into paragraphs. In fact, through computers we've learned that other presentation styles, such as visual data rather than verbal, which access different cognitive skills, are also valuable in training and deserve to be better utilized.

Learning to Learn

American Savings Bank in White Plains, New York, is addressing basic-skills training mainly to reduce the heavy turnover they've been experiencing in the teller area. While many tellers leave because of the usual reasons, American noted an upward trend in the number of individuals who were let go because they didn't perform well.

The failure rate costs the bank substantially—the cost of hiring, as well as the cost of additional recruitment. "At the lowest entry level," added Amy Rego, Director of Training, "we know that the great problem is an incapacity of some people to absorb knowledge through traditional schooling. In many cases, their basic-skills level is just good enough to get them that entry position, but not to succeed further. And even at that, their learning capacity is limited by their literacy level."

They noted that those asked to leave fell into two groups—those who were hired, but failed during the two-week training period; and those who graduated, but failed during the subsequent probationary period. To the bank, that meant that some were not capable of learning the material, while others could learn it but not integrate it into the day-to-day routine.

American Savings hired an outside consultant from a local community college to structure a program that would assist the tellers and other entry-level personnel. With that, they separated the potential candidates for the training into various groups:

- People with basic comprehension problems.
- People who have the intelligence but don't know how to learn.
- People who appear to need only remedial work in reading comprehension.

Each group required different treatment. The first and easiest step was to revise the current teller-training material to a lower level of comprehension. The second step was to give a reading comprehension test to the new hires to determine if they could still reach the reduced level. (They were surprised to find some college graduates among the comprehension failures.)

American Savings decided against the quick fix of remedial-reading training. They understand that those who cannot read well may suffer from an inability to learn and comprehend. So the program steps back to the point of introducing learning and comprehension skills before teaching the nuts and bolts. (Those of us who are not afflicted with comprehension problems probably cannot readily appreciate the problem.)

The "learning-to-learn" program, designed by the consultant, involves cognitive learning techniques and processes. It is designed to improve everyone's capacity to absorb and retain information. It involves both conventional training and doing exercises. The comprehension program is not altogether a stand-alone, but is rather integrated into the bank's specific training materials, such as the Basics of Negotiable Instruments. Writing skills, incorporating the same techniques, is also a part of the program.

National Westminster and American Savings are both willing to provide basic training to individuals who are "near-miss" employment candidates—commonly those who are returning to the workforce after raising children. Noted Rego, "The prehiring training also goes a long way in keeping employees. They are delighted to know that someone out there cares."

Getting the Most Out of Basic-Skills Training

The ABA has also developed a series of training materials that deal with basic-skills needs as relating to bank functions. Bill Browning at the ABA, who was involved with the materials development, notes that for any program to be most effective, a bank's basic-skills training needs to incorporate several principles.

• *Obtain senior management support:* If the bank wants employees to voluntarily participate in basic-skills training, senior management needs to communicate their support and assure employees that volunteering to participate in basic-skills programs does not put their jobs at risk. Otherwise, marginally skilled employees will cover up the problem and continue struggling to satisfy the demands of the job.

• *Base the program content on literacy task analyses:* A literacy task analysis determines the job-specific basic-skills requirements of banking jobs and whether the job incumbents are meeting them. The methods of conducting a literacy task analysis include observation, analysis of job materials, interviews, and customized tests.

• *Teach basic skills within the context of specific jobs:* The closer the match between the program's activities and actual job tasks, the more likely participants will be able to use skills learned on the job. A U.S. Army study found that participants retain twice as much from job-specific training. Furthermore, the Business Council for Effective Literacy reports that job-specific instruction can reduce the instructional time needed by up to two thirds.

To accomplish this objective, participants should be divided into classroom groups according to job tasks. For example, a module on basic oral communication and customer service may include tellers, CSRs, and bookkeepers, but not proof operators. One way to promote transfers is to use actual job materials, such as forms or manuals, in program activities. If you use outside materials or consultants, make sure that they do not teach academic concepts unrelated to the job, such as diagraming sentences or geometry.

• *Use active learning methods:* Remember, many participants may not easily transfer verbal learning to their jobs. On the other hand, participants may have strong social learning skills. Instructors should capitalize on these skills, using techniques such as role playing, paired learning, and small group exercises, allocating less time for lecture.

• *Link basic skills with thinking:* Basic-skills competencies anchored within an employee's knowledge of the job can be deployed flexibly to solve problems and adapt their skills to novel situations. Skills learned by rote drill often can only be used for rote functions, and not to accomplish more complex, changing tasks such as customer service or writing. When introducing new skills, use an employee's prior knowledge as a bridge for learning the new information. By teaching the *what* of a new skill along with the *how* and *why*, the employee will be better equipped to apply what was learned.

• *Build in constant feedback:* Often less confident in their learning ability, some basic-skills participants rely on the opinion of others, particularly the instructor, for cues on their performance in the program. Noncompetitive, ongoing, individualized feedback should be plugged in as often as possible: for example, written comments on exercises, one-on-one meetings, in-class praise, peer feedback, logbooks, pre- and post-tests, and on-the-job reinforcement of learning objectives by supervisors.

ONCE YOU HAVE FOUND THEM, NEVER LET THEM GO

In the 1990s, banks face the double problem of a declining workforce and one that is less well-educated and less reliable. Good workers will be more difficult to find. To increase productivity and lower costs, banks must reduce the high turnover of workers that exists today. Worker loyalty and morale can be enhanced by career-development programs, which train workers in all the skills needed to move ahead on a career path. Career counseling and assessment should be offered on a regular basis and opportunities for education in basic skills provided to the worker in need of remedial training. The motto of the 90s should be: *Obtain them; train them; retain them.*

REFERENCES

1. Greller, Martin M., and David M. Nee. *Baby Boom to Baby Bust.* New York: Addison-Wesley, 1989.
2. "Dealing with the Problem of a Disaffected and Unskilled Work Force." *Abtac Newsletter*, December 1989.
3. Farnham, Alan. "The Trust Gap." *Fortune*, December 4, 1989.
4. McQuigg-Martinetz, Beverly, and Edward E. Sutton. "New York Telephone Connects Training to Development." *Personnel Journal*, January 1990.
5. Chusmir, Leonard H. "A Shift in Values Is Squeezing Older People." *Personnel Journal*, January 1990.

ADDITIONAL READINGS

Kimmerling, George G. "The Future of HRD." *Training and Development Journal*, June 1989.
March, Joan, and Janet Bernhards. "Software for Training Administration." *Training and Development Journal*, June 1989.

CHAPTER 6

SALES AND SERVICE CULTURES: THE UNMAKING OF THE TRADITIONAL BANKER

"Senior executives must create the enthusiasm. Enthusiasm is like rain. If it does not start at the top, you will never find it at the bottom."—*Timothy Creedon, former Executive Vice President for Valley National Bank in Phoenix.*

RETAIL SALES AND SERVICE

"For years, the branch manager was really no more than a senior new-accounts person with a key to the front door," commented a retail banking executive, echoing the feelings of most of the banks in the United States. Creating an atmosphere amenable to selling and quality service has been the foremost task of everyone involved in keeping the branch system alive. Turning platform staff into something more than order-takers has been for the most part a wrenching experience, taking its toll on senior managers and platform personnel alike.

For years, many banks never even looked twice at the sales side of banking and even had a dimmer view of the value of the retail areas. John Porta, former President of Southeast Bank in Miami, noted, "Before we took hold of the problem, this place was a mess. You see, we used to be the the First National Bank of Miami and the premier corporate bank in the state. We attracted some of the best people, and our commercial-banking management training program was a breeding ground for many of the state's current bankers.

The dominant culture here was correspondent banking and corporate credit. Retail bankers had no clout."

When Florida changed its laws to allow multibank holding companies, Southeast began, like others, to acquire other banks. Suddenly, they had a number of various subcultures in the organization. To bring them into alignment with Southeast, they promoted corporate lenders from the main office as the heads of the new entities. The results were mixed. "They were entirely cut out of their element," added Porta. "These banks were not clones of the Miami bank. How could they be? This is a state of small businesses and consumer lending. The corporate people didn't fit at all."

Big, Ugly, and Difficult

The bankers discovered that their background in corporate training was strong in credit knowledge but weak in product-knowledge training and sales training. Not surprisingly, the lack of focus and the mix of cultures began to become a problem in the integration of the bank system. Added Porta,

> We were seen as big, ugly, and difficult by outsiders—not exactly the culture we had hoped to establish. Even our own people were complaining. We were a bank trying to posture ourselves as a corporate bank, when over 50% of our loans and over 75% of our deposits came from the community banking side. Once we decided to define ourselves for what we really were, to address the sales and service mentality (or more correctly, our lack thereof), then we stood a chance in the marketplace.

Used Cars and Bank Cards

Many banks have discovered, as Southeast did, that change doesn't always come easily to those involved. Comments such as "all of our old-time branch managers are gone" and "they went on early retirement when they heard about the sales quotas" are rife in the industry. Rather than struggling to rehabilitate 25-year people, many banks took the easier route of simply replacing them with those who could cope with the sales aspect of the job. Those who did stay were typically placed in product knowledge and sales and service-training courses, something that many had never been exposed to during their whole careers.

To many banks' dismay, however, they did not find the newly trained platform staff to be necessarily all hepped up about the opportunity to sell CDs to customers. Sales did increase after the training, but often tapered off within a short period. The enthusiasm simply wasn't there.

Why not? For the most part, the problem was far more deep-rooted than executives expected. Many platform personnel who superficially acknowledged that selling is an important aspect for getting the appropriate product to the consumer, deep down equated it with something less wholesome.

In their selling role, many saw themselves as the "Joe Isuzus" of the banking world, full of lies about the validity of their product. They were just a slightly more elite variety of the used-car huckster. "Hey, get a load of these interest rates! And if you wanna real beauty, we can get you a convertible account with dual savings and checking features, plus all the extras!"

At Least You *Can* Define Selling

Even if selling is not readily embraced by all, at least everyone knows when they are doing it. Service is less obvious. Service is like beauty; it's only in the eyes of the beholder. "Service is what the customer says it is. The customer's assessment of service quality is the only assessment that matters," noted Leonard Berry in his book on service quality.[1] Often, in service training, employees are asked to rate their own degree of service, which is compared to an independent survey. The discrepancy between the two ratings is often very wide—the employees rating themselves high and the survey rating them low. It wasn't that the employees were being self-serving: they honestly *thought* they were providing good service.

But since relationships are basically developed through salesmanship and good follow-through, the first aspect of any training agenda should be to have everyone probe his or her own beliefs and attitudes about selling and service. In particular, many people don't truly know what their feelings are towards selling because they've never had any experiences with it. Some may have had a taste of it in summer jobs, yet that might be deceptive because high performance was not critical. However, if the bank's future is dependent on how well the platform staff does (and which bank isn't?), then it should determine beforehand that no mental obstacles will prevent their success. Many have learned that you can train someone to death on these skills, yet the skills will never be applied if that employee believes that selling is inherently wrong, and service can be casually addressed.

First You've Got to Feel It

Even when participants have a positive attitude, banks have also learned that a once-over on product knowledge with a superficial coating of sales and service training is not adequate. A fundamental change in behaviors does not necessarily follow. More intense approaches to development are required.

Banks have found that to be successful, training programs must first address the underlying attitudes about selling and service. It became increasingly apparent to banks that academic training did not accomplish the necessary behavioral changes. A key ingredient now included in many programs is to expose the participants to "experiential" mode training so that they can begin to "feel" the need for sales and service.

An excellent example of experiential training occurs at Deposit Guaranty Bank in Jackson, Mississippi. Bank managers wanted their platform personnel to follow the golden banking rule of "treating customers as they would like to be treated themselves." Notes Sue Spitchley, in charge of the sales training there, "The only way to understand it is to experience it. We send individuals out to comparison shop with other banks. They are given specific roles to play. Some have extra funds; others are looking for money. Some act as married; some as single; some as unmarried couples. We want the subtleties in sales and service to really come out."

Participants must carefully note how well they were treated, how knowledgeable the staff was, whether they asked the "right" questions to come up with appropriate product suggestions. Participants then discuss who wins and loses when the level of salesmanship is low. Added Spitchley, "It makes people realize that product knowledge is more than knowing where the brochure can be found; sales is more than quoting the current CD rate; and service is more than big eyes and a bright smile."

The Nurturing Person

Banks are also beginning to realize that the type of person most likely sitting on the platform is not a high-powered "sales barracuda," but rather a person who likes the security banks have to offer. Typically, nonmanagement platform personnel are from the local area—females whose primary concern is the home, not the office.

"We're dealing with ESTJ," noted one trainer at a different bank, referring to the Myers-Briggs testing instrument that determines personality types, distinguishing people in general terms as drivers, amiables, expressives, and analytics. "These people most often test out as 'amiables.' They're warm and friendly. They want to be accepted as part of a group. They don't want to do anything that would hurt their perception or standing in the community."

That particular bank attempts to use its employees' psychological makeup rather than to submerge it. Individuals are encouraged to realize that they are not only *not* jeopardizing their friendship through sales and service, but actually performing a caring service—that is, helping neighbors utilize their money more effectively for their own ultimate good.

Deposit Guaranty Bank also uses personality analysis, but in another context: to determine how customers prefer being treated in a selling context. They apply a personality selection system that segregates people into dominant, information-oriented, steady, and compliant personality types. Participants learn to discern the different personality types of their customers and to modify their selling style to conform to those types' preferences.

First Union Bank, headquartered in Charlotte, North Carolina, is one of the more determined institutions addressing its sales and service needs. It established a retail branch training school, the Consumer Sales Academy, where employees attend a two-week off-site program focused on basic sales skills and product knowledge. The sequestering aspect serves to intensify the experience. Also, it ensures a level of attention to the training material that cannot be expected of employees when the training is given close to work and home. In addition, another three days prior to the start of the program were allotted for local market analysis. Attendees were asked to gather information about the competition—retail products, pricing, branch locations, marketing material, and so forth—to create a marketing plan for their own branch.

Fully Exposed

One trainer pointed out that the traditional platform employee, one with a narrow focus, is actually a *creation of* the bank by virtue of the bank's presumption that the employee is only "a platform type." This is an extension of what is known as the Pygmalion Effect: people *become* what is *expected* of them.

Banks have minimized that effect by exposing the individual to the broader aspects of banking early on. Some banks rotate their new retail branch management trainees throughout the whole bank on one- and two-week stints. Other banks arrange for presentations by managers from areas of the bank that platform people usually do not come in contact with, such as the comptroller's division. Another selects individuals to attend training programs for functions that are indirectly related to platform work, such as small-business credit analysis.

In essence, they are saying to the platform person, "We don't just want you to think in terms of CDs. Rather, we want you to be woven into the bank's whole fabric—thereby being better able to understand our philosophy." As one trainer put it, "Until the platform personnel can do that, they will see their role as that of the traditional deposit taker—not people who must take responsibility for helping the bank make its customers become stronger and more financially secure."

It Takes Two

Smart banks, such as First Union, do not truly expect to change the culture of the retail area only by running training programs. Experts note that cultural behaviors are not the function of what people are told to do, but rather what management expects and rewards them to do. Since rewards emanate from the top level, First Union addresses the attitudes of those people first. As the program is "bought" by the various subsidiary banks within the system, First Union spends as much energy in addressing the environmental elements as they do in the training.

First, the sales infrastructure was changed within a bank group so that sales information, reports, marketing plans, and meetings are all *consistently* handled through the system. People are also prepared for the anticipated change in attitude with additional presentations and directives. The president of the local subsidiary, as well as other bank executives who are effectively sponsoring the running of the program, are invited for a sneak preview—a two-day summary of the program so that they can not only understand the concepts being taught, but also integrate them into their strategies and communications.

Those that will actually be the sales managers are not only exposed to the program's contents, but are also trained independently to be sales managers. Since they will be the ones with the greatest impact on the learners, their attitudes are more closely assessed. The potential sales managers do an image profile in which they themselves, peers, and subordinates independently assess what the individual's capabilities as a sales manager currently are. Doing this allows them to focus in on the precise areas of deficiencies when they take the sales-management training.

Assessment tools are very helpful in determining shortcomings in abilities, but the impact that First Union is seeking is beyond that. The personal assessments draw individuals into personalizing the changes that are occurring around them, making them far more sensitive to the success or failure of the change. First Union realizes that simply telling someone to do something is not enough: that person has to have some personal responsibility for the success of the event for it to occur.

COMMERCIAL SALES CULTURE

Win Friends and Influence People

A calling officer 10 years ago was predominantly selling credit facilities, and the officer had nearly complete control as to the delivery of the product from the day of customer acceptance to the day of drawdown. Now, particularly with large corporate customers, the product lineup ranges from risk-management products to cash-management systems.

The relationship manager today, therefore, is one who must develop the customer's awareness about various noncredit product lines. In addition, the officer is likely to have to bring in the product expert on a sales call to do a joint calling effort. Afterwards, delivery of these products will transfer to the product's specialty area.

Despite the fact that many bank products are not emanating from the calling officers' specific department, these officers are still the ones who will be held responsible if they

(1) do not adequately stimulate the interest of the customer, (2) do not run a "good" joint call, and/or (3) do not assure the delivery of the product.

As much as banks must create a cadre of people to interact with customers (selling), they must create a cadre of people who can interact with the internal workforce (influence).

The Forum Corporation, a training firm located in Boston, lists nine characteristics that a relationship manager should have to be a top performer:

The Key Account Manager: The salesperson will have to be able to establish, cement, and sustain a select portfolio of key account relationships. Less critical accounts will not merit direct contact.

The Partner: As the point of contact in a sales partnership, the salesperson will be concentrating on representing the buyer's trust in the bank. More than that, the salesperson will be helping to redefine the buyer-seller relationship creatively, establishing joint ventures and strategic alliance.

The General Manager: The salesperson may also have to be his or her own sales managers, increasingly responsible for account profitability as well stop-line orders. More than ever, they will have to be able to sell internally, to negotiate positively, and to implement marketing strategies.

The Resource Manager: Relationship managers will have to be able to use their resources to create value for their customers and will need management skills to deliver that value. In large entities, the salesperson will have to be a leader, capable both of establishing permanent teams and of organizing temporary ones for particular applications.

The Marketer: As many banks decentralize their marketing locations, salespeople will be responsible for total territorial development, managing high-profile activities on their own, including product seminars, direct-mail efforts, and local advertising.

The Strategist: Salespeople will have to be able to look at the customer from the point of view of the customer's client and help determine how the customer can build competitive advantage.

The Pulse of the Bank: The skills of the relationship manager will be essential for differentiating products and services in the marketplace and for continually feeding back market information.

The Telemarketer: While most relationship managers will still spend most of their time in customer contact, much of it will not be face-to-face. Using the telephone, direct mail, and electronic media, the salesperson will actually be increasing contact with clients while reducing the cost of selling.

The Confidant: As a matter of routine, the salesperson will have such command of the client's problems, goals, and concerns that he or she will be trusted to perform part of the customer's job.

More Meaningful Relationships

Toward the end of the last decade, banks that had heavily stressed the sales culture began to see excellent results (30% average growth rates over five years were quite common). Nonetheless, many sensed that they were winning battles but losing wars. The focus had become so heavy on the transactional deal that the ideal of establishing a long-term customer relationship became misplaced.

Relationship banking became the new catch phrase, deemed by management as the great savior of their retail and commercial banking efforts. It meant that the customer was to be cultivated for the long term, and platform staff, particularly on the commercial banking side, were to handle the customer's whole array of financial needs, not just loans and credit.

However, banks have become aware that there is more to relationship management work than just appending product and sales workshops to the credit-training programs. They have discovered that if the bank expects to form a long-term relationship, then the account person must be able to convey more than just an interest in pushing a series of bank products. The bank's sincere interest in the customer's well-being must not only be established but maintained with vigor if the relationship is to withstand the competition.

Jill Flynn, SVP and Training Director of First Union Bank, which puts heavy emphasis on relationship management, commented, "We are placing an important investment in our account managers. But we've learned that even having skills to pitch products is not enough. In fact, if too much emphasis is placed on achieving product sales volume, the client may doubt our sincerity and ultimately defeat our primary goal of establishing a long-term relationship."

The difference between selling and developing a relationship is distinguished by the way the account manager handles a sale. Traditional selling skills direct the salesperson to conduct a probe in order to pick up comments or "cues" that lead him or her to the appropriate product suggestion. After that, the account manager elicits further comments as to the customer's opinion of the appropriateness of that suggestion. But, basically, the information sent or received is transmitted through a "filter" that screens out data that is unrelated to the bank's ability to service the customer. In other words, the banker is only interested in the information if it can ultimately help in the selling process.

See the Same Landscape

Banks now educate the employees to appreciate the needs of the customer as the customer perceives them, not just as a lead to use the bank's services. And the view must go beyond the immediate future, at least two or three years down the road. At the same time, the participants learn that, as account managers, they will have to be able to anticipate the actions of the competition and establish a strategic plan to deal with both the customers' financial concerns and the competitive forces.

The process is similar to looking down a telescope held by the customer. Too often, bankers are looking through the wrong end and seeing an enlarged aspect of the customer. What sets top performers apart is the ability to see the same landscape and horizon the customer sees. When they do that, they understand how banking fits into the picture from the customer's perspective.

A large Canadian bank also teaches the participants that a client company is not a monolithic structure standing on its own, but rather a conglomeration of individuals performing functions. The account managers must not only have a complete understanding of the company but also of the needs of the individual they are dealing with. Does that person have a particular concern that must be addressed, such as a need to gain approval from superiors on his or her performance? In the case studies, the bank intertwined comments from interviews with company executives to add an extra dimension of insight. It's the participants' responsibility to pick out these various subtle elements and to incorporate them in their selling practices.[2]

Their sales training program makes heavy use of simulation role-play and team selling. A scenario might call for four or five people within a meeting, representing people on both sides. Each side might be given 50 to 100 pages of role-play data about the company, which the account managers must elicit and integrate into their selling during the simulations.

The know-the-bank aspect is covered in a separate training session, called Product Application. It was specifically designed so that it went beyond traditional product-knowledge training: that is, only learning the features and benefits of a particular product. Information is presented from a market perspective, which shifts the emphasis from the technical to the marketing aspects of a product.

Account officers today do far more than arrange credit facilities: they control virtually all aspects of the relationship, that is, they must know how to draw on every product and resource available in the bank and ensure that they are being correctly applied.

Besides, It's Not Getting Any Cheaper

According to McGraw-Hill Research done in 1987, the cost of sending one salesperson in front of one customer for one call will approach $400 in the 1990s, double what it cost in 1983. The expense of having even a highly skilled sales force is rapidly escalating. The expense of having an untrained sales force is staggering, and the expense of having one that cannot effectively do follow-through and ensure delivery could be overwhelming.

This was more noticeably felt in the commercial-lending area, where well-developed banking relationships pay off more handsomely in the longer term, but to cover short-term expenses, account officers needed to do transactions to show current revenue. Worse, the focus on doing transactions left the bank giving each new lender equal weight, rather than emphasizing those whose business potential was greater. The result was too much attention paid to the near-term low earners and too little to the long-term, high-potential customers.

Banks are learning to develop an account manager who can first focus on the correct target market and then narrow that group even further to those providing the best results for the bank. A typical portfolio includes a mixture of mature accounts, those that are in the process of maturing, and ones that are being newly developed. The training aims to help the participants to determine which of those accounts will ultimately warrant the most attention and how to best allocate their time and resources.

Some familiar concepts of time-management skills come into play, but with a specific focus on improving sales productivity. Banks that are ultimately successful in maximizing revenue while minimizing costs will be those that did *not* train their officers to be all things to all companies, but rather to be the best account managers to those customers who could most fully utilize their services.

What Makes the Superman Super

Every coach's dream is to create a superior performer. In the sales field, the super salesperson is a legendary figure, and every large sales office seems to have one. The super salesperson is the one that hits the million dollar club, beats all the goals, or doubles the next highest hitter. "You wouldn't believe it to meet him; he seems like the least likely person," is a frequent comment heard about the super salesperson; or "I don't know what she's got that I don't have, but it sure works."

What does the super salesperson have? Books adorn shelves on what that "something" is—often more self-congratulatory than informative. Many fine consultants have also made good livings on identifying it. But, often, none of the generalizations of selling adequately apply to a bank's own specific work habits, organizational makeup, or product base.

But that doesn't mean a bank has to live in the dark, hoping to hire by chance that one natural salesperson who will singlehandedly bring up the branch's or department's average. The answer is already available *in the bank*; it only needs to be ferreted out.

Putting the Finger on It

The solution is simple: just ask the best performers what they do that is special and then train others to do the same thing. Sounds too ingenuous? Well, it does take a bit of a practiced hand to really put the finger on it because usually the best performers don't know what they are doing that's so special.

The technique is called *competency-based analysis*—an integral aspect in the development of any good training program. It requires spending time with those identified as superstars to get them to trace their activities and their emotional state as they performed various aspects of the function. It avoids broad questions such as "what qualities do you have that make you a good salesperson?" Rather, the questions are more specific: What comments or phrases do you use to open the conversation? How do you respond when you hear a specific objection? What are you thinking before you set up a call?"

The sum of the responses from the best can be compared to the responses that come from the average and worse performers to the same questions. Eventually, the differences can be sorted out. Once the superior elements are identified, then the others can be trained to understand and use the same elements. In addition, the same elements can be summarized and used in the selection process.

Coming On Strong
Aggressiveness is one quality that is often sought after in a salesperson. Frequently, the behavior is displayed in an interview because "the word is out" that coming on strong sharply increases the chances of being hired. In so doing, the personality trait is already reinforced, encouraging the new employee to continue acting aggressively. Sales training that emphasizes that the meek may inherit the earth, but they don't get sales, further encourages aggressiveness as an important behavioral trait.

Yet one institution that did competency-based analysis found that none of the super salespeople considered themselves aggressive. They had substituted enthusiasm and energy for aggressiveness and found that the customers appreciated that far better. In fact, the analysis determined that the poorer salespeople relied on aggressiveness the most, usually when it was apparent that they weren't going to make a sale. In short, the aggressive element was a "turn-off."

After discovering this (as well as many other behavioral aspects), the institution changed both its training and its hiring stance. It sought enthusiasm as part of the selection process, asking questions such as "what project, business, or personal project has interested you the most in the last few years, and precisely how were you involved." The training emphasized ways to draw out natural enthusiasm just prior to a call. Needless to say, sales substantially improved.

MANAGING SALES AND SERVICE

Sales Management Isn't Just Managing Selling

If the role of the salesperson has taken on continual added dimensions, then the role of sales manager has become even more complex. A great misconception is that the primary job of the sales manager is to administer the selling function: assign markets and territories, track volume, maintain the marketing function, and so forth. The old approach of taking the top producer and giving him or her administrative responsibilities is as shortsighted as it is popular. It's popular because it is the easiest way to select; no one can argue that so-and-so didn't deserve the additional salary boost. It's shortsighted because, in an attempt to avoid a possible confrontation about who should ascend, one can easily end up with the wrong person.

True, the sales manager has the sales expertise that others will want to *model*. The manager has to respect the challenge of selling and has to demonstrate superior ability to consistently meet the challenge. Yet, it's that very challenge that is the greatest hurdle to overcome.

Since many banks offer incentive plans that reward the greatest achievers, many platform personnel consider meeting goals the way one runs a marathon. They are seeking their "personal best"—competing against themselves as well as against the other runners. But the one who has made it to the position of manager is told to shed his or her "rugged individualism" and take on the role of "team player" instead. For many, it's a hard transition.

Besides, the best salespeople might make the worst sales managers for reasons other than the need to shift style. The selection of the sales manager is critical to the assurance of maintenance of a superior sales force. That encompasses far more than simply counting heads and giving an occasional rah-rah. It requires a whole new discipline, utilizing motivational, coaching, and reinforcement techniques. Sales managers must take over where sales training has left off.

Training Is Only a Beginning

Training the sales staff is probably the most critical aspect. No one can fulfill all the requirements of the job without formal training in sales skills. But training alone is inadequate for the long term. It has been estimated that the impact of initial sales training lasts approximately one week before the enthusiasm generated by the session begins to fall off. Sales success does not work in a vacuum.

Formal training is a catalyst. But, as in any catalytic action, there has to be a medium, the sales manager, through which to work. The sales manager should be seeking to combine the talents of the employee with the needs and expectations of the bank. If those needs and expectations are not clearly defined, the talents will be developed, but will ultimately languish in a sterile atmosphere.

Just What Do You Want?

Consider the typical platform employee returning to her desk after the completion of the sales-training program. First, she attends to the routine of the day—activities involving fixing problems, doing correspondence, checking account exemptions, and moving papers. Then comes the "let's-do-some-selling" feeling. OK. The next customer that walks in gets the treatment, with some success. Encouraged, she solicits another group of customers, but success varies: some respond favorably; some shrug and walk away. Meanwhile, activity items keep piling up on the desk: call about an overdraft, arrange money transfers, investigate a statement error, replace a lost credit card, and so on, ad infinitum. The impetus to do proactive selling loses it immediacy, and, by the time the week is over, is almost gone altogether. So the platform person continues to sell, but only when the customer invites it.

At this point, too many banks just reach for an incentive system thinking that incentives alone will keep the motivation up and get the employee to perform at acceptable performance levels. Incentives are often misused. *They should be used to reward superior performance, not mediocre perfor-mance.* The average person should already be performing at a relatively high level before having incentives. Otherwise, the bank is saying that we will reward you for being just average.

What is required then is a systematic approach to per-formance definition, recognition, measurement, and mainte-nance—in short, a performance management system. CORT, which stands for consistent, objective, regular, and timely, is the criteria for a systematic approach. *Consistent* means all comments agree and build on each other. *Objective* means that comments reflect "how I see your achieving the goal," not "how I see you." *Regular* refers to every day or week or month, as makes sense, but not at odd times or so rarely that the comment takes on undue importance. *Timely* means as soon after the performance as reasonable, but not so long af-ter that no one remembers the performance well enough to properly assess. (See the following chapter on Motivation for more insight into intangible and tangible motivational tech-niques.)

Training to Meet Expectations

Luke Helms, President, of Seafirst in Seattle, com-mented that the bank's biggest mistake in training was in not dealing with employee expectations.

> We were hiring them and telling them that with our new training program we were going to make them the best salespeople ever. They would become great successes. They loved the idea, but in the beginning we never translated the concept into anything concrete. What did one have to actually accomplish to be good?
>
> We realized that when the new hires hit the platform, they really didn't know what was expected of them, nor had we trained the branch manager on how to handle these great new "tools." Should they stand over employees? Or merely tell them to "keep in touch"? So, not surprisingly, employees couldn't translate the training into action. Were

they to sell 5 new accounts or 500? Should they push mortgages and forget accounts? If they sold two accounts a day, could they go home early?

Once we realized the problem, we really moved to correct it. The branch managers were provided with the training they needed to really use the staff. We taught them how to set defined standards and goals, so that the employees knew if their results were great, good, or lousy. We showed managers how to direct and motivate and generally keep the juices flowing. Once we realized that we needed to give people specific parameters—both the employees on what to do and the managers on how to make it happen—what a difference it made in the sales effort.

It All Leads Back to Training

In essence, systematically rewarding and directing employees is the daily embodiment of training. Sales managers who first become adept as trainers will be more comfortable with providing, and therefore more likely to provide, the necessary coaching on a day-to-day basis.

To do that, some banks have each line manager lead the three-day basic sales-skills training seminar, which requires two days of training-skills preparation. In these five days, not only do they learn the skills they will need in their coaching role, but they are also perceived as a "champion" of sales in the eyes of the participants, which helps improve their credibility in their subsequent coaching efforts.

Banks have come to learn that natural sales and service people can be "made"; they don't have to be born into it. But banks have also learned that it requires more than quick-fix training to create an employee who is enthusiastic and capable. In addition, the training should start from the top down, so that the managers are as ready to assist employees as the employees are eager to go. The need for managerial-level training, especially in motivational techniques, cannot be overemphasized—so much so that the following chapter addresses motivating employees independently.

REFERENCES

1. Berry, Leonard; David R. Bennett; and Carter W. Brown. *Service Quality: A Profit Strategy for Financial Institutions.* Homewood, Ill.: Dow Jones-Irwin, 1989.
2. "Relationship Management." *ABTAC Newsletter*, March 1989.

ADDITIONAL READINGS

Richardson, Linda. *101 Tips for Selling Financial Services.* New York: John Wiley & Sons, 1986.
———. *Bankers in the Selling Role,* 2nd ed. New York: John Wiley & Sons, 1987.
———. *Winning Negotiation Strategies for Bankers.* Homewood, Ill.: Dow Jones-Irwin, 1987.

CHAPTER 7

KEEPING 'EM MOTIVATED: FROM BACKSLAPS TO PAGO-PAGO

"Management's role is to give people a reason to come to work every day."—*Arthur Campbell, Executive Vice President, National State Bank, New Jersey.*

Wouldn't it be nice if a quick review of *Theory Y* and the *One Minute Manager* was all one would have to study to learn how to successfully motivate people. *Theory Y* says that people are basically happy campers at work, and that all the organization needs to do is to create the right campground. The *One Minute Manager* adds that the campers will remain happy if management gives them a simple goal (like putting up the tent) and then praises or reprimands their tent-making ability. With those two nostrums, campers would go on happily raising tents forever.

Quick fixes come and go, but people still jump at the chance to create yet another and reap the not inconsiderable benefits therefrom. Undoubtedly, before this decade is finished, we will be subjected to another untold number of simplistic ideas, often with one word or four letter acronyms, like MBWA (Management by Walking Around), which will provide the solution to all motivational problems in a single phrase.

Testimony to the fact that quick fixes don't work is the November 1984 article in *Business Week*, which noted the poor performance by many of the previously designated "excellent" companies. Apparently, many of these companies seemed to have ignored a long-term systematic approach, instead favoring a concept that was implemented "today" but petered out over time. Human nature being what it is, everyone will take a stab at something that practically "guarantees" creating a workforce that will march into the branches every morning whistling the dwarfs' theme song from *Snow White*. But, alas, solutions are just not going to come from a 50-page book.

Obviously solutions don't come that easily since nearly every bank will admit to still having deadwood employees. Most frequently, they refer to the deadwood in the retail area, but most likely that's because branch managers are in the most visible position undergoing change. Deadwood is scattered throughout the organization. Some interviewees have even nominated the senior management.

"They still do a 3-6-3 banking," referring to the old adage of the banker being able to take in deposits at 3%, lend them out at 6%, and hit the golf course at 3 P.M. "They just want to march to a 50s drum beat."

Although the image of deadwood being employees with their eyes on the clock rather than on the customers has some validity, most banks find that their deadwood is comprised of two types: those who couldn't understand the changes around them and chose to retreat, and others who have been shocked awake by change, but are incapable of comfortably functioning in the new environment. (Of course, every bank has found itself with a goldbrick or two. We're not referring to that type. We're referring to the ones whose productivity had been acceptable, even superior, in earlier years, but who now are marginal contributors.)

THE MARGINAL PRODUCER: YOU GET WHAT YOU EXPECT TO GET

In nature, wood becomes "dead" when the natural oils dry out, leaving only cellulose. To preserve wood in furniture, a layer of boiled linseed oil is applied and regularly reoiled to retain the natural oils. The analogy is apt in business.

Deadwood employees come into being when their natural enthusiasm dries out. It was once robust, but left to slowly drift away. The yearly performance appraisals reaffirmed the erosion, but did nothing to correct the situation. The resulting marginally effective employee base was inevitable. It is the American tragedy—the Willy Loman story repeated over and over again.

One well-known Japanese company, when faced with deadwood employees to whom they have assured lifelong employment, solves the problem in a unique way. They do what in U.S. culture would be almost inconceivable: they promote them.

They employ a theory generally known as the "Pygmalion Effect": that is, people work up to the expectations set for them. So the employee now has a new level of achievement to strive for. Promotion also reaffirms that individual's self-esteem, so any sense of worthlessness garnered on the previous job is dismissed.

Whether or not promotion is the appropriate, or just another quick-fix solution, the point is well taken. All too often in this country, the typical manager reaffirms during the yearly performance appraisal that the marginal employee is a low achiever. The manager may perhaps mumble something about more productivity, toss in a nominal raise, and send the employee back to the desk. Unstated, but nonetheless conveyed during the review, is the manager's expectation that things won't change. And not surprisingly, the employee lives up to the expectation.

Motivating employees requires many more elements than an occasional pat on the back or even throwing money at them. It requires a change in the employees' level of self-perception, a change in the relationship between manager and employees, and a change in the way the bank rewards employees.

The Cold Hard Realities of Work

"I think any worker takes pride in being prepared and capable," noted Julian Banton, President of SouthTrust in Alabama.

> There is a certain feeling one gets when a job is completed effectively in responding to customers' needs. In our

mind, our training gives them that capacity to be confident in their position. But we're not kidding ourselves. I've been on the line myself. I know that as a branch manager, you can sometimes get to the point of dreading opening those doors in the morning. Basically, it's just another day on the firing line.

Having a highly trained workforce does not necessarily mean a highly motivated one. To be sure, training and development serve to take away the obstacles that inhibit doing a good job, from lack of knowledge to lack of confidence. But once self-esteem issues have been satisfied (see Chapter 4 on empowerment), the stimulus to achieve has to be greater than just proving that one can do something well.

People suffer from burnout and boredom, from fear of success as much as from fear of failure. Attempting to create the ideal loan officer with the traditional annual this-is-how-yer-doin' and this-is-where-ya-oughta-change performance appraisal, however meaningful, is inadequate. (Adding certain specific elements will greatly improve their effectiveness. This will be discussed in more detail further in the chapter.) A far more powerful tool is *regular* recognition of the individual's contribution, combined with coaching and counseling, which can serve to move the individual in a real sense.

Title Inflation

Banks haven't ignored compensation as a motivating factor, but have most often used the yearly merit increase as a method of stimulation, in conjunction with the performance appraisal (most commonly stimulating workers two months prior to the anticipated yearly review). Most, if not all banks, have utilized job classifications that establish a salary range for a particular official level. As individuals pushed on the ceiling of the salary range of the title, the only remaining option for the next review was to promote them into another title. And when the bank ran out of titles, they created more. Thirty years ago, the next level above vice president was president and chairman. Now banks have senior vice president, executive vice president, junior executive vice president, senior executive vice president, vice chairman, divisional CEO, and ad infinitum.

The problem with title inflation is two-fold. First of all, title inflation, like monetary inflation, only ultimately leads to a debasing of its value. People who had been proud to be a vice president began to sense the meaninglessness of the achievement. VPs were regularly reminded of the old joke of supermarket titles, where there is not only a vice president in charge of prunes, but one for dried prunes and one for bulk prunes.

Secondly, and perhaps more important, is that the titles usually brought a greater range of responsibility, but generally less revenue-related productivity. Managers of commercial lending units generally did not have direct calling responsibility for a client base and accordingly saw the clients only on occasion. One step up, the geographic area manager usually saw even fewer clients, the divisional manager still fewer, and so on. Customer contact has become inversely proportional to official rank.

In fact, the implied reward of higher rank was that you would no longer be expected to have to deal directly with customers, except in special situations where a high-ranking individual's presence was thought to engender a certain panache. Therefore, dealing with customers had to be something one sought to remove oneself from; doing an exceptional job for the customer was *not* an implicit reward for the high-level bank officer. That productivity declined is reflected in the results of the banking industry. Earnings per employee has been on a downward shift, especially in earnings of exempt or official employees.

Nonetheless, the importance of title still remains strong. A number of banks today report that they expect the incoming 22- to 23-year-old management trainees to attain the rank of officer by age 24 to 25, AVP by 28 to 30, VP by 30 to 34, and SVP by 32 to 40. Since many of these banks report that 75% of their staff is under the age of 40, the implications for the older person who is a 50-year-old-VP-and-holding is minimized to a select few. A review of job postings (where positions and salary ranges are listed for internal fulfilling) also serves to show that title does not necessarily mean position. However, it begs the question of "Is there life after SVP?"

One, Two, Three—What Are We Working For?

We all know by now that money in and of itself doesn't satisfy our needs. Satisfaction comes from having a sense of self-worth, of peer recognition, and of personal achievement. Of course, money, while not being one of those rewards, does lead us to them. As our work will actually receive a value, we can achieve better creature comforts, peers recognize our contribution, and so forth. Title inflation does nicely fit into the formula; in fact, most experts feel that overall salaries in banking have tended to be lower because they are balanced off by greater psychic rewards through the title level.

The inability of banks to continue to provide special rewards through the debased titles has diminished the value of one of the great motivating factors. But it no longer retains its worth as something that distinguishes one individual from another. (It remains a negative motivator—essentially, if you can't make VP by 35, you're out.) If people worked for money, but lived for recognition, then another motivator had to emerge, preferably one that provided return for both the employee and the bank. The general merit-reward system of bumping the salary each year is inadequate, since most people feel that the pay increases are given for tenure and general dedication, not for real effort.

Keeping the Inspiration Alive–Nontangible Rewards

Many banks have realized that merit pay was inadequate and have added incentive compensation as a form of reward. A recent study shows that incentive planning is very much on the rise in banking.[1] Although breakout statistics are too complex to report, about 30% of the banks in the study reported offering incentives by an individual's functional area, while 70% of the banks reported offering incentives to senior management.

But what are banks "incenting"? More effort, more hard work, certainly, but for how long, and at what cost?

For instance, many banks have "sales campaigns," designed to whip up platform enthusiasm to sell individual retirement accounts (IRAs) or combo accounts or what have you. They may run for a month—some even for a year. At the end of the campaign, the employee with the most points gets a trip to Pago-Pago or some other exotic place, while the others share in a slew of lesser prizes. (Years ago, I personally was the recipient of two copper pots, still in use, after selling CDs to my relatives.)

Such campaigns are often successful in their short-term mission, but fail to achieve long-term success. The pots go in the cabinet and sales literature back in the desk drawer. Everyone relaxes and it's back to business as usual.

Sustain and Maintain

It's easy to confuse the primary objective behind using tangible incentives. It shouldn't be only used to raise revenue by getting employees to push more product. Campaigns with big payouts will undoubtedly generate a big sales boost, but the results are generally short-lived, when either the staff burns out and/or the CDs run off. *Incentives should come into play as a method of moving already high continuous sales or productivity averages of the employee group even higher—and keeping them there!*

If sales or service are low because the staff is poorly trained or undermanaged, the solution should be in more effective sales and management training, not in monetary handouts. That just increases the cost of motivation with uncertain results. It's another quick fix. Monetary incentives are most cost effective when they reward the employees for going beyond their "comfort zone," not for getting there in the first place.

Jeff Sucec of Financial Training Resources, in Lombard, Illinois, uses the illustration of a teller area as an example of appropriate use of incentives. Prior to training, the tellers were measured for the degree of customer service they were demonstrating. The ratings were done by two groups: a consulting group and the tellers themselves. The consulting group applied an average rating of 3 out of 10. However, the tellers scored themselves at an average of 8.

The tellers misjudged themselves because they really didn't know what specifically was required of customer service and how well they compared to it. The fault lay with the bank: it had not provided the employee with an adequate job description to know precisely what constituted good customer service: saying "hello" to the customer, mentioning the customer's name at least once, smiling, asking a question about the customer's needs, politely closing, and so forth. Fifty percent of effort necessary to improve the sales and service quality was simply defining it better.

The first step of the program, a combination of training plus a better job description, yielded an immediate improvement of the average up to 5 out of 10. A second stage of the program, generated through management training, provided the tellers more feedback, coaching, and other positive reinforcements. That improved the average to 7.5. The next step was establishing individual and branch goals that would bring recognition, such as names on the bulletin board or a mention at a meeting, but not tangible incentives. Those actions moved the average to 8.5.

Once that level had been reached, monetary incentives were brought into the picture. In fact, in this case, the incentives were defined by the tellers: they would draw up a "wish list," which ranged from weekends for two to having their house cleaned by a cleaning service. Using the incentive plan brought up the average to 9.5.

Monetary incentives should be used to maintain and sustain a quality of work that requires unusual or superlative effort on the part of the employees. Thus, all employees should already be performing at their highest comfort level. The incentives were adequately appealing to the tellers to motivate them to stretch further.[2]

The Role of Communication

Many so-called motivation problems do not stem from motivation issues at all, but from the lack of something basic —good communication. Organizations often fail to get the results they seek because they (1) never precisely told the employee what to do and/or (2) didn't tell the employee that what they were doing was correct and should be repeated. In fact, many motivational plans will fail, including those with strong monetary incentives, if good communication is lacking, and many motivational plans can succeed without monetary incentives simply through improved communications.

In short, people do not necessarily need monetary payoffs to be motivated. The "reward" can be consistent peer and manager approval and a strong sense of self, emanating from a well-executed job. In this regard, good communication is the binding element.

To those not familiar with this concept, it's surprising how effectively better communication can improve and stimulate motivation to performance. Listed below are three critical motivation tools in which better communication is the common thread.

Number One Simple, Overlooked Motivation Tool

Imagine playing a game with only vague rules. Let's take football. You know that getting the ball to the opposite side gets you points, but you don't know quite how many. Sometimes you get a lot, sometimes hardly any. And you often can't determine if you should go after the ball yourself or let others do it while you attend to something else. In addition, you have to overcome many obstacles put in your way. Should you meet them head on or circumvent them? You're not even sure whether you're winning the game or losing until the referree suddenly says the game is over and announces the winner.

If that were the case, football (or baseball or basketball) wouldn't be much of a game. It *is* a great game precisely because the rules and roles are so carefully defined, and the interrelationship between the role players so definitely honed. The same concepts apply in business. *One of the most obvious, yet consistently overlooked, motivation tools is having well-defined roles and goals: that is, job descriptions and performance goals and standards.* They are so taken for granted as a fact of bureaucratic life that they are almost never considered for their real purpose—to define the job adequately so that employees can understand what performance is expected of them and when they are doing well.

Simple clarity is the first issue. Consider the difference between a job description for a CSR that says "respond to customer inquiries on a timely basis" and "phone response to customer's inquiries within 24 hours of receipt of inquiry, follow up by written correspondence within one week if the amount exceeds $250 or at the customer's request." Which job description is more likely to generate the desired performance? It's no contest.

The second issue is the relative priority of each activity. If the job description for a relationship manager indicates cross-selling to current customers, monitoring credit status, updating the budget, and developing new relationships, which should be attended to first? Should the majority of time be spent on developing new customers or expanding relations with current customers?

Well-written job descriptions that communicate what each employee must do to successfully perform the job are powerful motivators. They tell the employee where the pay-off will be. When employees are clear on direction, they are more enthusiastic about performing the task because they know that the reward lies in doing what management wants.

Job descriptions can also assist in establishing development needs. Many banks are now asking employees to up date their own job descriptions, or at least the performance standards aspect, as part of the performance appraisal routine. It's a worthy time-investment because it requires the employees to focus on their roles and contributions to the bank. It also allows them to pinpoint how the job is evolving and to reestablish priorities.

The Handwriting on the Wall
One organization discovered that having employees exchange their job descriptions with others (either formally or in informal chats) greatly improved team-building efforts, particularly between the platform personnel and the operations areas. When employees understand the complexity of

the others' roles they became less critical of mistakes and foul-ups and more appreciative of the demand made on other groups. Most of all, exchanging job descriptions served to open up the employees' mind in considering where they were falling short (in conjunction with the performance appraisal) and the actions they should take to improve. Having the standards made known is the only way for the employee to do any kind of self-assessment—giving the employee a sense of achievement (in itself a powerful motivator). But, too often, goals and standards (assuming they have been determined) are poorly disseminated—hidden in a handbook or buried in the manager's desk file. Often, individuals do not get wind of their contribution until performance-appraisal time, when the manager points out shortfalls. "You're not very good at this, or you haven't been doing that," frequently to the surprise of the employee who thought that he or she had been doing an adequate, perhaps even superior, job.

Up against the Wall

Where should the standards and goals be noted? *Place them in the front of every sales manual. Better yet, post them on the wall.* Sure, every bank has a poster that says, "Our customer is the most important part of the business, and we should treat our customers with respect, blah, blah, blah." But what does that mean in day-to-day effort. Replace that poster with one that conveys the precise activity that represents superior performance: "At some point during every customer contact, we will inquire about the status of the customers' CDs: if they have any, when they mature, and whether they have considered other alternatives." Or, "We will make telephone contact with at least one customer a day in order to cross-sell." If you want solid performance, give clear directions.

At Southeast Bank in Miami, the performance-appraisal system was changed to improve the employee's awareness of what was expected. "Our old performance-appraisal form had four pages—you know, the typical standard form," notes Bob Day, Vice President in charge of sales and service in the community banking area.

One page discussed the employee's current productivity; the second page, the manager's comments; the third page, the what-needs-improvement and how the employee should go about it.

The last page used to be a "goals-and-objectives-for-the-coming-year" review, filled in by the employee. Sure, they are designed to provide the next year's objectives, but it was simply too broad a request. The responses ran the gamut. Some were very general, as in "I will work harder and be more thorough." Others were quite specific: "I will attempt to meet a quota of 300 new accounts." Judging employees the following year based on these types of expectations was obviously a problem and often unfair. Was the person who brought in 299 accounts to be penalized more than the person who only wanted to "work harder" and only brought in 100 new accounts?

Southeast changed the last page of the performance-appraisal form. No longer does it elicit vague or arbitrary goals. Rather, it specifically lays out what is expected of each person in the areas of sales and production, with the weighted importance of each function. For instance, 60% of the job should be devoted to selling, 30% to production items, and so forth.

This information is like a contractual "rider" to the job descriptions. The job descriptions are broadly formatted and remain basically the same from year to year. The goals and objectives sheet translates the job description into meaningful expectations, which vary each year according to the employees' capabilities, market conditions, bank strategies, and the like. (See Figure 7–1.)

"I couldn't believe the impact of this simple change," noted Day.

Of course, the other half was to make the right type of data available so that we could determine if the goals were being met. At first, we thought it would require revamping our information system; then, we found that the data was there all along—we only had to retrieve it. It's incredibly effective and so simple. I simply can't imagine how we got along without it all these years.

FIGURE 7–1
Personal Banker Performance Goals and Objectives

Banking center

Staff member

PERSONAL BANKER
Functional responsibility

19 _____ PERFORMANCE GOALS AND OBJECTIVES

SALES (Weight _____%) (not less than 70%)

1. Achieve _____% of total points of banking center, and a total point
   production of: _____ Qtr. 1
                  _____ Qtr. 2
                  _____ Qtr. 3
                  _____ Qtr. 4
                  _____ TOTAL

2. Participate in telemarketing program with existing customers to determine
   service level and identify future needs; monthly reports to be given to
   supervisor.

3. Attend at least one SEBC training program or product training by year-
   end.

4. Reflect satisfactory results by "mystery shopper."

5. Maintain knowledge of new and existing products and procedures to service customer needs, and review and submit daily the Closed Account
   Reports.

6. Maintain total sales point production in Sales Tracks that equals or exceeds the average sales production of people in your same capacity in
   Area II-A.

7. Maintain _____% of service charge reversal.

OPERATIONS (Weight _____%)

1. Receive zero valid customer complaints; all phone calls to be returned on
   the same day.

2. Ensure, within your area of responsibility, that operational audits are satisfactory, and assigned certifications are accurately and timely completed.

3. Timely reverse all overdrafts that result because of service charges, and
   which appear on the Demand Overdraft Journal prior to their attaining 30
   days. Control NSF/Service Charge Reversals by reviewing the Demand
   Overdraft Journal daily; mailing letters as needed; closing accounts as
   appropriate.

4. Maintain procedures to reflect:
   A. Return of signature cards, no more than _____ exceptions.
   B. Tax I.D. number on Business Accounts, no more than _____ excep-
      tions.

FIGURE 7–1 (concluded)

   C. Filing of customer records within 7 days.
   D. Q & E return applications not to exceed _____.
   E. New account documentation exceptions not to exceed _____.

5. Maintain security procedures to ensure zero operating losses.
6. Justify, by written report, to Management any account that has been in overdraft status of more than 15 days.
7. Meet all deadlines on special assignments, reports, verbal or written on or before due dates, unless approved by Supervisor.
8. Maintain operating charge-offs not to exceed $_____.
9. Provide timely follow-up to customer service unit phone calls, mail, etc.

Signature   Date

Source: Southeast Bank, Miami.

Count the Wins, Not the Losses

John Sponski, Corporate Executive Officer at Sovran Financial Corporation's operations area in Norfolk, instructs the managers to set the goals very carefully.

Everyone wants to be successful. Goals should be established based on that idea. For instance, let's say that we want everyone in a certain area to have a 20-second completed response rate for 95% of incoming internal customer information phone calls. (At least 5% of the phone calls will require greater analysis than can be achieved in 20 seconds.) But if the current rate is only 75%, we know that we would be overwhelming the morale of the employees to insist on 95%. So, instead, we speak in terms of a 10% increase, to 83%, which is much more attainable. When that occurs, we celebrate our victory with a big hoopla and then move on to another 10% improvement. That way, we can slowly get them to think in terms of 95%.

Sponski noted that Sovran's attitude towards training is the same.

We believe that success breeds success. We don't think in terms of testing what they don't know, but rather what they do. We aim to have everyone get the best results they can on the test; this way they will be encouraged to learn more. Our goal is not to weed out, but rather to build up.

Our ultimate success is in the eyes of the customer; in our case, primarily other Sovran departments. Our aim was to have them consider us completely reliable—so much so that the high quality of our performance is completely expected. Unfortunately, we don't receive any kudos for it anymore. For instance, our first conversion to a tandem data system went so smoothly that there was no notice of it when the second conversion came off as well.

But reward need not come from others. We establish our standard, devise a strategy to meet it, provide the means to attain it, and reward ourselves when we achieve it. That's all we need.

Number Two Simple, Overlooked Motivation Tool

The second tool is simply *recognition*. In the book, *The One Minute Manager*, the author is right in pointing out that the annual performance appraisals are not enough. If you want real results, you have to ap-"praise" daily. It can range from "nice job" to putting an article in the in-house bank magazine. Most managers provide recognition when they think of it or when something especially extraordinary occurs. This is unfortunate because the average-but-better-than-before performer also warrants attention for the effort in going one step further. After all, the goal is to get overall average performance to "notch" higher—not just to reward the superior performer.

As a result of managers' lack of emphasis on the continual pat-on-the-back, most employees feel their achievements are underrecognized, even though for the most part they feel that they are being properly evaluated. In the employee attitude surveys completed by the Bank Administration Institute, nearly 80% feel that their superiors give them an appropriate *evaluation* of their work. However, in the same surveys, less than half the employees feel that they get the appropriate *recognition* for their work. The difference is subtle: receiving an evaluation is expected; receiving recognition is special.

Recognition can be especially effective when small hurdles have been overcome. The employee who overcomes innate shyness for the first time and reaches for the telephone to make a call, even if he or she hangs up the phone before the customer answers, deserves recognition for having achieved even that little. It will help bring the next call to completion.

Praise done randomly tends to diminish the value of praise. A systematic approach is critical. Praise that is given "when I think of it," is usually "thought of" when there's another extraneous factor occurring, such as a big project that needs to be done. Employees are wise to this. They know that something triggered the event—that the praise did not arise spontaneously. The praised employee thinks Gee, the boss is in such a good mood; he must have gotten a raise, or, worse, I wonder what she wants now.

Not by Praise Alone

Of course, praise, although powerful, is not the only form of recognition. Other types of recognition abound, such as "the million dollar deposit club," "person of the month," or lapel buttons that say (in effect), "I'm a star performer." A bank in Ohio, which has 122 branches in 17 regions, introduces positive reinforcement through recognition and minor tangible awards. The first is by having a branch-of-the-district-of-the-quarter award. The branches that have exhibited the most "behaviors" correctly, such as attempts to cross-sell (even if the sales weren't made), win the awards. Everyone in the branch receives a prize, ranging from pen and pencils sets to cleverly designed beach blankets. The branches that have won awards get to join the President's Club, where additional prizes are doled out.

Perpetual Recognition

The bank incorporates recognition while doing training evaluations. Someone from the training area does spot-checks at the branches to determine effectiveness of recent training programs. They regularly watch a training alumnus in action with a customer. If everything is handled correctly, the trainer often passes out a prize on the spot, such as coupons to McDonald's or movie tickets.[3]

Perpetual Financial Corporation, based in Virginia, also recognizes the importance of the individual within the organization by offering service-quality awards to outstanding employees. In a unique move, though, Perpetual decided to honor all its employees publicly. On July 20, 1989, it took out a full-page advertisement in *The Washington Post* and several other local newspapers and magazines. The headline stated, "In accordance with federal regulations, Perpetual is publishing a list of its assets." The ad then listed the names of all 1,821 Perpetual employees. The ad copy continued, "Thanks to the 1,821 associates who helped make Perpetual a $6.5 million institution. There's a name for people like you: the best."[4]

The financial disclosure ad kicked off a day of surprises for the employees. After arriving at work, managers handed a package to each employee that included a poster-size reprint of the ad, a fortune cookie that contained a prize announcement, such as a set of mugs, a disposable camera, or a paid day off. Other prizes included wearable items, such as sweatshirts, golf hats, and visors. Everyone won some kind of prize. Banners were placed in every office with the headline from the ad. Visits were made by executives to personally thank the employees. Even the chairman hit as many offices as possible. Was this appreciated by the employees? Do you think that it succeeded as a motivational device? You bet.

Everyone Needs a System

Despite its potential impact, many managers shy away from using these recognition techniques for fear of being unfair, recognizing one person more frequently over another. It's true that partiality can easily creep in. One bank discovered that the best performance appraisals often went to the most extroverted, outspoken people whereas the quiet ones, who were equally effective on objective measurement standards, were often getting mixed results. (Nothing new. Experts point out that thin people are perceived to be smarter than fat ones, regardless of their IQ test scores.)

Southeast Bank's measurement system was designed to get managers back to doing systematic objective recognition. The bank provides the managers with monthly lists of the level of sales of each individual by name as well as his or her comparative ranking. The information is displayed in an open area in the branch, such as in the lounge or over the water cooler. As Bob Day commented, "There is no favoritism this way; it's out there for everyone to see."

Recognition can then be doled out by everyone—not only managers, but coworkers. Day remembers that at one award rally, the winner for the quarter was literally surrounded by his colleagues asking him specifically what he had done to bring in so many sales and how they could do the same thing.

Southeast scours the winning group to find the story that backs up their sales success and highlights them in the house newsletter. "For instance," Day added, "we had one woman who got on a bicycle on a Saturday, toured her own trailer park, and sold dozens of senior-citizens accounts to her own neighbors. They love it. We love it. We're still learning how it can be done."

In addition, the bank's then President, John Porta, regularly called the top producers to congratulate them. "When I got my call a few years back," added Day, "I milked it for months. You know, 'The other day, as I was speaking to John,' and that sort of thing. It's small, but it sure goes a long way."

The recognition works on both sides of the coin: Southeast recognizes the nonperformers as well as the performers.

> It's been a real motivator. No one really wants to see their name in last place (and if they don't care, then we know who to let go). I heard that one person, after seeing her name on the bottom, said, "I'm never going to let this happen to me again" and became top producer the next month. The president also calls the bottom performers, suggesting they give the top performers a call to get some selling hints. Believe me, that also goes a long way.

The Bank of Boston has a special service-training program called "Partners in Service Excellence." In it, they've paired branch managers with operations account managers. Each tours the other's departments, so they can see the problems their counterparts have to deal with and how important the service element is to customer satisfaction.

Just improving communication between the two areas went a long way in solving service issues. Each comes away with a much greater appreciation of the other's job, allowing them to find ways to support each other rather than to point fingers.

They also have established a Checkwriting for Service Excellence Recognition Program: an individual in a branch may reward operations personnel with checklike chits (see Figure 7–2). The pilot program, which was very successful, was run for two months between the bank's 107 branches and the deposit account managers. In essence, branch personnel were issued "checkbooks." Twenty-five hundred checks in all were distributed to the branches. Anyone in the branch could issue a "check" to whomever in the deposit area provided superior or consistently high service. That person accumulated the "award credits" given on the check. Those with the highest points received a cash bonus; those with fewer points received other types of awards.

FIGURE 7–2

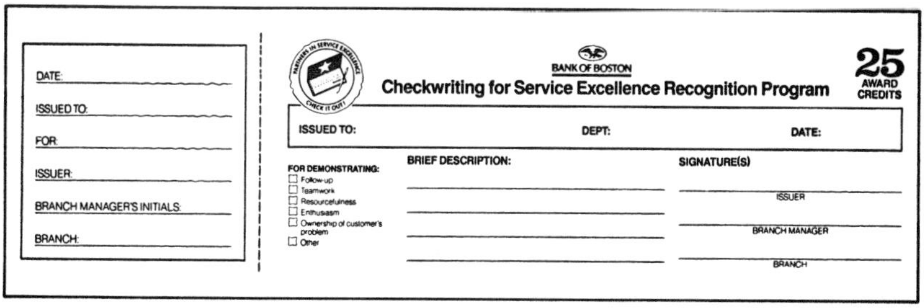
DATE:
ISSUED TO:
FOR:
ISSUER:
BRANCH MANAGER'S INITIALS:
BRANCH:

PARTNERS IN SERVICE EXCELLENCE — CHECK IT OUT!
BANK OF BOSTON
Checkwriting for Service Excellence Recognition Program
25 AWARD CREDITS

ISSUED TO: DEPT: DATE:

FOR DEMONSTRATING:
☐ Follow-up
☐ Teamwork
☐ Resourcefulness
☐ Enthusiasm
☐ Ownership of customer's problem
☐ Other

BRIEF DESCRIPTION:

SIGNATURE(S)
ISSUER
BRANCH MANAGER
BRANCH

Source: Bank of Boston.

Everyone receiving award credits was honored on the electronic bulletin board in the operations department so that they could be recognized by their peers as well. During the program's run, the bulletin board was always surrounded by employees watching the names as they came up.

Although, clearly, it's the operations personnel who directly benefited, the program was especially welcomed by the branch personnel—the *givers* of the chits—who were pleased to have a systematic way to recognize their service counterparts without feeling self-conscious. When the program was first introduced, it was feared that the branch personnel would feel burdened with "another thing" to do. The response was just the opposite. In one two-month period, over 1,000 checks were issued. It beats hands down the previous practice of cookies at Christmas.

Number Three Simple, Overlooked Motivation Tool

Name one successful sports team whose coach sat on the sidelines during all the practice sessions and never commented on the actions of the team members. After the big playoff, the coach pulls aside the team members and tells them what they did right or wrong during the whole season. Each team member thinks *Now* you tell me.

It is so ludicrous that it can't even be envisioned. We all know that coaching is critical in sports. Each game requires a highly complex set of activities and behaviors. Slight variations in these behaviors can cause the loss or win of a game.

The work environment is not a perfect extrapolation of the sports environment. Coaching opportunities are not as continuous as they are during football practice. But, even so, the less frequently coaching is done in the workplace, the harder it is to do because the activity seems so out of place. The BAI employee attitude survey referenced above supports the idea that managers are simply not providing enough feedback. At least 33% indicated that frequency of the feedback provided by their superiors was at an unacceptable level. And only 32% thought it was done often enough. (The rest were neutral.)

Perhaps because coaching requires an "I'm smart; you're not" posture by the coach that it is so infrequently done. One manager reported "feeling funny about always commenting on subordinates' work. I could treat my son's little league team like that, but when it came to employees, most of the time I just felt like I was hounding them." Nonetheless, the manager admitted that there was a definite improvement in the sales figures. "I got them to spend less time during a sales call talking about irrelevant stuff and to push towards the close. It was very useful there."

Coaching does not directly motivate employees to work harder any more than formal training does. But it assists the worker in being able to obtain additional recognition. Formal training usually removes the employee from the manager, so the manager cannot perceive the level of improvement. Coaching gives the employees an opportunity to improve their behavior before the eyes of the very person who will deliver the recognition and reward.

A Passion for Coaching

Tom Peters and Nancy Austin devote a full chapter to coaching in their book, *A Passion for Excellence.*[5] They note that even when coaching is done most casually, it's a complex skill. The tone between the coacher and the "player" has to be just right. The coacher cannot feel or act arrogantly; otherwise the player will be hurt or defensive.

Peters and Austin did *not* devote 65 tightly spaced pages to the coaching because it was already so well done by managers. They perceive an enormous hole in the manager's ability and comfort level to coach, as well as an insensitivity to what coaching should ultimately achieve. Its overall usage is generally limited to improving functional skills; for example, "Don't do it this way; do it that way." However, a superior coach can utilize the coaching opportunity to communicate more than just technical feedback, such as: enthusiasm, support, pride, encouragement, values, and motivation.

One simply cannot develop into being a superior coach

without superior training. You can read all about it in the self-help books, but, like sales training, actions will not automatically follow words, nor will a quick one-two review get you the desired results. Many managers have to overcome their natural resistance to nitpick employees, a significant behavioral change. After that, they must develop the timing, tone, posture, and verbal communication style to win over subordinates, not rub them the wrong way. Banks embarking on a sales-management program should make sure that they do not shortchange training for coaching capabilities.

"We take special care in how we develop our managers' coaching skills," noted a trainer at an East Coast regional bank. "Since this group is most responsive to positive reinforcement, we create homogeneous role-play groups, in which the peer members are asked to provide feedback. This continuous feedback process can then be more comfortably carried over to real situations on the job."

The trainer added that in her mind, the most critical concern for her group is assuring that their management supports their coaching efforts—particularly since the time spent coaching is time lost on personal achievement. Coaching must be perceived as a proactive aspect in developing the organization and not a punitive aspect of being a manager. Those who are successful in their coaching role should be rewarded. "Unfortunately, we cannot say that everyone here appreciates the value of coaching. And without the continuous support from the managers' superiors, we cannot guarantee that our training in coaching will be effective for the long term. Just like their subordinates, managers need to know that *they* are doing a good job too."

Bankers Just Wanna Have Fun

Despite all the emphasis on using these motivational techniques, they are not the only route to aiding employees achieving goals. Norwest looked for new ways to motivate its employees. "I asked myself the simple question of why people like to go to work," noted Richard Kovacevich, President of Norwest Corp., in response to a question about the quality of the training program. "The answer to me was the one I would give—because they want to have fun." (Yes, fun.)

"Now, attracting *good people* to our bank has never been a real problem. It never is if you dangle the right things in front of candidates. The hard part is *keeping the people good.* It doesn't take much to start losing interest and enthusiasm. And those attitudes radiate out. The new people learn it from the experienced ones. If they're not happy, no one else will be either."

Norwest should know the impact of attitude problems quite well, having experienced some serious losses in the mid-80s. "We know that business is a lagging indicator; employee attitude is the leading one. So we set up one goal for everyone—that work should be fun. If you don't like what you do, you're not going to be happy about doing it. I believe that employees want to do a good job and be proud of their achievement. We only had to give them direction."

Employees plan dozens of sales rallies, prepare videotape skits, and bring in entertainment, all to keep the enthusiasm (read *attitude*) high. At first, senior managers were active participants in designing the "fun." Now, the employees can do it well enough on their own. Kovacevich did much of the kickoff work himself. He even played the role (including singing) of one of the Beach Boys in a skit.

> I used to be actively involved in designing the videos and entertainment. I wanted to make sure the fun value was there. What's the point if people don't enjoy themselves. I'm happy to say others working on the entertainment soon figured the same thing out. Now, I only see the videos after they're finished. And they're all great.

Fun aside, Kovacevich knew that Norwest could improve the cultural attitudes as long as the value system they were imposing was similar to the one that the employees already had. He notes, "The right attitudes are already there; they always were. All the bank has to do is draw them out. People want to enjoy work and be proud of what they do. Just give them opportunity, and they will produce for you."

Fire That SOB

Not every banker so readily ascribes to the "Aw, let's just have fun at work" approach. Many bank managers, particularly those over 40, were raised in the "you're lucky you have a job, and don't you forget it" school. Someone pointed out that most managers over 40 did a stint in the military before the universal draft was repealed. As a result, they cannot understand someone else's *need* for positive motivators, much less ones that are *fun*.

"Nobody ever had to hold my hand, and look how far I got," is the typical feeling. Of course, part of that emotion is a reflection of the resentment of someone else now enjoying what was denied them. But a greater part is rooted in having to deal with a way of doing business that completely reverses what they had believed and acted on: work hard, and you'll climb the corporate ladder.

Is everyone at your bank having fun? A human resources director at one Midwest bank reported that he had conducted a cultural audit of the bank by sampling a number of professional employees. The results showed that they were not at all happy with the culture at the bank. The senior managers saw the results and figured, "Well, it must be the sample; you've asked the wrong people." So another cultural audit was done among all the middle managers. The results were equally damning, but now the senior manager couldn't deny the validity of the results. But rather than perceiving that they, the senior managers, were part of the problem, they attacked the middle managers. "These SOBs work here, and we pay them! Fire 'em."

The Thrill of the Chase

John Sponski, Corporate Executive Officer at Sovran Financial, neatly sums up the importance of turning goals and recognition into "fun" motivators.

> Ultimately, we are seeking to instill in our employees the "thrill of the chase." We want to feel that there is more to work than just showing up. They have to feel like a suc-

cess. To the extent that we can, we try to turn work into a game. After all, isn't a game just an activity where the goal is adequately defined so that you can know when you are winning? We make sure that everyone can be a winner. We reward winners with cash prizes in order to keep the game continuously interesting.

Their interest in winning stimulates them to go to greater heights. We are always there to provide them with the equipment they need, through training and coaching, to make sure they can attain the goal line. We'll even move the goal line if the challenge becomes stale. It's not just the winning; it's the striving that keeps everyone thrilled.

Doing What Comes Naturally

Does use of motivational techniques come naturally to managers? Only if they've been exposed to them from their own managers. As in parenting, people raise others the way they were raised. But most of us were "raised" in the old school—annual performance appraisals and an occasional pat on the back. The changing of the managers' motivational style, therefore, has to be slowly inculcated through training and example. Over time, such techniques will come naturally, as such actions become internalized and accepted as the norm. But until then, training must lead the way.

Once basic motivational techniques are adequately incorporated into daily operational procedures, then tangible incentives should come into play—but not as a quick fix. Too often the end result is that the cost of implementation and cost of administering outweighed expected results. Some shrewd thinking should precede any plan implementation.

INCENTIVE PLANS

Keep the Inspiration Alive—Tangible Rewards

Incentive programs help "keep the inspiration alive—something that will remind them of the value of being effective," in the words of SouthTrust Bank's President and CEO, Julian Banton. They use a mixed-based program typically employed at many banks: an across-the-board profit-sharing system is set up for all employees, plus various plans for the functional areas to provide individual incentives.

For instance, at SouthTrust, tellers might receive an incentive award for referrals, the bonus amount differing depending on the type of products sold. Branch staff can increase their salary 10% to 30% in that manner. Commercial development officers, who generate leads for other credit and noncredit products sold, can double their salary. The pressure on top executives is the heaviest because the incentives only kick in when exceptional goals are reached.

Some banks refine the incentive plan even further by utilizing either variable-incentive or variable-pay approaches for reward distribution. In variable incentive, the employees' total cash compensation is determined by a base salary, plus a formula-driven incentive. It may include a regular merit increase with capped incentives or minimal or no merit increases, but uncapped incentives. In the variable pay approach, large formula-driven incentives plus management driven incentives are calculated. A base salary amount is subtracted from the incentive amount. If the base salary is less than the incentive, the incentive is added to the cash compensation; if it is more, then the base salary is lowered. The latter system has the benefit of stimulating more effort from the high performers who can make out better and reduce the overall cost for the bank because it reduces payouts to poor performers.

Ready, Willing, and Able
To make an incentive system truly work—that is, impact the culture of a bank—the effort must be carefully crafted and sustained over a long period of time. It should reinforce the specific behaviors that the bank wants to see in the long term. The refinements aside, all incentive plans should follow four basic maxims to be successful: Be simple, be specific, be attainable, be measurable.[6] Three more maxims come into play prior to actual implementation: The bank

should know whether it is *ready* with the appropriate systems, whether the managers are *willing* to make the effort to support the system, and whether the employees are truly *capable* of achieving the defined goals and the awards.

Are You Really Ready?

The success of an incentive plan is based on numerous factors, from basic design elements to the appropriate payout-funding mechanism. Nonetheless, certain questions should be addressed prior to embarking on any incentive plan:

- What is the bank's culture?
- Is there a natural entrepreneurial spirit that will integrate well with incentives?
- Are the employees the types of individuals who can sense an opportunity to reach out to benefit both themselves and the organization?
- Most importantly, if the culture is not appropriate now, can it be changed?[7]

Turning this information into a grid approach, the illustration on page 188 gives a clearer view of the types of work habits that are best suited to utilizing an incentive plan. Clearly, the more the employee's job role is open and unconstrained, the more likely that employee will feel comfortable in pursuing the rewards offered by the incentives. Thus, the "Conventional" level is not recommended for an incentive system unless the "culture" can be changed to resemble that of primary "Level I" and preferably "Level II," where the job role allows more freedom to take advantage of the opportunities offered.

They're Ready and Willing, Now Make Them Able

Managerial skills and employee training play a large part in the program's success. Programs established without previously developing the employees' skills to perform the tasks as well as managers' skills to coach and support employees

Appropriate Use of Incentive Plans

Degree of
Personal Initiative
Encouraged

	A	B	C	D
Proactive and discretionary job role (4)				Phase III
Reactive and discretionary job role (3)			Phase II	
Reactive and prescribed job role (2)		Phase I		
Reactive and directed job role (1)	Conventional			
Base salary	A Salary at market	B Salary at market	C Reduced annual increases	D Reduced base salary
Incentives	No incentive	Budget incentive or gainsharing	Annual incentive increase	High incentive potential with annual incentive increase

Employee earnings potential

Source: Reprinted with permission from *Enterprise, An Organization-Wide Performance Pay System*, a training manual developed by William B. Abernathy and Associates, Memphis, Tenn., 1988.

are doomed to mediocre results, at best, and probably frustration and disgust as well.

But not only is the quantity of training an issue, but also how the training is perceived. When a new program starts, employees are sensitive to implications that they are somehow lacking, and therefore more training is required. The training smacks of being remedial because "they didn't know what they were doing." Hostility emerges, blocking training efforts and possibly the effect of the system.

Just as debilitating, employees can view the whole program as "another bright idea" fostered by some guru and bought by management as a salvation to all the bank's problems. Employees think, "Sure, sure, we do this for a while; then management sees it doesn't work as well as they wanted, or maybe it cost too much, so we quit and go on to the next thing."

Most of all, the rank-and-file employees disliked being singled out over other levels of management. The implication is that they were the only ones who were dumb; everyone in management must be smart because they don't need any training. "It really grinds me up," commented one CSR after a round of training. "They're teaching us all this stuff about sales techniques. But our branch manager, who couldn't sell space heaters to Eskimos, doesn't have to go." Not including everyone in the training sets up a we versus they attitude that is very difficult to undo.

Management Goes First

"It would be ridiculous to structure an incentive plan for the employees without giving them the proper training," commented Bill Plechaty, EVP at Southeast Bank. "You put so much effort into designing an incentive system and then ignore developing their ability to meet the goals. That wouldn't be smart."

But to be most effective, training has to go beyond the employee level, added Plechaty.

> It not just making the employees capable of meeting the goals. It's also a major tool for senior managers. We have to shape and formulate attitudes. Anyone who thinks they can do that simply by writing a memo to all employees is completely out of touch. Talking about it doesn't help either. You can have everyone on a ship looking off the starboard side, but that doesn't mean that the ship will change course.

Plechaty is very supportive of basic, conventional training. "One of the best media of communication is in the classroom. We can blatantly tell them what we want to occur and then show them how to do it. Even as I say it, you can understand how one part supports the other."

In Plechaty's mind, "attitude" has to come from senior management. "If we don't demonstrate what we say through our actions, then why should they? If we say selling is important, then everyone in those areas will do sales calls, including the president. If we say teamwork is important, then we cannot be caught backstabbing."

Southeast made a clear show of support from the senior managers by the way the training was scheduled. In the community banking area, the bank is "layered" first with platform personnel, then branch managers, their superiors, and yet a higher layer of executives. But rather than training the lowest layer first, they started top down.

Southeast knew that the top level had to understand the sales and sales-management process first to be able to convey the right attitude to those below. After that, the next layer down went for the sales-management training, followed by the branch manager layer. Lastly, the platform staff went for sales skills training. "If we hadn't done it this way," noted Plechaty, "the incentive system would have been just viewed as another gimmicky attempt to rev up sales. We've got to show employees that we mean business."

It's also important to make certain that all the aspects of the program are closely related. Banks have discovered that creating a simple, specific program is the easiest part. The real effort comes in the establishment of the measurement and attainability aspect. Most specifically, banks require a program that rolls out the sales-training program as the incentive program simultaneously brought out. The relationship of the training and the incentive plan must be made clear to the employees: "We want you to succeed, and we're giving you the tools to do so."

You Get What You Inspect, Not What You Expect
"That which gets measured gets done," quoted Bob Day at Southeast.

> You can talk about employees being salespeople all you want, but unless you tell them that they will be measured based on their sales productivity, nothing will occur. Our incentive system is really very straightforward. On the community-banking side, we reward branch employees when the branch exceeds its monthly quota or threshold level. We dole

out the rewards based on the prorata contribution of each employee within the branch. This encourages the employee both to push as an individual and to work as a team.

The reward aspect is really designed to reemphasize how very important exceeding the goals are to Southeast. So we measure achievement, we recognize their effort, and we reward them for going beyond expectations.

Southeast established 15 different reports. The individual is measured, the branch is measured, the region is measured, and so forth. Each employee is also ranked by branch, city or county, region, and state, as well as the branches cross-ranked by city or county, region, and state.

More Than Just Numbers

The difficulty comes more often in the measurement. The tracking of the numbers is relatively easy. However, a bank should be seeking answers to more probing questions as well:

- Are most people availing themselves of the opportunity?
- Are they using the techniques learned in their training to help achieve their goal?
- Are they consistent in their approach, or is luck playing a big factor?
- Are they continuously supported by their manager?
- Is it negatively affecting any other work?
- Does the incentive program only result in spurts of energy, or is there really a behavioral change in their overall attitude towards their position?
- Will their new attitude towards work impact their other work behaviors?
- What is the long-term impact in terms of quality of the workforce?

Several elements that show up in the numbers should address those questions. The individual's measurement data should show (1) consistent productivity throughout the quarter, (2) an increase in sales after the completion of any training, (3) the effort only occurring near the end of the incentive period, or throughout the period. Sharp and sustained increases in branch productivity show if the manager is making the effort to stimulate the platform people.

The annual performance appraisals are used to determine the impact on other work requirements and longer-term implications. "It doesn't help to bring in a new customer if at the same time we lose an old one," added Day. "Incentive programs should add pizzazz to work, but shouldn't knock the whole bank out of balance. Quality of service has to be maintained even if we don't immediately reward for it."

You Get Precisely What You Inspect

The emphasis on the sales culture and the ease in measuring sales efforts tend to skew incentive awards towards selling. But many banks are applying incentives to other areas as well. Unfortunately, not all incentive systems are well conceived the first time through.

Sovran Financial ran into problems with its operations area plan. Although pleased in the beginning, they began to discover that it did not reward an individual for better behavior. In fact, the specific behaviors necessary to achieve a reward were never quite clearly defined. Rather, it doled out rewards based on whether a certain base was exceeded; the reasons for success were not critical. The employees didn't believe that the concept worked; they personally were not doing anything differently, and rewards sometimes came for all the wrong reasons.

For instance, if telephone responses could be handled within a certain amount of time, the department would be eligible for an incentive reward. On paper, the idea sounded great, but it failed to take into account the speed of the responses when the computer went down. Rather than reflecting a slower response rate, the downed computer allowed them to simply say, "The computer is down," thereby creating a faster response time. Employees cheered whenever there was a computer problem because that meant a reward for them. That incentive system was soon scrapped.

It was replaced by one that was determined not by an outside entity, but by the employees and managers themselves. In fact, five separate systems were devised. They not only addressed the issue of rewarding for performance, not luck, but also the issue of having the employee understand precisely what must be done to have the performance be superior. Moreover, through group awards, teamwork was also rewarded. If one member of a group was overwhelmed, another could pick up the slack to assure the group's goals were met.

The incentive system was also heavily supported by training. Before being included in the incentive program, the new employees were given enough training to assure that they could attain the incentive base standard levels. Not only did they then feel confident enough to win an award, but their presence did not penalize the group.

BUILDING THE FIRE AND KEEPING IT LIT

Successfully motivating employees is one of the most important—and most difficult—of managerial tasks. The old days of handing out titles by the bushelful are gone, and a yearly appraisal and pat on the back are not enough to keep most employees performing at peak levels. Managers need training in motivational techniques. The tools of communication, recognitions, and coaching can be powerful motivating agents and easily inculcated through training and example. When these basic motivation techniques have become part of daily operational procedures, then tangible incentive programs can effectively be introduced.

REFERENCES

1. The American Bankers Association in conjunction with LOMA. *Incentive Compensation: Plan Design Features in Financial Services Companies,* March 1988.
2. Sucec, Jeff. "Using Various Motivational Tools to Improve Service Quality." *ABTAC Newsletter,* December 1989.
3. "Service Training: Placing the Customer First." *ABTAC Newsletter,* December 1989.

4. Koch, Jennifer. "Perpetual Thanks Its Assets." *Personnel Journal*, January 1990.
5. Peters, Tom and Nancy Austin. *A Passion for Excellence*. New York: Random House, 1985.
6. Cascio, Wayne F. *Managing Human Resources: Productivity, Quality of Work Life, Profits*. Second ed. New York: McGraw-Hill, 1989.
7. *Enterprise, An Organization-Wide Performance Pay System*, a training manual developed by William B. Abernathy and Associates, Memphis, Tenn., 1988.

CHAPTER 8

CREDIT AND TECHNICAL SKILLS: GETTING OUT OF GNOME MAN'S LAND

"Bankers used to be analysts who choked every time they said yes. Now they're salespeople who choke every time they say no. It's the eternal conflict between the gear heads and the fuzz heads."—*Jeff Judy, Director, Community Bank Training, Norwest Corp.*

What's the definition of a banker?

In the 60s, a banker was someone who took deposits, made loans, and cleared checks.

By the 70s, a banker was someone who took deposits, located other funds, made loans, invested funds, traded funds, moved funds, and cleared checks.

By the 80s, a banker was someone who took deposits, amassed funds, made loans, invested and placed funds, provided unfunded credit, traded funds and notional products, offered advice, moved funds, and, oh, cleared checks.

By the 90s—well, you get the picture.

Banking has changed, and so has its strategies. Training must continually be refined in order to support the strategy, and, in many cases, it has. Certainly, as new products have come on board, new training programs have been routinely introduced. However, sometimes training programs that had been successfully established early on do not always get the attention they require. This is especially true of credit and other technical skills.

TECHNICAL TRAINING: CREDIT SKILLS

Part One: Keeping the Right Emphasis

The continuous expansion of banking has shifted the influence of some very basic credit issues. Since the 70s, when banking was released from the constraints of limited liquidity through the opening of the domestic CD and the Eurodollar markets and the repeal of the Voluntary Credit Restraint Program, bankers have not had to face the problem of prioritizing lenders. Before all that, a bank had to select only the most creditworthy customers because the bank was limited to only a certain amount of loans on the books. The credit decision was the foremost factor involved in whether the bank brought in new business.

By the 70s, marginal cost was more the guiding decision factor than allocation: if the loan was creditworthy and generated in income more than the marginal cost of funds, well, why not? Doing the deal not only got you a loan on the books, it got you a foot in the door to sell other, profitable services. The concept was ultimately tested to its limits when capital-to-asset ratios fell below 4% in some notable cases—with consequences we're all familiar with. But the idea of doing the marginal deal still persists: making the credit decision is only one of several factors for taking on new business.

The ascendency of relationship banking and the related sales and service culture has shifted the priorities of skills at many banks from credit analysis to sales competency. In nearly every bank, the internal approval system as structured does eliminate the down and dirty loans. However, banks are often less effective when it comes to sorting among the incoming loans, in order to limit and diversify when one risk category, such as construction financing, has been used up. Rather, many banks continued to mine the mother lode (such as international lending, energy, real estate construction) until the walls of the mine collapsed around them.

Gear Heads versus the Fuzz Heads

"Bankers used to be analysts who choked every time they said yes. Now they're salespeople who choke every time they say no," noted Jeff Judy, Director, Community Bank Training, Norwest Corp. "It's the eternal conflict between the gear heads and the fuzz heads."

"It's much easier to take a liberal arts major and teach him or her analytical skills, than to take a finance major and teach interpersonal skills"—a sentiment oft repeated by managers when asked about recruitment preferences. "We are looking for relationship managers," read a Citibank recruitment ad in *The Wall Street Journal.* (The *Journal* found the phrase "relationship manager" so striking that it noted that particular ad in the "Briefs" column on the first page.) "Someone with strong marketing skills to call on middle-market companies in the area. Three years experience required. Also, knowledge of credit and loan structure important."

"Wanted," read another ad. "Someone with superior analytical and marketing skills." What is the likelihood of finding that person—someone who has both *superior* analytical and marketing skills. Ned Hermann, in his book about personality dominance,[1] reports the results of personality testing on over 500,000 people based on left- and right-brain dominance, which determines proclivity towards good analytical skills and/or interpersonal skills, among others. The tests determined that only 8% of the population have scored high in having dominance in both opposing brain functions. The majority of the population have their strong suits in one or the other side of the brain.

Even if the "fuzz heads" can be developed into decent "gear heads," their personalities are still split by the banking system. The rewards for volume come today; the rewards for booking quality credit comes tomorrow when the loan is repaid. Even when incentives are slightly penalized for lower-grade loans, the risk-reward payoff clearly favors doing as much loan volume now to waiting for the better deals

to come through. So being a fuzz head is much more personally rewarding than being a gear head.

Easy to Lose but So Hard to Replace
As Jeff Judy put it:

> We train them about credit, but all they hear is sell, sell,
> sell. Sure, they do enough analysis to put on "bankable"
> loans, but they can't see the problem with only bringing in
> marginal deals. They think that as long as the deal is good
> enough to pass inspection, they should do it.
>
> Pretty soon, they've got a whole portfolio full of nothing but
> marginal deals. In fact, they're all excited because they can
> price these deals 1% and 2% more than the quality loans, so
> they think that they are really raking it in. But the thing is,
> they're so busy selling and selling that they don't have the
> time to monitor these credits. Then, some of them go bad. And
> when marginal deals are bad, they're real bad.
>
> We try to get them to see that for every bad loss, they've got
> to find *at least 50 good loans in the same year* just to get back
> in interest income the amount of the principal that went
> down the tubes. No matter how you slice it, that's a lot of
> running around. It would've been a hell of a lot easier to do
> the analysis and the monitoring right in the first place.

So What Do You Recommend?
Why didn't they do it right? Because a lot of forces pull in
different directions. The problem rarely redounds to the
quality of the credit training. Most banks have good, and
some even have intense, training programs that put trainees
through the paces. (Every so often, though, I hear of a bank
that doesn't have any, and shades of Penn Square Bank
dance in my head.)

So the issue is not whether bankers are competent at
credit analysis. Rather it's whether bankers are focused on
credit or focused on sales—because the two have seriously
contradictory aspects.

Unfortunately, the dilemma of quality over volume will
not ease until competitive forces disappear. Even banks who
10 years ago would have been loathe to do certain business
(such as highly leveraged transactions) now find themselves

backed into joining because they can no longer fight. And since banks reward employees more for deals done versus deals rejected, employees will naturally push to have marginal deals approved.

The problem is further exacerbated by the general feeling that the credit analysis is a "negative activity": one is looking for the company's faults rather than at its good side. Further, analysis is a passive activity: reports are written, passed around, and then filed (except for negative reports that only serve to create distress). Even the most enthusiastic "gear head" can become disheartened by the long periods of crunching numbers if the work only results in shattering others' expectations of a company's creditworthiness.

So, by the time trainees hit the platform, they know that the sales effort elicits backslaps and good cheer, while the credit effort generates stubby pencils and snarls. No wonder their impressions of the importance of credit analysis has diminished over the last few decades.

You *Can* Have Loan Volume and Quality Loans

Some banks have been able to maintain a high portfolio and strong loan growth. South Carolina National Bank (SCNB) averaged a 15% increase in commercial loans during the last half of the 1980s, giving them a market penetration of 33% of all commercial loans in the state. Nonetheless, their average charge-off to total loan ratio averaged about .35%, about 20% less than their competitors.

They attribute the high quality to good credit policy and a strong monitoring system. Officers are directly responsible for their portfolio and are evaluated quarterly and just prior to their performance appraisal. The guidelines are that no commercial loan portfolio will have more than 1% past due beyond 30 days, or more than a .25% loss ratio for the previous 12 months. (Similar standards apply to installment loans.)

"If we see a particular portfolio slipping, our first question is to determine if the problems were within the officer's control or not," noted Bill Barksdale, Senior Credit Officer at South Carolina National Bank.

> I sit down with the officers to discuss what went wrong and how they are attempting to deal with it. If the officer was negligent, then we find out whether it is a question of too little training or a question of competency. The training issue we deal with as soon as possible. The competency causes us to think twice about the person.
>
> If they are not up to snuff, their career advancement opportunities are severely limited. Most know to vote with their feet and quit. The others can proceed along the training development path laid out. I guess you could say that one of the rewards for maintaining a strong portfolio is the privilege of being further trained and developed.

Banker as Doctor

With the continual monitoring of the officers' credit performance, the bank is sending the signal that quality is a critical issue. Part of getting employees interested and focused on the analysis side of lending is to improve the perception of its importance. "Banks are guilty of creating heightened expectations," added Barksdale. "That's because so many credit programs put all the interpersonal skills into sales training and took them out of credit analysis. So trainees see sales as all fun and credit, all work. That's wrong. Interpersonal skills are really at the center of credit analysis."

Like other banks, SCNB places credit training at the center of the curricula, but, unlike others, it attempts to add another dimension. "We try to make the participants realize that credit is not a chore—a hoop you have to jump through in order to get the loan proposal approved. Rather, we get them to think of it as an opportunity to get to know their customers better."

To keep that sentiment from sounding like merely a platitude, Barksdale does a comparison to the medical profession.

> Think of doing an analysis as if you were a doctor looking at a patient. First, the doctor gathers all the basic data, tem-

perature, blood pressure, and runs a blood test, and so forth. Then, if he spots any number out of line, a more in-depth analysis is made. Meanwhile, of course, the doctor's asking lots of questions about how the patient feels, so that the information from the tests is put into proper context.

Barksdale continued his comparison. Do doctors consider this part of the discussion dull and boring? Of course not: diagnosing a problem and solving it is their profession. That's the fun part. "Of course, many patients don't even know they have a problem until the test results are in. It's the same with companies. Often, by the time the managers realize there's a problem, it's almost terminal. An analyst's role is to catch the problem before it's too far gone, for the good of everyone."

As homey as the example sounds, it adds a whole new dimension to credit analysis for the trainees. It serves to move their attitude towards credit from being a reactive (order-taker) to a proactive (diagnostician). "You know, lots of people hate doing credit analysis, not just because it's tedious, but because they're afraid of finding out bad news. Just as in medicine, finding 'bad news' should mean that the doctor has done a good job."

The allusion also adds to the stature and importance of the analytical function. "We try to get them to think of themselves as the company's internist. So every time our bankers make a call, we want them to use the opportunity to check the company's pulse rate and to peer down its throat. Too many people are afraid to ask questions. That is all wrong. Most companies love the attention."

Credit training should be an involved process in which individuals can sense their own personal involvement in the ultimate success. Just how is that accomplished? Several ideas follow.

The Trees and the Forest

Credit training should teach everyone how to look at forests as much as it teaches about the trees. Many trainers are older credit people who have been through a lot in the past 20 or 30 years. They've seen the big picture.

But that's not what is addressed in credit-training classes. We talk about ratios, cash flow, industry comparisons. Topics that trainers know well are easy to discuss: a current ratio is such and such; cash flow is defined as this and that—the trees. When it comes to talking about the forest, trainers often are a little less articulate. They presume that the trainee can integrate and extrapolate from their comments. Probably less than half the loan officers and trainees today have been through a recession. They haven't really seen the impact that a bad loan can have.

It's a common problem. Trainers think they have taught trainees everything they need to know when they have really only taught them only the basics. Even many so-called advanced credit courses often only address basic information, but in a specialized field, like lease financing or construction lending.

Worse is using self-study manuals or CBT as the sole source of credit training. Don't misunderstand: many consultant- and internally-designed self-study materials are superior in the approach to training, especially since they can dramatically reduce conventional training time and costs. (See further discussion at end of chapter.) But their message is limited to the learning style employed, which communicates knowledge-based "facts" far better than "intuitive" or inductive reasoning. A specific program should be designed that touches on the nonfact-based issues, and someone with high credibility must personally deliver the message.

In the Long Run We're Dead

Loan volume may impact earnings in the short run, but that credit quality will make or break the bank in the long run. The evolution of "service" in the banking industry has brought a motto on the walls of nearly every bank's cafeteria: "We've committed to servicing the customer." I suppose adding the phrase "as long as in doing so we do not take risks that exceed levels that a bank seeking to protect its shareholders' and depositors' funds would consider prudent and appropriate in the face of external and internal factors" rather weakens the impact. In short, bad loans break banks.

As mentioned above, that message is communicated within the confines of the classroom too little as it is and even less frequently outside it. Like a battery, the unreinforced message will lose power over time if not constantly recharged.

Bedside Manner

Good loan officers are as much financial doctors as they are salespeople, and good "relationship banking" behaviors should include actively plying those skills, not burying them. But again, the constant conflict between "servicing" and "offending" the customer comes into play. For fear of losing the business opportunity, bankers are more inclined to pull punches than to deliver them.

Much of the problem lies in the way relationship managers are taught to acquire information. "If you see a problem, call up the customer and ask why. Why are sales declining? Why are the financials late? Why is cash low?"

Communication experts know that any question beginning with the word *why* is an immediate offender. A training exercise consists of having two strangers holding a conversation, with the restriction that all sentences begin with the word *why*, such as why is the sky blue? or why are you wearing a brown shirt? These conversations usually switch rapidly from abstract questions about the sky to personal ones with the word *you*. The *you* combined with the *why* is an almost innate irritant for most people, and within minutes the atmosphere turns hostile.

In fact, many relationship managers preface asking their customers questions by explaining that the credit committee has asked for this information, just in order to deflect some of the annoyance.

If we want to develop financial doctors as much as financial analysts, then more bedside-manner training is required. In the best scenario, the bank-company relationship would not be seen as adversarial. Rather, the banker would display the same type of empathy and deference a doctor would with a client. Having established rapport, the banker would then be able to probe more comfortably and deeply into the customer's symptoms through a series of questions phrased to encourage response rather than to arouse hostility.

Most banks spend dollars and hours on teaching salespeople to question and probe in a manner that draws in the prospect. The same behavioral skills should be translated in the credit world (where getting the "right" response at the right time could be more valuable to the bank than any sales pitch).

The Most Fun Is at the End
Booking loans is "fun." Seeing them paid off is even more "fun." When sales volume quotas are made or exceeded, the individual or department may win an award, perhaps attend a sales dinner, or become a member of the President's circle. Compare that array of recognition with what typically occurs after the internal loan auditors review the loan portfolio and classify all of the loans as healthy. Awards, prizes, firecrackers perhaps? Dinners with the president? Forget it!

Many banks have devised state-of-the-art computer monitoring systems for tracking sales and service behaviors. By comparison, *loan* monitoring systems are still in the age of green eyeshades and columnar paper. The most unloved people in the bank are the auditors: their coming usually brings on scowls and cringes.

You get what you reward. Measure and reward loan volume, and you'll get more loan volume. Measure and reward loan quality, and you'll get loan quality. Granted, some incentive systems have built in a loan-quality factor (the lower the risk rating of the loan, the less the reward, and no reward at all for "unbankable deals"). However, the system does not encourage higher loan quality; it merely defines the lower limits. The system has no reward at all for loan-quality maintenance or for early detection of loan deterioration.

Getting Personal
Credit is more than the sum of its numerical elements: it encompasses an understanding of the human aspect of client companies' management. They are, after all, the decision-making forces behind the company. But since we prefer to

teach concrete data—and the credit discipline offers so much to work with—often, the nonfactual side is dismissed as so much fluff. Alternately, the discussion is reduced to the concept of "character," meaning, I guess, that one shouldn't lend to known pikers and felons.

The neglect of the human aspect of lending has led banks down the path with many notable overleveraged failures of the 80s because the real purpose in borrowing was arguably to satisfy an inner craving for greed and glory rather than the pure financial needs of their companies. Personality issues must be taught with the same intensity as industry ratios and cash flow.

Nonetheless, lending is still a process whose basis is foretold by numbers. Those who are not competent with the numbers (many attempt to justify their analytical shortcomings with good gut feelings) are doing the bank a disservice. Remember, only 8% are good at both interpersonal skills and analysis.

Dual Track

Several banks employ dual-career tracks—one for relationship managers and one for analysts—thereby relieving the account manager of the technical aspects and centralizing the analysis function with a more highly trained staff. This way, job requirements are realigned in order to focus people on doing what they are best-suited for, rather than having everyone do a bit of everything. In addition, it offers a better delivery system of bank products, with fewer middle managers and more "producers."

Under this structure, the analytical function is performed by a specialist, allowing the relationship managers to concentrate more on customer service. The training is distinguished for the two career paths—a relationship track and an analytical track.

Because it does not require as much cross-training, the time spent in entry-level training is shortened considerably (as much as half). The analyst position will require approximately only six months of training. Both groups receive the basic academic core skills, but the analytical track requires more rigorous credit courses.

Analysts are typically subjected to more knowledge-based testing, with a mastery of one area being a condition prior to proceeding to the next. In addition, the rotation periods through loan administration, loan review, and field examination department are extended.

A Horizontal Approach

When Seafirst Bank changed the organizational structure at Seafirst, they also changed their approach to credit training. Specifically, the bank removed the traditional vertical organizational design and replaced it with a more flexible, dynamic structure. For instance, in the commercial banking area, lending officers are grouped into teams which include three functional levels: team leader, officer, and senior officer.

The result of leveling out the organization was that individuals now had more autonomy in their activities, and to self-manage their development. "As a result, fewer 'touchstones' for training exist," commented Rodney Cornwall, Manager of Credit Training. "We realized that it made more sense to provide a training curricula which aims at improving productivity, rather than being centered around rank or titles.

Previously, Seafirst offered a relatively heavy entry-level curricula, followed by some training at the post entry, junior officer, and senior officer level. They reduced the amount of entry-level training, and replaced it with "core" training which new hires receive when they're closer to their ultimate assignment. "Journeyman" level training is available when an individual can accomplish 80% of their work without direct supervision. Ultimately, there is an "expertise level," designed to hone in on an individual's already advanced level of skill in a particular area.

"To make our training most effective," added Cornwall, "our focus is on functional tasks performed by individuals rather than on traditional areas of training." The structure of the training areas reflects that distinction. Separate training areas exist; for example, credit, trust, operations/computers, and personal banking. In credit training, Seafirst developed programs for just not the commercial lending, but community banking and installment lending as well. Cornwall continued:

> In that way, I can identify common learning needs of various departments and group them into a particular program. For instance, those who need to understand personal financial statements might be in commercial or retail banking areas. A training program is set up to meet the common requirements of both jobs, rather than having one course for commercial lenders and one for retail. Thus, our training is less geared around "career paths" and more towards "job sequences." People are being provided with building blocks of knowledge which they can transfer into the different functional areas within the bank.

When possible, Seafirst attempts to blend the training together into a progression of knowledge and skills advancement. While wary of over-homogenizing training, to standardize training, they seek to identify the most critical elements in their job tasks.

"Nice-to-know training is not a realistic option for us," commented Cornwall. "Our bank's incentive-pay structure induces people to stay closer to the customer than to sign up for 'away-for-a-day' activities. So to make our offerings beneficial, we design our training to relate directly towards performance improvement."

"In essence, we teach them the absolutes and ignore the grays. We then show them how to best apply these absolutes on the job. This is partly a result of having reduced our training to the most significant elements and partly a reflection of the bank's attitude towards credit—we would rather seek out one squarely centered borrower than concern ourselves with two on the fringes."

Part Two: Keeping Abreast

Many bankers, having been so well trained in credit in earlier decades, believe that the elements of basic credit analysis remain constant and tend to ignore the possibility that credit-analysis methodology may have changed since their introduction to it. "You'd be surprised how many banks still have not adopted cash-flow analysis as the basic point from which to determine repayment ability," noted Michael Pimley, who serves as the 1989–90 Chairman of the Professional Development Division Council at Robert Morris Associates (RMA), the Philadelphia-based national association of bank loan and credit officers which, in 1982, helped pioneer training to the banking industry based on cash flow.

> They still think the so-called five Cs of credit (character, collateral, capital, capacity, and conditions) cover it all. Many still believe that the only good loan is one backed by real estate. Of course, all those elements are pertinent, but it's cash flow, not capital, that assures the bank of being repaid on the loan's maturity.
>
> So when RMA teaches credit-analysis courses, I hear of many attendees complaining that they "know" that they could never get their own senior credit officials to accept a cash-flow-based analytical system. Well, what good is teaching a sophisticated approach if the participants won't, or can't, use it?

RMA, as well as many other credit-training organizations, has been bumping into this problem throughout the last decade when cash-flow analytical techniques started to become more prevalent.

> The credit scene is constantly in flux. Banks have to think in terms of providing training for the senior credit officers as well as the new hires. In fact, so many new credit issues have recently come down the pike, such as leveraged buy-out financing, that every bank needs a continuous education system if only to have a forum to discuss the validity of their own internal credit parameters. In fact, credit *training* can actually aid in shaping a bank's credit culture because the train-

ing by its nature is an examination of the elements that comprise credit decision making.

But, for a culture to be constantly in sharp focus, the decision makers must be active in the training, either as participants or as leaders. Credit officers cannot comfortably distance themselves from communication of the credit information, as either the sender or the recipient, and expect a strong unified credit culture to be maintained. Once the loan officers are at odds with senior credit officers' decision bases, conflict is bound to follow.

Continue the Education
Many banks have taken deliberate steps to assure that all of their officers are kept up to snuff. "The last thing we want," noted a trainer at an East Coast bank, "is to presume that once trained, all is learned.

> Even someone who went through the basic training program five years ago would be woefully ignorant about capital markets, the fastest-growing part of regional banks. Our vision is to constantly be enhancing the skills of the banker through continuing education programs. This way they can work with the more financially sophisticated transactions we do.[2]

This particular bank had gone through a series of mergers, causing a need for a revamp of the management-training program, if only to achieve a greater consistency in the quality of training among the eight different banks in the system. But, as the bank began to articulate the important goals of our training, it became apparent that more was at issue than just a uniform training curriculum. Particularly in a constantly shifting financial environment, banks need to maintain a high degree of professional knowledge and skills among all of their commercial lenders, at all levels, not just among the new hires.

The East Coast bank has, as have many banks facing similar dilemmas, established a defined, continuous education program aimed at keeping their officers current, well informed, and competitive. Typically, there is a specific number of courses that officers must attend. The East Coast bank expects that their officers will attend at least 20 hours a year of training. They have about 15 in-house seminars that they developed, covering general banking, technical and credit, and marketing skills. They will be adding more as the program expands. Employees are not restricted to these programs only. They recognize that various outside courses provided by banking associations, consultants, and colleges may sometimes work better in meeting an individual's needs.

Not Just for Education's Sake

As in the case of the East Coast bank, training and education are not the only goals. The other issues include corporate culture and personal interaction. For instance, that bank has the Loan Structuring seminar taught by a team of three people from different banks in the organization. This gives the attendees the opportunity to learn and develop a unified approach to banking, as well as create relationships among their peers from other banks in the holding company.

The reaction at the East Coast bank to the new programs was very gratifying: registrations started coming in the day the catalogs were made available. Attendees ranged from junior officers to senior vice presidents. Their response sent a very clear message—that we are addressing the officers' own perception of their needs for professional advancement.

There's no doubt that in the long run the personal growth of the individual will translate to growth of the corporation. Management's commitment to continuing education cannot help but aid in recruiting the most attractive candidates and retain a highly professional staff whose performance will favorably impact the bottom line.

Certifiably Knowledgeable

Not all banks are relying on occasional continuing education programs to make sure that the trainers are up to snuff—some managers are more adamant about making certain that their lending staffs are adequately prepared. For instance, at The Huntington National Bank in Columbus obtaining and *retaining* commercial lending authority is contingent on having completed the required courses given by the bank through their recently created training center, The Huntington Institute. The courses range in nature from financial accounting and credit analysis to negotiation skills. The amount of training necessary is commensurate with the level of lending authority. Even those who are already officers are required to revisit the training courses, or pass an proficiency exam or check. Ultimately, every lending officer within the bank will have "certification" for their commercial lending responsibilities.

Back to School

If anything, the greatest problem with continuing education is the inherent stigma of having to go back to school. Most trainers are reluctant to approach senior management to suggest their presence at credit and technical training programs for fear of the implied suggestion that they need to "hit the books" again. Other training directors have learned that it is not what's inside, but the way it is packaged that can distinguish an insult from a gift.

Right or wrong, a senior manager showing up at a seminar attended by lower-ranking officers is distressing both to the executive and to the junior staff. Even if the senior groups are not embarrassed (the material is so new, how could the executive have been expected to know it?), learning is stymied because neither level is willing to express itself in front of the other.

SouthTrust has taken the high road in order to keep its official staff informed on credit issues, noted Bill Schoel in the HR Development Area. He schedules credit seiminars on a regular basis for the senior officials. "In fact," added Schoel, "advanced credit training used to be done within a school setting, which ran for two four-day periods." SouthTrust dropped the format when it became problematic for the executives to be away for that length of time. The idea of variable length seminars was substituted, each running from one-half day to no longer than two days.

The subjects are determined by taking a poll of the senior officials, such as the banks' chairman, CEOs, and senior lending officers, but also by eliciting the opinion of the chairman of the finance department at Georgia State. Most commonly, "hot" topics are listed. These offer a sense of something new and urgent to the training, but "refresher" training is also added to the curricula. Recent topics have included Interpreting the Quality of Earnings, Assets and Equity, Lending to Companies under Cash-Flow Stress, Managing Bank Credit in an LBO, Real Estate Lending—all topics designed to look at the basics from another angle.

A Change in Strategy

Sometimes, a change in a bank's approach to continuous education was prompted by a change in strategy. After its trauma in the early 80s, Continental Bank in Chicago had taken the opportunity to redefine themselves so that they could rebuild their future. "Within a few months after the arrival of Tom Theobald, the new CEO, he developed a new set of strategic plans," commented Michael Pimley, who was head of the Professional Development Group at the time. "Those plans inevitably required a new focus in the training function, not just for the new hires, but for employees at all levels of the bank, from the executive level on downward."

Continental's strategy was to move its market focus toward the more sophisticated corporate end, which would entail having a cadre of highly trained and knowledgeable corporate relationship managers and product specialists. Pimley continued, "Restructuring the program for the incoming trainees would be relatively simple. However, the current official staff needed to be brought up to speed as well. It was an issue we couldn't and wouldn't sidestep; in fact, we gave it primary focus."

After determining which programs would be most appropriate to support the new strategy, the bank then set about organizing training sessions for the senior executives first. Top executives, including Mr. Theobald, were among the first to attend, and that set the tone for the rest of the staff. The response was remarkable. In fact, regular attendance at training programs is now part of an executive's routine; the bank targets an average of 10 days a year for them.

Pimley concluded,

> There's no doubt in my mind that the success of the senior management training program was a result of the top executives' obvious commitment to training. We cannot underestimate the value of good example: it eliminated the stigma of being retrained almost immediately. And needless to say, our growing success with the new strategic thrust was very gratifying.

TECHNICAL TRAINING—TREASURY SKILLS

The growth of the financial markets within banks has crept up so slowly that many bankers are continually astounded to see the enormous impact that they have had on the bottom line. In the 60s, the Euromarkets were just starting to emerge. In 1970, the trading of treasury securities was still occasional; foreign exchange currencies only began to "float" in 1972. The swap market didn't hit stride until the early 80s, as did other derivative products; and dealing in corporate securities didn't start until 1989 with the de facto collapse of the Glass-Steagall Act.

Department heads—much less anyone in training— could barely keep pace with the changes. Not surprisingly, formal training lagged way behind; not only did the subject matter change constantly but subject matter experts changed even more frequently as bigger salaries constantly sucked them into greener pastures. In any case, the financial departments were often independent of the training loop, relying, for good or bad, on on-the-job training (OJT). (A probably more typical-than-not account of sink-or-swim training at a money center bank is recounted in *Trading Up*, where the heroine takes over the FX currency options desk two weeks after starting the job when her bosses suddenly quit.)

On-the-job training for trading positions has many strong points. The job has a relatively low knowledge-based requirement, but high behavioral one (quick decision making), which can best be learned by doing. Unfortunately, many banks have found out the hard way that certain members of the trading staff have not mastered the decision-making technique. Even ignoring decision-making bloopers, OJT still remains costly, because the individual must spend a certain amount of time observing prior to doing, racking up salary expense without comcomitant productivity.

The Trading Mystique

Many believe that it's impossible to establish formal training systems for traders and others active in the capital markets. Like salespeople, most traders believe that they are born, not made. They believe that you can't be *taught* to make hairsplitting decisions. Either you can, or you can't—period.

Many traders, whose fast minds and urge for instant gratification kept them out of graduate schools and, very often, college, have a special consideration for those who did spend time pushing for an advanced degree: they can't stand them. ("Can't trade their way out of a paper bag." "So dumb they couldn't get arrested.") In the same vein, telling them that they will now be subject to the same "sit and listen" that they avoided for so long and which is a trademark of the very group they disdain, is rarely well received, especially if it takes away from trading hours.

Who can blame them? If the training does not achieve making them better traders, why do it? *Knowing* about a market has nothing to do with *trading* in it. (Otherwise, every finance professor would be a millionaire.) Thus, any training program must specifically be designed to achieve certain criteria:

- It should not rely on text or theory to convey knowledge.

- It should integrate all information into real-world scenarios.
- It should hone decision-making skills.
- It should serve to shorten the time between hire into the department and actual trading.
- It should be able to select out those whose decision-making skills are weak.
- It should be interactive, involving the participant as much as possible in the learning process.

Technological Training for Technical Skills

Self-paced learning, whether it be at the computer-based (CBT) or pen-and-pencil technological level, is just beginning to truly find its niche in training programs. Lots of trial and error have demonstrated that it is at its most productive when knowledge-based learning is involved, and it is well integrated into the bank's cultural issues, usually through the use of conventional, stand-up training.

CBT tends to be far less valuable as a training tool when either of those two aspects is lacking. The use of CBT for behavioral training, as in negotiation skills, is generally limited. The individual may productively learn "principles of negotiation" on a computer, but the actual modification of the behaviors is much more complex to achieve when the participant is only facing text on a screen.

The newer technology of interactive videodiscs (IV) holds more promise for us in behavioral situations. The technology involves utilizing a videodisc player (similar to a TV screen) as well as a computer. The participants respond to situations by selecting an appropriate answer. In turn, the videodisc will respond to the participant's decision by playing an appropriate scenario.

In general, however, self-study training performs best when factual information is being presented, such as the features and benefits of deposit-based products. However, self-study can be most efficient when applied to complex knowledge-based learning situations—those in which comprehension time may vary from participant to participant, such as in learning about capital and derivative markets.

In particular, CBT has a special edge over conventional training in presenting complex data because the participants can pull up "help" screens more readily and more frequently than they would be comfortable asking questions. In addition, it can "manage" more data, allowing the participants to cross-reference more easily. Thus, the quick studies can move right along, while dimmer lights can spend as much time as necessary to master the basics.

The other advantages of self-study learning, especially CBT, can be equally compelling.

- It solves logistical problems: one person in the West Cowpie branch can be as easily taught information as the 100 located at Big City headquarters.
- Learning can begin immediately after hire into a position: there is no need to wait for a critical mass to accumulate.
- Even at the slowest pace, the time expended at the computer is far less than in conventional classroom training.
- It obviates the need for classroom space, as most CBT and certainly all written self-study can be accessed at the desk.
- Learning can occur (and reoccur) at the point of need. Employees who have, say, learned about and forgotten the basics of interest rate swaps can readily reacquaint themselves by accessing either the original texts or any reference or job aids that usually accompany the texts.

Credit trainers have been one of the earliest groups to take advantage of CBT, particularly for accounting, financial mathematics, financial statement analysis, and credit analysis basics.

Not by CBT Alone

CBT—actually all self-study learning techniques—tend to suffer when employed in a strictly stand-alone capacity. For one thing, the use of self-study relies on the participant's self-motivation and discipline. Granted, the motivation level of the management trainee, especially the MBA, is very high. (One trainer reports seeing her trainees hold competitions to see who can finish their CBT modules first.) The motivation level is less intense with other groups—those who are already on the job and pressured with their immediate work, their families, or other activities.

Secondly, the quality of the training format is critical for maintaining interest. Straight text is monotonous. Making the text clever and full of well-executed visuals can be expensive, although the cost of developing a new, high-quality CBT program has moderated in recent years. (Allow 50 to 250 man-hours of development for every 1 hour of training time.)

Enter the Conventional Trainer

Equally important is the issue of personal involvement in the material learned. The more closely it is related to the work that will be immediately performed (such as deposit-products training for platform staff), the more the material will be internalized. On the other hand, information that is either relatively esoteric or tangential to the employee's main job function (such as capital-markets training for commercial lenders), the more likely the material will land in a type of learning limbo. It may never quite get connected to the "real world."

To counter that problem, enter the conventional, stand-up trainer. Ostensibly, the role of this person is to answer any questions related to the self-study training, but the real role is to assist the participant in integrating the material into his or her ability to perform better.

Thus, it's easy to underestimate the importance of the stand-up trainer. The temptation is to bring in a subject-matter expert who comes "for free" from the area of the bank the training addressed. Many times, however, that person is not focused on anything beyond the "any questions" stage—in fact, may not even be good at drawing out questions. The participant then hears a brief review of the same material and leaves the presentation still uncertain of the applicability to his or her job. In short, money wasted.

TECHNICAL TRAINING—OPERATIONS AND SYSTEMS PERSONNEL

Not surprisingly, the most prevalent use of computer-assisted training is in the departments that are most computer-oriented—operations and systems. "The problem with computer-based training for these areas is that programs can be so easily purchased. And so much quality design is already on a CBT format that we rarely consider alternative delivery systems," noted Tom Kraack, VP of Securities Services at Norwest Bank Minnesota. "As a result, you get lulled into assuming that you are meeting needs."

Technical training generally falls into two categories: computer and technical skills training for the bank as a whole and training for the bank's systems personnel. With regards to the first group, training often is spotty and unfocused: some banks may offer courses, others rely on the equipment vendor to provide training, and yet others consider training only when problems arise. Only the more farsighted banks have established programs to assure that all employees using computer equipment are fully literate prior to using it.

As an example, Mellon Bank in Pittsburgh established its technical training program seven years ago, as the bank began a major equipment acquisition program. It centralized the training effort, which allowed the bank to get away from scattershot training and offer a complete hands-on program available to all employees. A "guru" from the systems area acted as the subject matter expert when the training department developed the courses.

Access and Follow-up

Mellon offers assessment testing to participants to determine the level at which they should start training. CBT and interactive video training can serve both as introduction and brush-up courseware. But the bank doesn't rely on CBT exclusively: they do extensive convention training in our computer workshops to make employees feel as comfortable as possible with the equipment.

"Our experience taught us not to 'double up' on equipment," noted Connie Ruhl, who helped develop the curricula. "We found that one misguided person can lead the other one way off track. Rather, we give as much individualized instruction as possible. We also do follow-up evaluations with the attendees' managers to make sure the learning is applied immediately and not allowed to slip back into the mind's recesses."

Mellon also invested in equipment that could be readily upgraded, thereby lasting for the years since the program began. "Think long term when purchasing," cautioned Ruhl. "And maintain good relations with the vendors. They can be a great adjunct in developing and delivering programs. We even have a hot line to them that we use when we run into computer-training glitches."

A Better System for Systems Personnel

The training developed for systems personnel is the most likely to be perfunctory and least likely to include programs that are not job specific. Curriculum designs are often heavily oriented towards such topics as Advanced MVS/XA Dump Analysis and limited on anything more broadly based. The problem is that systems people are too often viewed as project workers rather than as long-term employees.

"Do we just want to train people who will do a job for us until a better position comes along?" asked Kraack at Norwest.

> Or do we want to engender these people with the bank's value system and attitudes, just as we would for a relationship or a branch manager? Of course, we want to develop in them a positive attitude, good team spirit, and create an atmosphere for reaching out to other resources within the organization—in other words, people who are as committed to the bank as they are committed to their careers.

No Critical Mass

Norwest Bank officials realized that under their old training structure, incorporating such values would be difficult to do.

> The training design needed better attention, but the programs were scattered all over the bank. When the programs are "owned" in diverse areas, one area alone does not have enough of a critical mass to warrant a training specialist. So we created an umbrella organization, the Norwest Institute of Technology (NIT), which would handle all the technical training and management training for systems personnel and for certain operations and clerical staff, as well as end-user PC training for all employees.
>
> Certainly, if nothing else, the establishment of NIT created a better synergistic efficiency. Overlapping programs were eliminated. The development of CBT programs became far more cost-effective and, with our far-flung bank subsidiary network, solved a major logistical program. Also, we could draw more readily on resident expertise.
>
> But we did not create NIT only to consolidate activity. We also wanted it as a vehicle for achieving our other goal of developing committed employees. To do that, we design many of the technical programs to have a personal aspect, often part CBT, part classroom training. In addition, we utilize internal people as much as possible as trainers. Not only can they relay a better sense of team spirit, it also provides us with an opportunity to discuss mutual values and expectations.
>
> In pulling together NIT, we also addressed the career concerns of this group. Typically, few systems people rise to, or, for that matter, are particularly aiming at management positions. Yet many see themselves as having "plateaued," either because they have nowhere to go if they don't become managers or because they are stuck behind someone who has more seniority, but not necessarily more talent. Such organizational structures, in my mind, tend to preserve mediocrity—particularly if the good ones leave for more challenging positions.

To counter that, organizations, such as Norwest, have deliberately set forth to create an atmosphere that prizes the superior technical specialist. Their aim is to develop the systems employee into the world-class level, which both enhances their own self-image and provides them with the ability to move around the organization into other appealing positions. The training aspect is the hub of the career directive: the more prepared systems people are for future positions, the more likely they will reach them.

Integrated Approaches

Too many banks place technical training—credit skills, treasury and systems knowledge—on a separate educational plane. The implication is that technical training is somehow independent of banking and/or that it should be held distinct from other involvement in the organization. Such thinking either serves to segregate the technical function, or it diminishes the value of what is learned. Technical training is not a stand-alone, nor are the technicians. Every aspect of the training needs to be fully integrated into the banking experience.

REFERENCES

1. Hermann, Ned. *The Creative Brain*. Lake Lure, N.C.: Brain Books, 1989.
2. "Continuous Education." *ABTAC Newsletter*, April 1989.

CHAPTER 9

MANAGEMENT TRAINING PROGRAMS: THE BEST AND THE BRIGHTEST

"Where do they train these people anyway"—advertising copy from a Norwest Banks' television ad comparing the quality of staff at other banks with Norwest. The Norwest University is prominently featured as an important reason to do business at Norwest Banks.

Ah, the management trainees—that elite corps that enters most every bank in the summer months, bringing the promise of the future. Their designation provides them with a passport throughout the bank and special cachet at cocktail parties. They are expected to meet high-performance standards and generally live up to expectations. Training funds are readily available and rarely diminished, except under the most exacting of times. In short, the value of the program and the trainees is undisputed.

If anything, the general acceptance of the program's worth may have done it a disservice. The sense that the program will never be touched tends to keep it from regular critical review. Granted, courses and seminars are changed to meet changing times. But, once established, the program's underlying purpose and mission are rarely re-examined.

What's to question? The trainees come in; they are taught the basics of banking and exposed to the working of the bank; then they hit the platform. In most every bank, the tour averages 18 months, with the advanced trainees and M.B.A.s making it in 12 and the brought-up-through-the ranks employee sometimes taking a longer period.

A discussion of the training program with bank managers, surprisingly reveals that many are vague about the

222

nature of the program. The *features* of the program are easily delineated: so many hours of coursework followed by such and such rotational assignments, and so forth, but the underlying *point* of the program is rarely well articulated. One hears explanations such as "planning for the future," "a good program aids in our recruitment effort." I'm certain that in many of the cases, "the point of it" has never been questioned at all, its existence having been so well entrenched in the bank's tradition.

DEFINING TRADITION

Actually, many banks are not really sure why they run a management trainee program. Tradition (as in "that's the way we've always done it") plays as much a role as analysis. Yet the lack of clear definition has an insidious impact. Left without a specific goal, many of the programs are left to drift to the most convenient direction rather than to the most meaningful course. Nor is there any guiding force that keeps the direction clear, such as a board of regents or an external examination group (such as the National Association of Securities Dealers that administers tests for the stock brokerage industry). As a result, programs range from bank to bank to the highly structured, extremely technical, collegiate level to very unstructured, heavily dependent on OJT "rotations" punctuated by talking-head presentations.

Any bank that is just setting up a program (and there are still some out there), and checks with other banks will probably come away very confused. The bank should back up and first question: *what precisely are we trying to achieve?* How will the program address these issues:

1. *Specialists versus generalists.* What is the specific goal of the program? Is the focus near term or longer term? If it is near term, then the bank's aim is to develop specialists—those that can enter into the designated position readily, such as a commercial lending officer. If a longer-term view is held, then the program should also be laying groundwork for future positions by developing generalists, with an overlay of the specialists' program.

2. *Impact on hiring and recruiting.* Will the program's design and purpose help the bank to attract better candidates? Will they be satisfied with the program or quit during its tenure? Will they stay after the program is completed, or does the culture in the "real life" bank fall short of expectations, leaving them as easy pickings for headhunters?

3. *Impact on current employees.* Will the program be an opportunity for all employees or solely for those brought in from the outside? Will it ultimately serve to create an elite group, whose presence will threaten or cause current employees to become disaffected and leave? Would such an occurrence be a positive or negative for the bank? Are there other programs that will raise the quality of the bank's current employees?

Generalists versus Specialists

In the early 70s, when many of the programs gained their toehold, the generic title of the program was "management-training programs," reflecting the assumption that all trainees coming through would eventually end up somewhere on the hierarchical ladder as managers. As time passed, other programs leading to managerial positions sprang up, as in the audit or operations areas, so that many banks switched the verbiage to be "the loan-officer development program" or something that reflected the true intent of the program.

Nonetheless, the program remains at the core of most banks. Banks have essentially broken into camps as to the program's entire purpose—to train as specialists or to train as generalists. Essentially, one approach says prepare now; you never know when you will need it, and you will not have enough time to fully prepare when you do need it. The other says prepare when you do need it; otherwise you might end up spending too much on too many too soon. Each camp has an equal number of rational theories to back up its decision.

The Specialists' Program
The specialists' program trains the individual to have a deep understanding of the chosen area of specialty. The largest

group typically goes into commercial- or corporate-lending areas; however, more emphasis is now placed on retail banking, operations, systems, and finance. The talent match occurs prior to joining the bank; thus, either the individual successfully completes the training program or is likely to be out on the street. The training effort brings into play only those aspects that are most likely to be part of the job within five years of entry. Minimal concern is given relative to the positions that might be held afterward.

Banks that prefer the specialists' program do so because

- The training effort best reflects what the trainees will be doing immediately after they complete their stint, rather than what they may be doing in the future. Therefore, no training hours are wasted.
- The industry and the organization are so rapidly changing that to expend the effort now for future positions is counterproductive. What is operative now may be completely obsolete in 10 years.
- Highly motivated trainees are typically eager to get going and don't want to be stuck doing something that does not have immediate impact.

Most banks offer the specialists' training through a decentralized training structure: the credit area is responsible for the lending program; the operations area for future back-office managers and so forth.

The Generalists' Program

In the generalists' program, the effort is focused on two main objectives: essentially, to develop individuals who have a broad understanding of the financial services industry and how the various areas of the bank function and to determine during the training period what specialty area best suits the individual and scope out the remaining training program to best meet the needs of that field.

The theory behind it takes a longer view of development.

- The bank will never quite know when the individual is likely to shift from one area to another.
- It takes best advantage of the individual's talents: the

bank can best determine an individual's true skills profile after several months have passed, and the individual can best judge for himself or herself which direction should be taken.

In most banks the generalists' program is managed out of a centralized training structure, usually the Training and Development Department or the Human Resources area.

Making the Decision

The strategic decision to have a generalist or a specialist program should come as a result of the strategic decision the bank makes based on its true needs, not on tradition or even monetary cost, since clearly the generalist program will be far more expensive. Some elements that should impact the decision are:

• *Timing considerations:* How long will it take to bring the trainees up to the level under consideration? For instance, if the division needs first-level officers within two years, can the bank afford the time of developing a broad training program and/or of having the designated individuals complete the program.

• *Expertise considerations:* Do the trainees receive adequate basic expertise required to actually work in different areas of the bank, or will the area have to do extensive additional training anyway? For instance, if the retail-banking trainee is transferred into a commercial department, can the trainee simply receive refresher courses, or is a whole new training program still required?

• *Degree of training considerations:* How is the training going to be organized in order to effectively develop the most important aspects with the least job disruption and cost? Will rotational periods be truly productive for both the department and the trainee, or are the skills so demanding that the trainee would not be in a position to participate?

• *Maintenance considerations:* How will the decision to go with a generalist program impact the current business lines or current employees? Will there be an even greater emphasis on their value and productivity, requiring the skills of the rest of the workforce to be continually honed.

• *Cultural considerations:* How will any strategic changes impact the current cultural environment? For instance, will trainees be considered outsiders and resented for their special situation? What additional management courses might be necessary to smooth out these issues?

First American Corporation in Washington, D.C., now an $11 billion bank holding company faced some of these issues. Robert Altman, its President, tells about how he saw the bank when the investors took it over in the mid-80s.

> Our plan was to have the entity grow. Then we were $2 billion in assets. Although not insubstantial, our view was that a smaller number of larger banks would dominate the market, and our size was not large enough to allow us to be one of the major players. Becoming a bigger entity is relatively easy if accomplished through acquisitions. However, we had not just a larger organization, but a more complex one. It's not just that a $10 billion bank needs five times as many managers as a $2 billion one; the whole business is different. The managerial skills had to change as well.
>
> Since "people" suddenly became a priority, our first step was to centralize the HR area into the holding company and to structure a uniform HR approach for the banking subs. We then took a three-part approach. As part of the overall scheme to attract and retain the best talent, we strengthened the incentive plan, improved our recruitment effort, and placed a major focus on training. For our future management needs, 5 to 10 years out, we entirely revamped the entry-management training program: all trainees from all the subsidiary banks are now trained uniformly at the headquarters in Washington.

Bringing the trainees to a central location for training is costly, but First American has very specific reasons for doing so. Altman continued, "Most banks train their talent for the specific position. Our strategy is different. First, we train them as bankers; then we focus on their specialty. We know we will need managerial talent, but since we cannot predict where, we're developing the well-rounded banker who can adapt to any area."

For their most immediate managerial needs, the bank

established The First American Management Institute, an in-residency program at Wharton School. The curriculum there was customized specifically for the bank, designed to develop leaders with applied knowledge of First American, not just generalized banking theory.

No Predetermination

First American's Manager of Training and Development, Bill Donahue, noted that at the beginning of the training program he asked how many of the new recruits would prefer retail banking to commercial banking. Very few raised their hands. "Commercial banking," according to Donahue, "is always the winner. It seems to be the more glamorous of the banking positions, and everyone wants to be associated with it. But by the time many of the recruits have finished their rotational period through both the retail and the commercial banking area, their attitudes have changed. The number of recruits that ultimately opt for retail banking jumps to over 60%."

The Huntington Bank in Columbus, which also hires on a non-predetermined basis, found that 100% of the trainees surveyed felt that being able to choose at the end was one of the most positive features of the program. Both banks use this aspect as one of their most visible recruiting sales points.

Short Run versus Long Run

The characteristics of "train-it-now" include many elements that will not be put into effect until later. At National State Bank in New Jersey, community banking trainees rotate through all the major banking areas, including loan administration, trust, finance and money, and the human resource area. The tour is not just "look-see." For instance, they will be tested on their understanding of salary administration and benefits. They must read a number of publications on topics related to managerial concepts, such as *From Control to Chaos* and *Decision Making Trickles Down to the Troops*, topics that are only of value if the trainees ultimately land in managerial positions.

Clearly, National State expects the trainees to hit a

managerial position at some point. During the time between now and then, they presume that if the trainees are cognizant of various banking issues, they will be more keenly aware of how managerial concepts are currently used or impact the bank and how they, the trainees, will integrate the concepts into their own style when the time comes. Also, in the smaller banks, the likelihood is greater that a particular employee trained in one area will be beckoned for another area—anywhere from 2 years to 10 years down the road.

Many of the larger banks have the luxury of relying fairly heavily on formal delivery during the broad training period. First American Bankshares does basic banking training in its professional development phase out of its Washington, D.C., headquarters. All participants are housed locally before being assigned around the subsidiary banks throughout the East. Over five months, the courses range from principles of banking to asset-liability management and communication skills. Term project assignments are done for the subsidiary banks on topics from researching a new branch location to developing a new product. During this period, trainees also attend a career management workshop to teach them how to set short- and long-term career goals and develop strategies to achieve them.

The Huntington Bank in Columbus has a similarly structured program: that is, the new hires are given 8 months of broad-based training prior to doing a 3-month stint in credit analysis. After that, the trainees reach Interview Career Point I, at which time they are sorted into various career tracks, including retail and trust areas.

An Unstructured Disappointment

A large Midwestern bank had shied away from a structured training program—mainly because one of its major competitors was in the process of instituting a highly structured one, against which the bank felt incapable of competing head-on. Instead, the bank offered a training program that was primarily rotational and on-the-job. By dispensing with time-consuming training rigors, the recruits were on the platform and given titles in a much shorter period.

The recruitment results were excellent, which led management to believe that it had the formula for attracting talent. Unfortunately, the follow-up results were quite the reverse. An unusually high number of trainees left the bank soon after becoming "operational." The title that they had earned enabled them to move to better positions with smaller banks. Ultimately, the bank's position proved to be "penny wise and pound foolish," since it cost them dearly when the trainees left.[1]

Not for Lenders Only

Similarly, several banks, particularly the larger ones, have put more emphasis on broad-based training for the nonlending areas—such as the operations area—than on the ability merely to be able to run a specific department. The Professional Phase I of the First American Bank Program also relies heavily on classroom study preceding the operations training program. A major city bank has the operations trainees do four project assignments that would cover a six-month period in topics such as supervision, budgeting, technical skills, and project management. In addition, they each must make a formal presentation, attend senior management briefings, and attend courses relating to each of these four assignments.

The Beauty of Being a Specialist

One of the main advantages of the specialist's training program is that it can turn raw recruits into productive employees in relatively short order. Certainly, dispensing with the more broadly-based training courses to focus on the immediate job needs will cut weeks—even months—out of the training curricula. In addition, the specialist-type programing has allowed some banks to shorten even further the time spent in entry training by restructuring the phases in which learning will occur.

Most management-training programs, particularly for the generalist's program, typically "front-end load" the training, meaning that the majority of the training is accomplished within the first two years. Training then substantially tapers off, down to zero in some unfortunate situations.

Some institutions have realized several flaws in that system. First of all, trainees will have been overwhelmed with information dumped on them in the early stages, with the result of everything being "learned," but nothing being mastered.

Secondly, trainees learn information beyond what can be immediately used and have to relearn at the point of need. For instance, highly technical training such as corporate finance, is, like French, difficult to retain if the learning is not immediately applied. Even such basics as selling skills diminish the longer the trainee is away from the marketplace.

Providing training that is soon forgotten is expensive. The expense is even greater if the trainee quits the bank not long after completing the program, and insult is heaped on the injury if the trainee lands at a competitor. Granted, large banks have been for years a feedline system, often providing basic training to employees who go off to banks that cannot afford such training, bringing the experience of the more sophisticated bank with them. While this has been a boon to the overall banking system, the cost factor laid on the big banks is becoming prohibitive.

Lastly, up-front training presumes that the industry is static, and data once learned will always be relevant. The 80s disproved that: the number, type, style, and structure of nearly every product a bank offers dramatically changed along with the bank's strategy, goals, and expectations. Most bankers were expected to keep up on their own or from quickie reviews. The "expensive" knowledge was lost; the new important information was provided almost as an afterthought.

Just-in-Time Training
Some banks have decided to realign their specialist training program by adopting the "just-in-time" approach. Just-in-

time (JIT) most commonly is used to describe an inventory system in a manufacturing plant, where the raw and semi-finished product is completed and delivered only days, sometimes only hours, prior to being needed. The great savings is in reduced inventory financing, as well as the ability to make last-minute order or design changes.

The same technique is applied to specialist training. The first stage of the trainee program is reduced to a very short time, while the intensity of the program is increased. The trainee learns only what is needed to be able to perform the next immediate function—say, financial analysis for a credit analyst or product knowledge and customer service for a platform assistant. After having been in an entry position for a period of time, typically anywhere from 6 to 18 months, the trainee is then sent for additional training to learn the skills needed on the next position—say, that of a junior relationship manager.

Although the length of the training tapers off over time, the program continues throughout the trainee's career. Banks usually expect 10 to 20 days per year of training, each series of courses either being more advanced or specific to the new level of responsibilities.

Metamorphosis

Continental Bank in Chicago changed its trainee program in the 80s from the more traditional across-the-board structure to a just-in-time format. The bank was going through several changes in management and strategy, and the time was ideal for introducing a different approach to training. "We used to have a 9-month program before the trainee would hit the platform," noted Michael Pimley, VP at the bank and previously in charge of the Professional Development Group.

> We decided to shorten that to 8 weeks at a maximum. Training during that initial stage is much more concentrated—a boot camp for officers.
>
> Not only did we step up intensity, we also upgraded quality. We made certain that all our subject-matter experts

also had good presentation skills, or we hired consultants from the outside. We also relied more heavily on self-study programs, which trainees can complete during given hours or on their own time, considerably shortening classroom time. We are selective about the training: we don't teach them any nice-to-knows at this level. Our goal is to have them be productive as soon as possible, so they are taught precisely what they need to know in the depth they need it.

We made a deal, if you will, with our trainees when they entered the bank. We told them that we will shorten their up-front training and get them going as soon as possible. But we weren't going to shortchange their training; we were only going to change the shape of their learning curve. Instead of everything at the front end, it will be more evenly spread over the course of their career at the bank. Instead of the 2 days or so a year of additional training that officers were typically exposed to, we would give them 10 days or more. And we keep close track of their historical and current progress, so we know precisely what additional coursework they need and how well they are faring.

Overall, it's been very successful. We get the person just at the appropriate point in time. And the trainees know that they will always be up-to-speed in their level of knowledge. We will give them the ability to be at a world-class level. That appeals to both of us—the bank and the employee.

Wide and Shallow or Narrow and Deep

The greatest advantage from the bank's point of view is in the dollar expense saved by having the right training performed at the right time. But just saving money is not a good enough reason if the program's design does not ultimately meet needs. Like the generalist program, it has its pitfalls. The most obvious is that the trainees generally have little concept of the functions of the "rest of the bank." Their knowledge is circumscribed by job at hand. Their value to other areas of the bank is limited, and the ability to transfer a trainee to another area of the bank that needs recruits is sharply diminished. So, should the bank find that it has too much personnel in one area, moving the employees to another area would require a complete "retooling."

Secondly, the individual is unable to perform at a higher level of responsibility without the additional training. So the credit analyst cannot assist in making sales calls, and the platform assistant cannot do credit checks. And just as the JIT inventory system fails when the raw materials don't arrive on schedule, the bank must wait until the additional training is done before the trainee can be of much use in the next level position.

"It's a question of wide and shallow or narrow and deep," noted one human resource director of a large community bank which supports a "generalist" type program.

> Can the bank readily draw recruits from the outside if those inside aren't available? Does the bank even know precisely how many people it will need in a specific area? Is it big enough to afford the time and money for cross-training, or would it, like us, be scrambling for people if it ever had a major change of direction. Specialists are luxury items. I've seen some really superior talent turned out in specialists programs; we've been lucky enough to hire some ourselves. But we believe it will cost us less in the long run by spending a larger amount of money up front.

Recruiting the Best and the Brightest

One common thread throughout the whole concept of the structure of any management-training program is the bank's basic ability to recruit. In simplest terms,

- A bank without an attractive training program cannot select the best candidates graduating from college.
- A bank without a strong reputation cannot headhunt the best candidates further down the career link.

Getting 'Em Down on the Farm
The Merrill Lynch advertising campaign of a couple of years ago showed two eager beavers in the 50s (no yuppies then)

saying that they knew they had a future with Merrill because the firm's philosophy was "to hire the best and train them well." Now, would the beavers have been as eager if the "train them well" aspect wasn't there?

Everyone knows that filling personnel needs by relying on walk-ins doesn't work. The qualifications today require something more than they did 30 years ago, when affability, good grooming, and (maybe) a college degree generally fit the bill. Now the banks must rely on critical selection. Since most college grads would like to know where they will be in five years and how they are going to get there, the training program is one of the critical deciding factors to any financial institution's recruitment policy, perhaps excluding investment banks. (The Salomon Brothers' training program, as described by Michael Lewis in *Liar's Poker*, seemed far more well intended than well executed. Besides, any program that doesn't disqualify trainees immediately when they throw spitballs at the speakers leaves a lot of open questions.)

Banks have also been adjusting their selection criteria. As the analytical demands grew stronger, more recruits came from finance and accounting backgrounds. As the notion of relationship banking became more prevalent, banks found them to be excellent analysts, but generally weak on interpersonal relationships. An alternative approach was to select B.A.s, whose qualifications are usually just the opposite. (One bank noted that they prefer B.A.s with certain disciplines, such as psychology, which suggests interpersonal and analytical abilities.)

Training: A Rotational Plum

At the Bank of Boston, the management-training program was formalized in the early 70s by Lin Morison, who is now an Executive Vice President and Group Executive of the National Banking Group there. The program, which is technically oriented, heavily relies on in-house trainers rotating from the line.

In the early years, most of the line people who transferred in were predominantly those whom the line managers were happy to dispense with. For them, we provided an easy solution for what to do with marginal workers.

But that didn't match with our goal. We want the best people to be teachers—not the worst. They will only pass on their mistakes and shortcomings to the trainees. But it was in the line managers' best interests to keep their superstars and pass the others on to us. Appealing to them in terms of "this is best for the bank in the long term" didn't work. Years passed without my being able to staff the trainer-advisor positions with the people I wanted.

In the early 80s, I changed tack and directly appealed to the potential transferees themselves. With senior management's blessing, I held out a carrot to them. "Rotate through the training area as an advisor, and, if you've done good work, when your stint is up, we will make sure you move to the department of your choice." For a while, that resulted in a lot of pondering, until one of the "superstars" stepped up to the plate.

That broke the ice. More and more highly qualified people began to see the benefit of rotating through this area, especially after the superstar got a plum assignment in London. Now we have a waiting list of line people who want to serve as advisors. We now have 12 people, which works out to approximately 1 for every 15 trainees or, more precisely, 1 for every 6 trainees who are still in the formal training aspect of the program.

Don't misunderstand me. Acting as a trainer-advisor is not merely a "holding area" until better things can occur. We go out of our way to make sure that the experience is worthwhile. To begin, we organize a number of seminars and programs that are for this group, focusing on the leadership skills and personal development that they are not typically exposed to on the job. The positions have high visibility with executives; in fact, the bank president occasionally drops in for a brown-bag lunch meeting. We look to them for new ideas and value their experimentation and intrapreneurship.

Eventually, the popularity of the position convinced the line managers that they could not steer their people away from it. But they also realized the value: while they were losing a high producer, they would ultimately be gaining others as they came off the program and moved up. In fact, the program was assuring a continuation of the "stars" they had. And as the stars moved out into other areas of the bank, the whole bank was strengthened, and a greater unity prevailed. In short, line managers began to "globalize" their thinking. It took us a while to get to this point, but in the end it was well worth the struggle.

Make It Just like College

Essentially, most graduates prefer structured environments that ease them into the working arena. It's true that a trainee can fall into the rut of "if it's Tuesday, this must be the checks processing" learning. The present emphasis on a highly structured management training program may seem out of sync with the real, immediate needs of a bank.

One mid-Atlantic state bank attempted to change the structured environment with disastrous results. When the bank decentralized its business lines, the management-training program, which had a structured format and a central location, also moved to decentralization. Rather than having the trainees nestled around a central group, they were assigned directly to various departments after the core skills were addressed.

Management was sure the program would appeal to recruits who wanted the opportunity to shine in an open, unfettered environment. In fact, the graduates were turned off by the managers' inability to verbalize during interviews exactly what the training program was trying to achieve. A former recruiting "hit" rate of 100% dropped to one in five. Potential recruits who rejected this bank stated that one reason for declining was that the other banks' training programs were better defined and more appealing.

Those who did join the bank showed signs of malaise during the 9-month training period. The most highly regarded recruit left to join another bank. Reasons for the discontent were varied and broad. Most trainees disliked the uneven work flow. They felt they were simply filling in departments' work gaps, rather than learning. Some trainees were pleased with their mentors, but others, particularly those who were less extroverted, felt ignored. In the end, few felt that interesting opportunities came their way, much less those that would allow them to shine.

Equally upsetting to the human resources managers were the end results. At the end of the 9-month training period, they discovered they had employees with ill-defined characteristics and skills. They had no way of knowing if the trainees had received the necessary bits of information that they had expected the managers to impart. They noticed that the outgoing and amiable recruits tend to be rated higher than the quieter, more introspective ones, whatever their real work contribution.[2]

Just Tell Us What You Want

Recruiting succeeds when the real world of banking matches the expectation of the candidates. Most financial institutions (except perhaps investment banks) are not expected to have a "baseball team" culture, where training is meager, but you get big rewards when the bat makes contact with the ball. Rather, banks typically offer the "academy" culture, consistent and patterned training followed by a consistent and patterned career path—in short, an extension of the academic environment they already know and (apparently) love.

Managers have a tendency to forget that. They look back and discount their college years the way we all have already discounted high school. They think that new hires are full adults, ready to assume the full mantle of responsibility. More commonly, trainees are in the transition period going into adulthood. It requires a bit of hand-holding on the part of the bank, much to most banks' dismay.

Many managers even wonder why they should go through the hand-holding period at all. "If we need people, we'll buy 'em." Not a bad idea, assuming some basic issues: for instance,

1. Is that bank truly capable of attracting superior talent, or, like a would-be bride, is it a Plain Jane or a Locational Hunchback? And how does that compare to the size of the dowry the bank is likely to offer?
2. Is the bank's culture unique, or, in any case, unlikely

to blend with candidates that come from likely sources? Will a go-go guy from a big-city bank be content with a laid-back country style?

3. Is the selection system superior? Does the bank have a good ability to ascertain a candidate's real skills and potential using question and answer selection tools, interviewing skills, and assessment analysis? Or does the bank generally rely on "gut feel" and old school ties?

4. What will the job market be like in the bank's specific area for the bank's specific need? Is it looking for electronic systems analysts in San Francisco or for interest-rate swap specialists in Missoula, Montana?

Every bank should score high on all questions before it rejects taking the long view of developing talent in-house.

TRAINING FOR ALL

A number of banks have realized that the everyone in a professional position, not just those that were brought in as "trainees," should be fully trained and developed. The Huntington National Bank created The Huntington Institute of Banking; Norwest Corp. has the College of Credit and the Norwest Institute of Technology; Seafirst Bank has the Seafirst College, among others.

Frank Wobst, a German who now is Chairman and CEO of Huntington Bancshares, commented that "the German banks, such as Deutsche and Dresdner Banks, are all noted for their superior training of their staff; I've heard that they often have 300 applicants for every one position."

Meeting the quality of the foreign banks is not the reason for establishing The Huntington Institute—at least not a primary reason. "The only thing we have for sale is the quality of our people. To be a survivor, excellence has to be consistently above average—at all levels."

> We used to think that we could train some and hire in the rest. It doesn't work. At best, 50% of those brought in from the outside will work out. We know now that if we want a

certain level of quality in our employees, we have to develop them ourselves.

My aim was to not only create a person that was technically knowledgeable, but also flexible. This is very important to me. In the last two to three decades, we have seen the whole industry radically change—in the types of products, deregulation, geographic areas, competition, technological advances, international approach, everything.

In order to adapt, a person needs an open mind: common sense ought to prevail. Minds are opened up through education and training. It helps develop people who can think past their immediate job and look with greater perspective.

Training Across (and Up) the Board

In order to achieve the broadly focused person, Bob Albright, in establishing the program, looked towards technical, service, and leadership skills.

Ultimately, the program at The Huntington Institute utilized a double-matrix approach. An individual can receive a specialist certificate by progressing *up* the matrices of technical knowledge and training. These matrices include customer service (retail and corporate), technical (consumer lending, commercial lending, and general banking), and leadership skills. The specialist certificates are offered at two levels, the fundamental level and the mastery level.

The individual can also receive a diploma in relationship banking by moving *across* the specialty matrices. So by fulfilling all the requirements in the service, technical, and leadership categories, the employee can earn either a relationship-bank fundamental diploma or a mastery diploma.

However, just making a series of programs available doesn't assure getting the people with the right skills at the right time. Albright noted, "We had to figure out a way to address all three areas, but have the employee focus on the most relevant first. We need people with leadership skills, but they should understand how to properly serve the customer first. For the most part, we only have an employee for five years. That's the average length of service. So they've got to learn first things first."

In order to do that, a certain study path is recommended for each employee. For instance, a commercial lending representative, levels I and II, would first receive certificates in customer service and technical training. At level III, he or she would also add obtaining mastery certificates in customer service, technical and fundamental certificates in leadership, and would qualify for a Fundamental Diploma. Those at levels IV and V would add the mastery level of leadership, thereby qualifying for a mastery diploma. (See Figure 9–1.)

Albright continued,

> If all our employees were new, we would just bring them through the programs the way one routes a trainee through. Of course, that's not the case. Many of our professional people have been here for a number of years, but have only had spotty training. It's those people we want to bring back into the mainstream. Preferably, we want everyone to be a "certified" professional, and over the next decade we may make the training mandatory.
>
> Naturally, many of our employees are already quite familiar with the material, and we give them credit through proficiency testing, which exempts them from the training. None of the material in our training programs was arbitrarily pulled together; it's all either designed by the line and/or developed in conjunction with them. So it relates to the experiences that the employee either has or will have. In fact, in our minds, this is the main driving force of the Institute: it is by, for, and of the line employee.
>
> The employees were apparently very responsive to the concept. During its first full year of operation, 1,800 employees (37% of the bank's employees) took over 3,500 courses through the Institute—some even achieving full diplomas on an accelerated basis. Huntington carefully tracks all the employees using a computerized system, which notes not only the courses that they have taken, but also the ones they should consider in the future. The systematic approach allows them to provide full details to the employees' managers and supervisors.

FIGURE 9–1
The Huntington Institute of Banking Certificate and Diploma Programs

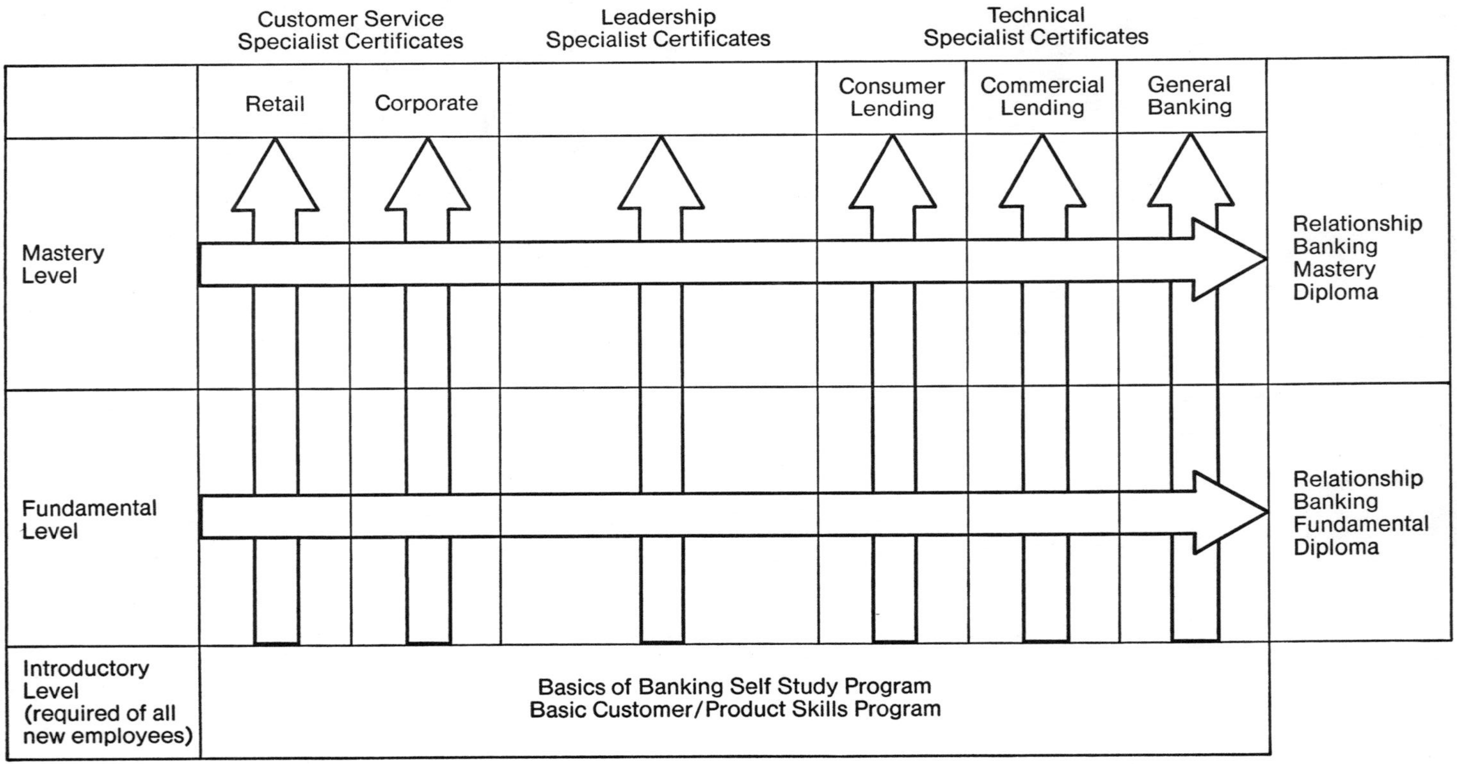

Source: Used with permission of The Huntington National Bank.

Don't Miss the Point

"But don't forget," added Wobst, Huntington's Chairman, "our object is not just to 'certify' people, but also to provide a forum for idea exchange and expansion of thought."

We also want to relay to our employees that learning never ends. Banking has changed—is changing—so you don't get to one level, and then you know all you'll have to know for the remainder of your career. It doesn't work that way.

Look, none of us likes upheavals or change. But change will come anyway. We need people who are flexible and can deal with it. Sure, we want the best of the college graduates, but ones who also have good judgment. Some banks learned the hard way that it's easy to bring in technical experts—lots of MBAs and all that—but it didn't guarantee people with good common sense.

I suppose that you can't *teach* common sense, but you can create an atmosphere in which it will flourish. The best way to do it is through the classroom. It allows us to reestablish our standards and allows others to express and modify their ideas in an open forum. Our bank has a very long history of quality and ethical standards. It's important to us to have that continually reinforced through example and discussion.

Cost Control

The discussion of extensive training programs causes most executives to see dollar signs fleeting in front of their eyes, especially when outside consultants are brought in to do an aspect of the training session, such as the design, development, or delivery. For all of you getting a queasy feeling about the expense involved in any program, let's discuss costs. The two primary costs are (1) the salary expense of those on the payroll but not yet producing, and (2) the actual cost of running the program.

Cost pressures are everywhere. Nonetheless, every bank executive has been tempted to revert to either a pared-down program or the least expensive aspect of training.

"Why don't we just use the people we have in-house? They know their topic as well as anyone, and they're free."

Or, "They give this course at the local school. Why are we spending money to develop it in-house?" Every manager contemplating a training program has pressed these questions at least once in his or her career. The counter reply often is the equally poor "you get what you pay for." Granted, many things for sale are mispriced; more expensive does not always assure the best results any more than less expensive precludes it. The chapter on cost-benefit issues addresses an analytical approach to determining the most cost effectiveness in more detail, but the following discussion enumerates the pros and cons of various lower-cost training formats.

On-the-Job Training

OJT to most people is the classic "sit next to Joe, and do what he does" approach. It boils down to an experienced employee explaining to an inexperienced one how to perform the job.

In its simplest and most generic form, this format has been widely regarded as inadequate mainly because there is little way to insure that all the bits and pieces necessary for the learning process have been relayed. Often, due to the casual approach to training, both well-defined objectives and measurement systems to determine what should and has been learned are also nonexistent. Lacking these, neither the trainee nor the trainer can be held responsible for the failure in learning, since neither had any clear idea of what had to be achieved.

Limitations such as these may be overcome and have been most effectively handled in the teller-training area. As a result of the continuous need for tellers at most banks, the art of OJT teller training has been well refined. Most banks require the OJT teller trainer to be certified; that is, attend an in-house or off-site course that demonstrates the appropriate training style and amount of information that must be conveyed.

For the more professional areas, such as platform work, the approach to OJT generally has been less formalized, with considerably less likelihood of certified trainers. Consequently, OJT frequently reverts back to the "sit here and absorb" style, often with no specified, much less certified, trainer and the department manager only has a vague sense of what the newcomer does or needs to know. Banks that have come to realize that this approach is too hit or miss have made certain steps to assure that learning occurs. For instance:

> *Buddy-buddy system:* One specific person is assigned the role of being the newcomer's mentor, so that the trainee always has someone to talk to when a question or problem arises.
>
> *Designated trainer:* This person's secondary function (or sometimes primary function) is to train new hires. Training techniques, learning objectives, material availability, and resources are addressed so that the trainer has a precise sense of what is to be accomplished. The designated trainer is a step below a certified trainer. The certified trainer will generally have completed a very specialized course in the topic to be trained.
>
> *Learning checklists:* The department manager and the trainee are provided a list of specific learning objectives (usually drawn up by a training and development area) that must be accomplished within a specified time frame. The checklist is routinely updated and sent to a control person in the human resources office that monitors the trainees' progress.
>
> *Learning contracts:* Learning contracts take the checklist concept one step further by establishing a formal, signed arrangement between the manager and the trainee. They are especially useful for trainees on rotation through various departments, where the managers do not have vested interests in the quality of learning that occurs. The monitoring of the contracts may be done at the human resources level or by the trainees themselves.

In its ideal form, the manager presents the trainee with an outline of exactly what learning will occur in the department: what skills will be learned, how they are to be applied, what methodology the manager will use to train those skills, and what productivity levels are expected. A typical contract clause might read:

> *Objective:* Be able to review and analyze monthly budget variance statements. *Format:* The first month, the trainee will discuss with the manager the elements that went into the budget review and analysis. The second month, the trainee will write a review and analysis, along with a more experienced department member. The third month, the trainee will write one independently that the staff member will edit. *Production:* After the training period is complete, the trainee will be expected to do three more budget analyses within the next year.

Off-Site and Open-Enrollment Training

The names most frequently associated with training are the industry and trade associations that count banking and financial institutions among their members. The best known are the American Institute of Banking (affiliated with the American Bankers Association), the Robert Morris Associates, the Bank Administration Institute, the National Council of Savings Institutions, the U.S. League of Savings Institutions, the Mortgage Bankers Association, the Consumer Banking Association, the American Management Association, as well as the independent state banking associations. In addition, numerous other private organizations and consulting groups hold seminars and courses on bank-related issues. The directory of open-enrollment seminars that ABTAC publishes semiannually typically lists over 500 seminars that seek to draw attendees nationally; countless more are offered by the local AIB chapters and other state and trade associations.

The obvious advantage to these offerings is that the presenting group has developed or created a program that meets the constituent banks' training needs, thereby relieving them of the requirement to do the same. The only costs the bank must incur are those of registration and the attendees' loss of time at the bank. For instance, The Institute at The Huntington National Bank relies on the local AIB to handle most of the course for their General Banking certificate, taking advantage of the evening offerings. Only when a large number of people are to be trained does it make economic sense to consider reverting to in-house. (Most off-site groups have in-house options.)

Of course, *inexpensive* doesn't necessarily mean *good*. Yet because of the associations' or the consulting groups' reputation, they often can locate quality and present the best. Accordingly, many programs have been rated very good or excellent by the attendees. With such a track record, why aren't they used exclusively?

There are several reasons. By definition, the programs must be designed as "generic," meaning that they cannot adequately incorporate the bits and pieces of information that distinguish one bank from another. As such, those programs are at a distinct disadvantage in creating a unified cultural standard or in being able to develop any "bonding" between the attendee and the bank.

In addition, it is difficult to do developmental or behavioral training: the scope or format of the course often doesn't allow enough time to change behavioral patterns. In addition, the participants cannot be monitored in their office situation, so, while the behaviors might be improved in the classroom, application is uncertain.

Lastly, evaluation and measurement of the success of the program are generally not done. Occasionally, especially for technical course work, tests are given, sometimes leading to certificates. But, more commonly, the evaluation is done on the instructor and not on the participant. (If the participant had "a nice day," then learning is presumed.) Rarely is any measurement of either knowledge of topic or increased productivity done at the bank for a program that was given off-site. Hence, effectiveness is an unknown.

Even so, not every program in a bank's training curriculum needs to be specifically tailored to the bank or have a complex measurement system. Programs such as Overview of the Banking Industry, Basic Credit Training, and Documentation are good examples. The best uses of the off-site programs are generally (but hardly exclusively) those that are predominantly knowledge-based and at the introductory level. Banks can then attach other tailored or more advanced programs to them to incorporate the necessary cultural, behavioral, and evaluation elements.

Using In-House Expertise

Use the in-house experts as presenters, and you can get all the training you want for free—or, at least, so the conventional wisdom goes. Undoubtedly, one of the best sources of information usually resides somewhere in the bank. But one should be careful about making the leap of assuming that one only has to identify that person and give him or her a flipchart and a colored marker. All of us have experienced a presentation by an expert that has been deadly dry. What goes wrong?

The answer lies in our notions that learning occurs when people who know something about a topic tell us what they know. That's how we learned in all of our school years—a concept that is only now starting to be challenged in educational circles. That type of learning presumes that the participant is interested, or even listening, has the cognitive skills to interpret the data, and is able to apply it to situations on the job. If educators are still grappling with these theories, it is unlikely that the average line expert will have any particular insight, or even exposure, to them.

As a result, many programs created or delivered by subject-matter experts are often curiously lacking in quality from the participants' point of view, although the most obvious problem is usually that of poor presentation skills. But even a great presenter may not achieve the goals of assuring tnat learning has occurred: the content may be misguided, the material sloppily integrated, or the exercises too extreme or unrealistic. When design element is poor, attendees know there is a problem with the program, but have greater difficulty putting their finger on it. So the program evaluations never really get at the problem, a fact that makes solutions difficult.

Thus, to insure that the program is simply not a waste of time, the analysis, design, development, and delivery work should be done in conjunction with a training expert. When all the time utilized in the program's development is accounted for, the program is no longer "free." (Perhaps on an out-of-pocket cost basis, the expense is minimal, but to calculate a true cost basis, the hours and days expended by the experts should be included.)

If having a training expert involved is not feasible, then it's important that a subject-matter expert be selected very carefully. The person who handles the design and development (but does not necessarily do the presentation) should be able to determine the precise learning need or problem and be familiar with a wide-range teaching media, as well as be able to create good written materials and visual aids.

Presenters need either to have the natural presentation skills or the time and inclination to take the necessary courses to develop it. Banks trying to save money sometimes only succeed in short-circuiting the learning process. The ultimate result can be far more expensive than the bank bargained for.

One Florida bank has developed a compensation system for the line managers who become involved in the training process. First, managers are expected, as part of their job descriptions, to allocate time for training. Even so, those that do are rewarded with letters sent to their superiors and to their personnel files recognizing their efforts.

In addition, the managers are compensated with "in-kind" credits—dollars specifically allocated to the manager's internal-training budgets. Thus, the managers can send their own subordinates to training programs offered within the system, using those credits to offset against the allocated cost. This way, the managers don't feel that they are giving their time up "for free."

THE PAY-OFF

Good training programs enhance banks' performance and reputation. Appealing and well-designed management training programs attract the best college graduates. Whether these programs take a specialist or a generalist approach, they must offer a structured environment and have clearly defined objectives. Some banks are acting on the realization that everyone in a professional position should be fully trained in order to achieve both high technical skills and the flexibility to handle change. These training programs reinforce the quality of employees' performance and ethical standards.

REFERENCES

1. Keene, Margaret. "Training, a Powerful Recruiting Tool." *ABA Banking Journal*, September 1987.
2. Ibid.

ADDITIONAL READINGS

Dixon, George. *What Works at Work: Lessons from the Masters.* Minneapolis: Lakewood Books, 1988.
Johnson, Dale A. "Training by Television." *Training & Development*, August 1989.

CHAPTER 10

DETERMINING VALUE: THE COST OF MAINTAINING APPRECIATING ASSETS

"How much can you really lose by spending money on a better training program?"—*Luke Helms, President, Seafirst Bank.*

People hate being thought of as "assets." They abhor the notion that they should be selected and judged like inanimate objects—by their production capacity, durability, and future value. Perhaps the time when the most people came to think comfortably of themselves in "measured" terms was when the word *personnel* was commonly replaced by the words *human resources.* But if one claims that an investment in employee training offers potential rewards, potential revenue, and income rewards, then it follows that employees are assets and should be subject to the same tests of value as other items on the balance sheet.

Granted, reducing people to rigid accounting standards is a ludicrous concept. While a good accountant can determine the worth of the bank by its assets—cash, securities and investment, loan portfolio, and so forth—including "employees" as just another line item would be presumptuous.

Yet there is universal agreement that the workforce is a bank's most important asset. And, if we think in broad accounting terms and financial theory, human assets have at least as good a payback capacity as most financial portfolios, as great a likelihood of appreciating over time as real estate, and a durability factor that often allows them to withstand greater periods of stress and hardship over longer periods than many machines. In fact, it is the only asset whose productivity has the capacity to increase rather than decline with time.

Indeed, the irony is that by *not* thinking in accounting terms, corporations are actually doing a disservice to the very individuals whose "human" image they are trying to protect. When corporations determine the monetary or specific worth of material assets, they are willing to "invest" in them, both at the time of acquisition and during the life of the asset. Items that haven't been attributed a value typically aren't "invested" in and are left to lie fallow or decline over time.

So we will treat employees as accounting assets, at least within the context of this chapter, for the sake of clarifying the importance of their value in the ultimate worth of the bank.

THE ONE REMAINING CONTROLLABLE FACTOR

As discussed so far, when it comes to obtaining and retaining the best human assets, the two most critical factors are proper selection and proper development. Unfortunately, banks only have limited amount of control over selection. External factors, such as the location of the bank, the demographics of the people living in that location, the public and private educational resources in that area, the local economy, and related level of employment play as much a part as the bank's ability to utilize an effective selection system.

In addition, the selection process is further pressured if there is great urgency to fill a position. Banks that have continually ignored cross-training and development, career pathing, and/or succession planning are the most likely candidates for having to recruit from outside, even when it would be preferable to promote from within. The bank is then subjected to the likelihood of an outside hiring failure: at least one third of "experienced" recruits fail to pan out. If recruitment cannot guarantee finding the ideal employee, no matter how good the bank's selection techniques, then it follows that the only remaining controllable factor is to create the ideal employee through training. The cost of training investment is not an issue, per se, because no other option exists.

Example: At Sovran Financial Corporation in Virginia, due to local workforce factors, the average turnover for an entry-level operations employee is 50% (partly due to the extensive job-posting system), with even higher averages being reported in Northern Virginia and the Washington, D.C., area. (They joke that anyone who stays beyond 90 days gets a gold watch.) Recruitment, therefore, is continuous and highly reliant on the local talent pool. For Sovran, then, the only way to assure having a quality workforce is through training.

Since the training time frame is short (employees must be at their highest productivity levels quickly) Sovran has a heavy front-end expenditure. Their ratio of employees to trainer is 50 to 1 (more commonly, it is 200 to 1). Prior to starting on the job, every new hire or transfer must go through a two-day orientation program, which lays out the bank's mission of quality service. Notes John Sponski, Corporate Executive Officer and the head of the 2,600 employees, "The cost of the training program is *not* the critical variable. What is critical is creating the type of worker who can provide the type of service we need in as fast a time as possible."

Good Enough?

Should all training cost analysis be thrown to the wind, substituting unrestrained spending? Tom Peters' recommendation in his book *Thriving on Chaos* suggests that companies should simply "train everyone—lavishly." He has taken perhaps a bit of literary license. Since most companies' training budgets are minimal, any additional training is likely to be a major improvement. In recommending *lavish* to many CEOs, Peters probably presumes that by the time it filters through all the committees, the word *lavish* will be translated into *a tad*.

The real question is whether the cost of creating a quality workforce is worth the benefits derived. Unfortunately, there are no hard and fast data that provide an answer. As a result, many managers make the conservative choice of accepting training that is just adequate. Doing that leads to a second question of whether "adequate" is good enough.

"There is no such thing as an 'average' training program," noted Luke Helms, President of Seafirst in Seattle. "Either it's excellent, or it's bad. Either you're achieving all your goals, or you're entirely wasting your money."

The answer to "good enough" then is whether the training impacts the bottom line. Seafirst's recent expansion of its retail-training effort *quadrupled* the previous level of expenditure to get the programs they considered "good enough." But the impact was to sharply increase earnings, as well as the total market share, which moved by five percentage points, from 25% to 30% in two years. In Helms' mind, the previous program could not have contributed to achieving those returns, and although the program had been deemed "good enough" at the time, it clearly wasn't.

I Know It When I See It

Of course, it would be wonderful to be able to determine the precise impact of the training on return on investment (ROI) calculations. Realistically, the issue is more complex because the value of the training will be impacted by other factors such as local economic conditions, competition, and salary scale, among others. This is particularly true if the analysis is done on an *average* basis—the average number of dollars spent to the average increase in earnings.

However, some bank managers aren't concerned about the precision of the analysis. How much can you really lose by spending money on a better training program? is Helms' question. The amount of money risked is not significant to the potential gain. To these managers, the answer is in seeing results at all—not in attempting to determine the worth of every dollar spent.

Example: SouthTrust Bank of Alabama intuitively relies on training and development to meet its goals. "Our workforce is drawn locally," noted Julian Banton, its President and CEO. "Being in Birmingham, we don't have the advantage of the New York and Chicago locations, which can more readily attract top-quality people. We knew our weakness versus the competition, but we were not going to rely on luck to see us through. We established a training program to overcome our limitations."

"We created a precise profile of an ideal officer," added Banton, "and we set about pulling together the necessary training to create a workforce as close to that profile as possible. I estimate that we spend 25 to 50% more than other banks on training. And since we squeeze our pennies real hard, that number represents very little by the way of travel to a glamorous off-site location for high-priced seminars."

The ROI analysis done by SouthTrust Bank reflected the aggregate analysis: we spend more than banks our size on training, but, look at the impact on our bottom line. In 1988, SouthTrust was ranked 169th in assets in 1988, but it ranked 14th in overall performance and 11th in overall asset and profitability growth rates, based on a *United States Banker* report of the top 100 banks in the country.[1]

Macro and Micro

However, doing analysis, based on macroindicators lends itself to criticism and detractors. A bank's returns may be up, but how were those returns impacted by external factors, such as the economy, the incentive plan, the new hire program, the new menu in the cafeteria, Auburn beating Alabama State (or vice versa), and so forth.

For all those reasons, determining the average return on the average investment in training may be a wasted exercise. There are just too many factors to convince those who are not already predisposed to training, and the effort is unnecessary for those who already are.

However, a *marginal* analysis approach, which looks at each of the major programs on a microbasis can be far more valuable. In addition, there is more flexibility in the analytical approach: it can be done strictly through financial analysis or a combination of the more complex financial analysis and a less complex nonfinancial evaluation. The levels of complexity are broken down below.

> *First level:* Ask the participant if the program was meaningful to him or her, usually through a pencil-and-paper questionnaire completed immediately after the program ends—commonly called a "smile sheet."
>
> *Second level:* Test the participant to see if the material was learned. This is usually done as a series of test questions immediately after the program ends.
>
> *Third level:* Track participants to see if learned material is being applied to the job. This is usually done by noting differences in productivity levels and/or through the manager's observation of participant's performance, generally three to six months after training is completed.
>
> *Fourth level:* Determine the impact on the "bottom line," through tracking the improved revenues and/or reduced costs that occur within one, three, six, or twelve months after the completion of the program.

These evaluation methods are the basic standards in the training industry.

Easy to Say; Tedious to Do

A survey done by *ABTAC* among its members on evaluation techniques revealed that on the average, 78% did level-one evaluation: that is, obtaining a smile sheet. Only 48% of the banks did level-two evaluation: that is, testing for knowledge learned. A negligible number of banks did level-three tracking of productivity or behavioral changes for the training in *nonsales* skills. For *sales* skills training, 16% of the banks did either behavioral tracking or bottom-line analysis. Lastly, only one of the banks responding to the questionnaire indicated that it made any attempt to determine the bottom-line impact of its nonsales-related training program. Should bank trainers be chastised for a lax attitude towards doing evaluations? Not really. A study reported in the *Harvard Business Review* determined that 30% of all corporations conduct no formal evaluation of their T&D programs.[2] The reasons for not doing so are many.

1. *Difficulty of creating a valid measuring system.* How does one determine if the impact on, say, sales revenues was caused solely by the training and not by the new manager, a better incentive program, improved products, or just better morale in the ranks?

2. *The effort versus the benefit.* If a program *seems* to be effective, is it worth setting up a complex measuring system, which can take hours of time, to prove what everyone generally senses?

3. *The ultimate value of the information.* Even if the effectiveness of the measured program is shown to be only marginally effective, the next step is rarely obvious. Should the program be scrapped or radically changed (even if the participants found great value in it)? Or should another measurement be found to validate the data collected from the first measurement, which could have been corrupted by external factors, such as the appointment of a new manager?

Despite the obstacles, banks should not too readily shrug off the effort of doing more advanced marginal analysis. Admittedly, doing a complete overhaul of the evaluative approach could be daunting. The problem is mitigated when it is broken down into selecting individual programs for review and ignoring others. This way, the training concerns can be prioritized, and the obstacles noted above can be dealt with on a case-by-case basis.

Matricize and Prioritize

One way to prioritize programs for further marginal analysis is to utilize zero-based budgeting. That is, a bank determines the value of each program individually each year. Since every program must be viewed with a critical eye annually, it provides the decision makers an opportunity to select programs for more advanced analysis. A decision can be made to select, say, 10% of the programs for further analysis. Not only is it a reasonable sort of system, but it helps prevent the common problem of zero-based budgeting of automatically resetting the budget unless someone has a forceful reason for crossing it off the list. This way, a specific focus must be placed on all the programs to be able to widely select those for further study.

Zero-based budgeting, at least in its most basic format, is catching on. A recent ABTAC survey of bank members indicated that approximately 25% of the respondents use the zero-based approach or a near variant of it. Thus, utilizing the system for analytical selection would be a relatively minor improvement.

Another approach in determining priority is to establish a matrix similar to that used in financial-project analysis.

Projects and investments are sorted on a matrix, in which they are represented as either stars, dogs, cash cows or undrilled oil wells (unknown value). In financial analysis, decisions to hold, consider expansion, or divest are often based on the project's place in the matrix.

The same approach can be applied to determining which training programs should be subject to further scrutiny. Training projects can be categorized as low to high importance (commonly in terms of numbers of people attending) and low to high cost. The low-importance, low-cost programs (dogs) are ignored; the high-importance, high-cost programs (stars) and unknown-importance, high-cost programs (the oil wells) are analyzed; the cash cows are placed second in priority. (See Figure 10–1.)

Indeed, any consistent system that allows the user to select the training requiring further evaluation is appropriate. Consider the IBM example which follows.

Example: Traditionally, IBM has had one of the largest budgets for training and development and great pride in its programing. Cost pressure in the late 80s caused IBM to give closer scrutiny to the training expense, then approximately $900 million. First, the training programs were sorted by degree of importance.

IBM first pinpointed 80 major job functions within the organization and from that list selected the most important jobs and their related training. To begin the analysis, the tasks relating each major job function were ascertained. Then, they compared the training that was being done to the tasks being performed. The training had to demonstrate that it either improved performance or reduced problems. In addition, there had to be evidence that the training was actually

FIGURE 10–1
Priority Matrix for Determining Cust/Benefit Analysis Candidates

	Inexpensive	Expensive
Large Population	*Cash Cow* Hold As Is	*Star* Do Analysis
Small Population	*Dog* Ignore	*Oil Well* Do Analysis

Example

	Inexpensive	Expensive
Large Population	*Commercial Documentation* Course Satisfactory Hold As Is	*Sales Skills* Course Critical Do Analysis
Small Population	*Writing Skills* Course Not Critical Ignore or Kill	*Capital Markets* Importance Uncertain Do Analysis

being applied on the job. If IBM determined that the current training did not meet these criteria, IBM did one of two things. If the expected benefits still outweighed the cost of training, the content was changed and the training reinstated. If the cost would not outweigh the benefits, the course was scratched.

In some cases, IBM used measurable standards by which to determine the differential. One way was to compare 50 trained new hires to 50 untrained ones. If a comparison of the results showed less productivity in the untrained ones, either through downgraded services or the need for extra people, which ultimately cost the company more than the training expense (including the cost of reputation), then they considered the training appropriate.

If the training were to be retained or amended, the next step was to consider which methods of program development and delivery would be most cost effective. They started by estimating how many participants were likely to attend over a specific period of time, then compared the per person delivery cost of training by means of conventional stand-up versus self-study (say, $350 versus $75). If they were dealing with 500 people over a three-year period, then the savings on delivery costs would be over $400,000.

From that point, IBM reviewed developmental costs. Their basic question was how much of the savings in delivery would be offset by the generally higher cost of self-study development. In the example given, if the development costs were only, say, $300,000, IBM's cost reduction would be over $100,000.[3]

While there was a substantial time and money cost in doing the analysis project, the positive impact was even greater. In the end, IBM was to reduce the training budget over $150 million a year. IBM's approach not only prioritized the most valuable jobs first, but their complete process allowed them to address three major issues:

- What precisely were the benefits of the training done?
- Do the benefits exceed training costs?
- What is the least expensive way to structure the training function in order to do the training?

The following three sections will address the benefits, costs, and alternative delivery systems.

Part 1—Benefits Analysis: The Bolts

The decision to do all-out, full-blown, no-holds-barred analysis on the whole training function as it currently stands may be, resourcewise, daunting. On the other hand, the decision to do it for any new program under consideration should be automatic—especially if the point of the program is directly related to the bottom line, such as sales training or service quality.

For such programs, it is critical to determine if the training is specifically impacting behavior adequately to improve revenue. At the minimum, a tracking system for the overall change—such as the level of product sales—is required. However, more finely tuned tracking systems will provide data as to whether new trained behaviors are being appropriately applied and consistently used.

Example: "We set up over 30 tracking systems," noted Chuck Lussenhop, VP of Training and Education at Southeast Bank in Miami, referring to their sales training program and incentive plan. "They cover everything from increase of sales of a particular product to the level of sales referrals." Southeast knew that the incentive program itself would impact sales levels whether or not training programs were implemented, so they also set up separate tracking systems to evaluate training elements independently.

Southeast has a specific approach to the training analysis: First, there are the participants' evaluation forms—the so-called smile sheets—which typically ask: Do you think that you have learned something, and will it be applied to your job? Now, most level one evaluation, although valuable, is subject to the "enjoyment factor" of the day (hence the name). Amusing speakers always rate higher than dry ones, but learning may or may not occur.

Pre- and post-testing get around the smile factor, focusing on what was known before the program compared to what was known after. Such testing is also critical to program evaluation, but there is no guaranty that any of the knowledge will be applied.

Southeast pursues the evaluation further. Level three analysis requires determining if the training is being used. The increase in sales volume will reveal that, but does not state whether the increase occurred because of luck or random sales effort or because of the better grounding in selling skills?

To determine that, managers are being asked 90 days after the program is over if the training had any impact on *consistent sales behavior*—as in routinely contacting customers, following up on leads, and looking for sales opportunities.

All Training Can Be Measured
Clearly, evaluation cannot be successful if the measuring stick is not valid. Prior to establishing the program, it's eas-

iest first to determine the measurement system and then design the training so that the two are integrated. People erroneously make the presumption that you can only apply numeric measurements, such as level of sales or number of items processed.

Not true.

Even training for the "soft" skills can be validated. Credit judgment, service quality, managerial skills training all can be measured, if an appropriate yardstick is laid out ahead of time. For instance, at many companies, if an employee has a problem that he or she believes is not being appropriately addressed by the department manager, that employee can circumvent the manager to reach a higher-level person, who will begin an investigation. That option is called the "open-door" policy. One measurement for a manager's ability to deal with personnel problems is the number of open-door investigations that have occurred.

Nearly all *skills-based* programs, no matter how apparently "soft," have some trackable feature. Consider some of the elements that can be measured in a customer-service program in the branches:

- Number of referrals (from teller to CSR, CSR to mortgage department, etc.).
- Number of lost customers.
- Number of mistakes in completion of new account forms.
- Number of variances from overdraft credit policy.
- Number of complaints.

Quality service improvement can also be observed by the number of times an employee smiles at the customer or uses the customer's name. Measurement criteria must simply be sought out. If banks want to spend wisely, they must be able to measure the impact.

Example: One West Coast bank applied a behavioral type of evaluation to a training program held on construction lending, attended by all 90 members of the department, irrespective of their previous knowledge. The bank was aware that some of the participants did not need as much training as others, but, in order to assure a uniform knowledge base, all were required to participate.

The participants' impressions of the course were immediately given after the training, and the feedback was used to fine-tune future presentations. But due to the uneven knowledge base, more reliance was placed on the evaluation of how each participant's performance improved.

Participants' managers were surveyed approximately three months after the course was completed as to their opinion of (1) whether their subordinates were meeting the goals of the course and (2) what degree of change they saw in each subordinate's performance.

For the latter, the managers filled out a separate questionnaire in which they rated both the subordinate's performance before and after the training and to what degree the change could be attributed to the training, based on a scale of one to five. The participants also filled out a similar questionnaire regarding their own performance, as well as rating various modules of the program. Although the procedure is open to bias, the bank found it to be the easiest and best way to determine if the program was effective in improving the employees' performance.

Is the Training Needed in the First Place
A good tracking and measuring system will determine if the training was effective. However, the problem may not lie with the lack of training in the first place. Often, problems in other areas—poor communication, poor pay systems, lack of appropriate motivational techniques—are the real culprits. However, training is often sent in as a quick-fix solution, with the predictable unsatisfactory resolution.

Example: A community bank in a southern state had a decline in the overall level of new retail accounts opened within the branch system, even though its interest rates were competitive. A consulting group established a cross-selling training for the tellers to take advantage of the current broad customer base. The tracking system used after the introduction of the sales training program showed little improvement. The training was an apparent waste, and the consulting group was let go.

But was the initial problem an inability to cross-sell products? A good up-front study or *needs analysis*, which was later done by another consulting group, pointed up the real problem. In fact, prior to the training, the staff was making a reasonable amount of "teller referrals." The second consulting group determined that the problem lay in the physical layout of the branches themselves. To begin, they had not been refurbished in 10 years, so the walls were dingy and the floors and counters worn. Years of accumulated papers, basically from a lack of filing space, had built up. The physical layout required a customer to go to the back of the branch in order to learn about the new products that were being referred. And when they got back there, no one person, a receptionist or CSR, was available to direct inquiries. Everything about each branch seemed to suggest leaving it was more pleasant than staying. The lack of training was clearly not the problem; therefore, training could not have cured it.

Education Is Not Training

Measure everything? What about accounting programs and bank simulation games? How about an overview of the banking industry or the secondary mortgage market? They can't be measured for their impact on the bottom line. Clearly, programs such as these would quickly fall off any training curriculum (or worse, never get on).

In this instance, we must be careful to distinguish *education* from *training*. Training develops skills and improves the knowledge base for performing a task. Education provides background information from which one can build a better understanding of the job that he or she is involved in. It is a foundation block for being able to achieve something that will overall be better in the future. It is based on the same premise that we may never use our knowledge of history or algebra, yet having an understanding of what preceded us or what can be determined through an appropriate alignment of numbers can only deepen our decision-making capacity.

Still, it poses a problem for the training director: How

should educational courses be treated? Which should be maintained and which eliminated? In revamping its programs, IBM faced a similar dilemma. As a solution, it listed 150 "education" programs on a survey, sent it out to employees, and asked them to select which programs were of *unquestioned* value to them. The list narrowed to 28 core programs. All others were subject to review.

Busy Enough Already

Despite the many benefits of doing advanced evaluation, many training personnel are understandably reluctant to take on additional workload. It's also fair to say that new program development is demanding enough without having to add a whole series of evaluation measures. In many cases, the department is so understaffed it would stretch limited resources unbearably.

In addition, there is a psychological resistance as well, based on the premise that if everyone believes that any reasonably well thought-out training is better than none at all, then why go out of the way to do something that wasn't asked for? If it proves the point, there is no value to the effort, and if it doesn't, then T&D will only look incompetent.

Unfortunately, this reasoning ignores the fact that in today's climate few banks can afford the luxury of assuming that everything is OK. Just as IBM discovered, even the most sophisticated of training programs can benefit from critical analysis. Without it a bank can not determine:

- What's right and retain it.
- What's wrong and reject it.
- What almost works and strengthen it.
- What's especially effective and run with it.

In addition, training directors themselves will directly benefit. Armed with good data, they will be able to more effectively "sell" to bank management:

- The need for new programs.
- The need for changed programs.

- The need for new resources.
- The real value of training and development.

Example: First Union Corp., headquartered in Charlotte, had always used evaluation techniques to determine the validity of its programs. But they stepped up their efforts when they instituted their sales "academies," which run for two weeks at various times throughout their bank system in the southeastern United States. Both the basic cost of the program and the various bank subsidiaries that sponsored the programs warranted validation of the program's worth.

First Union uses several techniques to do so. The first one is to query the attendees after the completion of the program as to whether they felt the program was worthwhile (level-one smile sheets). The participants are also frequently tested during the program to make sure that they have mastered product knowledge and other basics (level two).

The second is to determine if the program is actually changing behaviors. Six weeks after the participants finish the academy, they are asked to respond to 40 questions about their professional sales behavior. A sample question might be: "Do you make telephone sales calls more frequently, as frequently, less frequently than before?" The respondents' managers would also rate their subordinates on the same questions based on their observations of the employees (level three).

Lastly, they track the level of deposits, loans, and products per sale of the participant's branches prior to, during, and for 3 to 9 months after the program. They also note if any major external events are occurring—a dramatic reversal in the stock market, for instance (level four).

The data collected has been proved invaluable. Overall, the data showed the program to be decidedly worth the investment. Beyond that, First Union derived some very specific unexpected results: it was able to identify certain behaviors that were *not* being impacted by the program (despite expectation) and took measures to strengthen those particular program modules. In addition, the changes in the level of sales over time after the program give a good indication of how long the motivational effect lasts.

It Still Don't Mean a Thing, if It Ain't Got That . . .

Management support. A million statistics can be gathered and disseminated without the least bit of value if one critical factor is missing: a client who cares about the end result and supports the newly learned activity in the department. If a program is on a roster, the natural tendency is to assume that someone felt strongly enough about the program to request it and that that person continues to sponsor it. Not necessarily true. Many programs are offered "because": "because" all curricula have a such-and-such course; "because" someone years ago requested it; "because" the materials were developed.

Example: A Midwestern bank offers a training program through a corporate training area covering commercial loan documentation. Attendees, predominantly first-level officers from all parts of the bank, self-nominate or are nominated by their manager for participation. The one and one-half day course, basically in lecture and case study format, is given by an experienced loan officer with good presentation skills. In the level one evaluations (smile sheets), participants consistently give the presentation high ratings.

Is this program a candidate for further in-depth evaluation? No, it would be a waste of time. But *not* because the course is already apparently successful—*in fact, it probably is not a successful course*. It would be a waste because no one would care.

This is a case of a *program without a client*: no one senior manager or area supports it. It's a classic catalog course: the sponsorship and rationale behind the course, no matter how valid at the time, has passed into history. The result is that it now belongs to the faceless and nameless bureaucracy.

Why isn't the course successful? The course's shortcomings are numerous: (1) the attendees are not trained to be able to assemble the loan documentation; rather, they only learn about them, (2) there is no test to determine the degree to which even that learning occurred, (3) the cases tend to be academic in nature, not applied issues.

An appropriate type evaluation might be related to the presumed end goal for the course—reduction of documentation exceptions. A likely method of evaluation, therefore, is to measure exceptions beforehand, and then afterwards, or analysis along those lines.

However, where is the motivation to bother? If the course was found deficient, who would support the revamp? More to the point, does the bank even value the employee's precision in loan documentation? If you are inclined to say, "It must, absolutely; millions are lost every year due to improperly documented loans," then (1) why is the program not taken immediately by an employee who has any loan responsibility, rather than "at some point as a junior officer"? (2) why isn't testing mandatory, with all those who flunk required to take it again? Are their jobs on the line if they cannot do loan documentation correctly?

Indeed, what is the presumption about the importance of loan documentation within that banks, and how seriously should the attendee dedicate himself or herself to learning during those one and one-half days? (A teller whose drawer is consistently off stands to be fired, even if the amount only totals in the hundreds. An officer who misdocuments a loan puts the bank at risk for hundreds of thousands, maybe millions, but that error often receives less "to-do" than the teller's.)[1]

Who's on First

When the training is not validated, it is the fault of two people—the line area manager requiring the training and the training professional who does not insist upon doing it.

Tom Peters is more direct than most when it comes to training departments' effectiveness. While we advocate zero-base budgeting for training programs, he advocates zero-base budgeting for training personnel. Is the department run by trained professionals or basically by line people who landed up there after the fickle finger of fate pointed in their direction?

Using line people per se is not the problem, but using line people who do not understand training is. True, many who are rotated into the training area after being bankers can bring insight and expertise that cannot be achieved by the training specialists. In addition, the business skills can be invaluable.

Unfortunately, the ex-line people are often not exposed to good training and development theory and practice. So, in doing the best they can, they are not aware of the limitations of their offering. Seeing that the training personnel receive the same "care and feeding" as the line personnel is of utmost importance. The same theories of employee development that apply to banking personnel apply to training personnel.

Part 2—Cost Analyses: The Nuts

One executive commented, "I hate the HR department. Whenever I see them, I know it's only going to cost me. Training, bonuses, benefits—it's more for them and less for me." An American Bankers Association study shows that training costs for all banks responding to the survey averaged $200 per employee per annum.[4] (By contrast, IBM averages approximately $2,000 per person.)

Actually, in most banks, the cost accounting system is very crude. Accountants are rarely heard in the cafeteria discussing the subtleties of training costs, yet there are many worth considering. A survey done by ABTAC in 1990 revealed that while most (but not all!) banks included out-of-pocket expenditures as costs, the inclusion of personnel and attendees' time costs, allocated costs, and facilities costs varied all over the place. Costing data was not only not comparable bank to bank, but almost too dubious for use as a basis in a cost-benefit analysis.

The marginal costs of training should be broken down into several categories: namely

1. *Development*—the effort expended to conceptualize, design, and develop the materials used during a program, including out-of-pockets as well as the time allocation for the effort of the in-house staff.
2. *Delivery*—the cost of actually putting on the program, including out-of-pocket costs as well as time allocation of the attendees.
3. *Overhead*—the cost of maintaining the T&D function, exclusive of development and delivery costs.

During the budget process, cost analyses most often combine all three aspects (e.g., next year, our department will spend $1 million dollars). When a request is made for a new program, the program is discussed most often in terms of the out-of-pocket costs of development and/or delivery. In short, the overall budget may not be adequately broken down, and the marginal cost analysis (cost per new program) may not be adequately inclusive.

Another cost issue that receives inadequate attention is whether the developmental costs should be expensed or capitalized (if not for the benefit of the shareholders, at least for the purpose of better internal analysis). Many programs have a shelf life beyond a year, yet when costs are analyzed, the development costs are often lumped both into the annual budget and into any marginal cost analysis as if the first delivery use will be the only one.

Cash on the Barrelhead and Other Phobias
The rather limited ability of most T&D areas to accurately cost their programs is most dramatically manifested when comparing computer-based training (CBT) to conventional stand-up training. It is not atypical for the development costs of a CBT program to run in the hundreds of thousands, causing most people to stop considering this alternative immediately, generally as they see the last set of 000s. This leads to what I call "cash on the barrelhead" analysis: that is, only the out-of-pocket expenditures are taken into consideration.

It's not unlike asking which is better—buying a house

outright for cash or taking a mortgage? (For most of us who do not have the funds available to plunk down cash, the question is moot.) However, we have been so conditioned to thinking "mortgage," that even for the cash rich, buying outright is unthinkable. Yet the cash, if we held on to it, may only earn us 7% a year, while the mortgage costs 10% (taxes notwithstanding). Clearly, the cash route is better, yet the enormity of the number is a natural deterrent. (The analysis is even less favorable when we think in terms of renting versus all cash, but we all suffer from fear of big-numbers phobia.)

Similarly, large up-front training expenditures tend to dissuade the client from even pursuing doing a full analysis, thus possibly tossing out the cat with the kitty litter. Courses developed by outside firms tend to be the greatest victims of this shortsightedness, because with them the out-of-pocket expenditure tends to be highest. On a comparable cost basis, which would include time cost and allocated costs, the expense might be seen as much more reasonable.

Example: At a large East Coast bank, managers of the systems department felt that it would be very useful to have training on the operations and function of the capital markets department, for which many of the systems people were designing programs. The line managers determined, for many good reasons, that computer-based training would be ideal. The corporate training area set about to determine the out-of-pocket cost of developing such a program, which ended up at just under $100,000. Astounded at the size of the number, the line managers switched to stand-up conventional training using an outside consultant. The basic cost of the conventional training was estimated at $30,000, but ended up costing approximately $48,000 per year because of the need for repeat performances in distant locations.

Actually, the approach to the costing was incorrect since it did not take into account the shelf life of the program. If the CBT program had lasted three to five years, the per annum cost would have diminished to approximately $33 to $20 thousand (plus the time value of the money, if you wish to be precise).

A second set of considerations was the costs that would be saved if CBT were utilized:

- The reduced costs of the amount of the students' time CBT needs as a learning medium versus conventional class time.
- The eliminated cost of the instructor's time.
- Travel costs.
- The eliminated cost of providing facilities and food.
- The reduced or eliminated costs of printed materials.
- The reduced or eliminated costs of the support staff.

This list is not to suggest that CBT is always the better training alternative (indeed, it has very definitive advantages and disadvantages), rather that good cost analysis is basic to decision making and absolutely critical to doing a thorough cost-benefit analysis.

Below is a listing of the costs associated with the production of a training program. It includes such critical noncash costs such as the participants' time, the staff's time, direct allocated overhead, and administration costs.

Although this particular cost analysis basis ignores whether any of the costs should be capitalized and amortized, it does break out those costs into a separate category (developmental costs). The cost of time is calculated by taking the individuals' per diem salary plus benefits and multiplying by the number of days related to training.

Developmental Costs:
　　a. Cost of purchase of training materials, or
　　b. Cost of in-house designer's time, and
　　c. Cost of subject matter experts' time, and
　　d. Cost of leader/manager/liaison time, and
　　e. Cost of clerical staff time, and
　　f. Production costs, and
　　g. Other materials costs, and
　　h. Evaluation costs.

Delivery Costs:
　　i. Cost of outside instructors' time, or
　　j. Cost of in-house presenters' time, and

    k. Cost of participants' time, and
    l. Cost of monitors' time, and
  m. Travel costs, and
    n. Facilities costs, and
    o. Equipment, and
    p. Food, and
    q. Marketing costs, plus
    r. Allocated department overhead

Alternative Delivery Systems

Good cost analysis also provides opportunities to reassess the pricing of current programs. However, it should be noted that not every issue is dollar related, and the least expensive method is not always the best. The basic training criteria must first be established: what should the employee be able to do after the program is completed? All issues should be taken into account and then weighed against the advantages of a diminished cost.

    Example: A New York bank, in doing a cost-benefit analysis of a capital-markets training program, had several issues to deal with. To begin, the program delivered by a consultant in conventional stand-up style was moderately effective, judging from the responses on the smile sheets. The participants felt they were learning (verified by pre- and post-testing), but that the material was reviewed too fast, they could not immediately appreciate how it would be applied, and the notebooks were too cumbersome as reference guides.

    The bank decided that just tweaking the training format would be insufficient. Besides, overseas delivery of the program was another problem in terms of cost, logistics, and language, which could not be solved by improving the stand-up delivery in New York.

    Alternative delivery styles—in this case, computer-based training, were investigated. The benefits were defined as more flexible: slower learners could spend more time on the material, and a greater variety of problems integrated into the workplace could be addressed. Further, the overseas problems were eased, as well as similar logistics problems dealing with domestic nonentry-level staff. And, in New

York, the stand-up training could be integrated with the CBT for those who had a greater need for more in-depth knowledge.

The question then begged itself: How much would the bank be willing to pay to add CBT training to the program to reap the benefits? If the analysis would have been done based solely on the additional cost of developing a CBT program (which generally requires high up-front expenditure) plus the production of the training/reference books, the request for additional funding might have been staggering. Full analysis of cost-benefit was far more revealing.

To begin, the training consultant's time was brought down from 14 days overall to 4 to 5 days. Secondly, since the overseas people did not need to gather in one location, travel costs were virtually eliminated. In addition, the costs related to the training space were minimized.

As a result, it turned out that rather than costing money, expenditures were actually reduced. And even more surprisingly, benefits exceeded those initially anticipated. It took an overall shorter time period to reach the required level of comprehension, and the quality and types of questions asked during class-time reflected a greater depth of understanding.[5]

STRUCTURING THE DEPARTMENT FOR COST EFFICIENCY

Program-Wise and Structure-Foolish

Even the most efficient per-program analysis is ineffective if the structure of the training function within the bank is inefficient. Dollars saved on developing an optimal program are also dollars lost if there is a duplication of effort in another department or inefficient use of the program throughout the bank. Unfortunately, there is no one ideal structure. As the overall organizational structure varies from bank to bank, so will the structure of the training function, each having its strengths and shortcomings.

In particular, there is a constant tug-of-war between fans of centralization and those of decentralization in every institution that has more than one division. Typically, the decision will rest on which organizational structure will allow the bank to serve its customers the most expeditiously. With regards to training, the same issues arise—only in this case the customer is the internal line manager.

Centralized Training
In general, centralizing the training efforts has several advantages:

- One reporting system to management can be established, so that they can determine training's status and effectiveness.
- Control can be more readily maintained, assuring programs meeting quality and cultural standards.
- Better utilization of resources—not just the time and staff of the control department—but also more effective use of the outside consultants as well.
- Duplication of effort is minimized.
- Budgeting process is simpler.
- It minimizes "turf wars."

Centralizing has its drawbacks as well. By nature a democratic system, it must meet the needs of the majority first. Smaller departments and specialty areas get ignored or stuck with programs too broad or generic for their needs.

Despite its drawbacks, many financial institutions prefer the centralized approach and have even refined it further by the establishment of in-house learning centers, usually designated as a separate aspect of the bank by being called academies, institutes, colleges, and other similar pedagogical titles.

Decentralized Training
Decentralizing the training function often results in erratic quality levels, extra and overlapping resource requirements, and greater complexity in reporting and budgeting. But its advantages are substantial:

- The training area related to a functional department can develop its own tailored training programs more clearly focused on the area's needs.
- Because it is less generic and better related to the employees' own situations, the training is usually more effective.
- Training needs are generally more quickly determined, and, because of the proximity to subject matter experts, programs can be more rapidly implemented.

Training for the major business lines are organized under separate areas. The designation can be related to the type of knowledge or for the main product areas. For instance, some banks have separate learning centers for retail banking and for commercial banking. Others have it organized by competencies or learning groups: credit and finance, sales and services, and management and professional development. In the end, the decision about which way to go is based on the best allocation of resources possible.

Matrix Structure

Blending the best of the centralized and decentralized approach is the a matrix structure. Essentially, at the corporate or bank-holding company level, the bankwide generic and orientation programs are developed, while the divisional area creates programs which are area specific. Training personnel within the division report on a solid-line basis to the division managers, but on a dotted-line basis to the corporate training area.

Thus, the corporate-training department is responsible for precluding duplication of effort and for assuring that the quality and cultural elements are appropriately addressed. The obvious disadvantage is the complexity of the reporting system and the time and manpower needed for the additional review and program adjustments. In addition, there is the additional cost to the division of having to maintain a separate training staff.

"We use a matrix system here," noted Dottie Imhoff, formerly head of corporate training at Mellon Bank. "It works well, but we have come to learn one thing—that it is as good as the people involved. It requires an unwritten agreement on the part of the managers to ultimately defer to the judgment of the training area. If the managers support it, it will work. However, if managers only want their own way, then it's too complex. The training professionals will be pulled apart in their loyalties."

Rent-a-Consultant

An alternative to the matrix structure is having a centralized unit with a "rent-a-training-consultant" option. In this, the centralized corporate area maintains a cadre of training personnel that are made available to the different divisions. "Rental" options can include a full-time person, a one-half time person, even a one-third or one-fourth time person. Technically, the leased person reports to the corporate-training area, but receives feedback from the line areas, informally and formally in the leased person's annual review.

The obvious advantages are that the line areas get the tailoring and design they require, while the corporate-training area is assured of quality and maximum utilization of resources. However, as with all leased products, the lessor must settle for the available "merchandise"—which may or may not meet the lessor's preferences. Also, the corporate area must maintain an adequate number of internal consultants on the staff to meet demand, which, as in all businesses, will ebb and flow.

Internal versus External

Despite the discussion about the in-house training area, I am not necessarily advocating maintaining a large training department. Many fine programs are offered by the various banking associations, which were listed on page 246, as well as a large variety of private consulting companies and institutes.

It begs the question of how much should be done in-house and how much should be left to open enrollment training. The ABA has determined that about 30% of the banks' training dollar is allocated to outside training. The overall answer lies in the evaluation of goals versus the costs. But a more general guideline can be established by analyzing the nature of the training involved and whether there is adequate transfer of the learned material to the job. (See discussion of adult learning on page 95.)

DYI or Call in a Pro

Assuming that a decision is taken to handle the training in-house, the next consideration is whether the training staff actually develop the material in-house or should an outside professional be involved. The first consideration is always the out-of-pocket cost. However, just comparing numbers can be misleading. There are four basic nonmonetary considerations that should be included in the decision:

- *Time requirement:* How soon does it need to be implemented? Is the time available to perform the job, or will it require foregoing another project to complete this one?
- *Level of expertise:* Is adequate in-house expertise available?
- *Level of development:* Will the in-house developers be recreating the wheel or starting from scratch?
- *Allocation of resources:* Is this the optimal way for the in-house staff to operate? Are there other more valuable projects that require attention?

For many training departments, the ultimate question is whether they are *production* shops or *consulting* shops. Most banks feel it is better to act as full-time consultants dealing with substantive issues and call in outside production people as the need arises. This way banks can avoid the "activity trap," in which one is so busy "doing" that the point of activity is often forgotten.

Investing in Assets

We started by suggesting that people should be deemed to be assets, worthy of being listed on the balance sheet, not "priceless" humans. With more precise cost systems (cost of hire, cost of training), we could evaluate a human worth better—*hopefully leading to better investment in developing and maintaining the asset.* Until organizations see how paltry their investment in employees is by comparison to other successful entities, they will never be convinced of the virtue of training and development.

A comment by Jack Bowsher, the retired Director of Education External Programs at IBM, which has a training budget near $1 billion, speaks squarely to that point: "People misconstrue the information regarding our training budget. They think we can afford to spend so much on training because we are so large. But actually, it is the other way around. We are so large because we have spent so much on training."

APPENDIX

The following is a full cost-benefit analysis for a hypothetical program.[6]

AN EXAMPLE OF FULL COST-BENEFIT ANALYSIS

Current Situation: Of total retail deposit portfolio, IRAs and Combo accounts are currently 12% and 18%. A new course in retail deposit products knowledge is being considered to emphasize the benefits of IRAs and Combo accounts (higher yield than other deposit accounts). The bank would need to train 180 people over the next three years.

Cost Analysis:

Total Cost for Conventional Training Methods
Development cost = $9,000 ($3,000 per annum)
Delivery and other = $23,000 = $128 per person ($7,700 p.a.)
Total per annum cost = $10,300

Total Costs for Self-Study Training Method:
Development costs = $18,000 ($6,000 per annum)
Delivery and other costs = $ 6,500 = $35 p. p. ($2,100 p.a.)
Total per annum cost = $7,100

Benefits Analysis:

Desired Behavioral Change: More product presentation regarding benefits of IRAs and Combo accounts.

Desired Bottom Line Impact: Increase in percentage of these products relative to total portfolio.

Actual Results:

Behavioral Change Analysis Observed after One Year:
Conventional Method: More comfort discussing IRAs and Combo account.

Self-Study Method: Generally more comfort discussing accounts, but less perceived enthusiasm.

Actual Bottom Line Impact after One Year:

Current Conventional Method: IRAs and Combo accounts now, 15% and 22% of total portfolio. Dollar value of portfolio change, estimated $14,000.

$14,000 ÷ $10,300 = 136% return on investment

Self-Study Method: IRA's and Combo's accounts now, 14% and 20% of total portfolio. Dollar value of portfolio change, estimated $11,000.

$11,000 ÷ $7,100 = 155% return on investment

REFERENCES

1. "Old Kent Grabs the Prize." *United States Banker*, July 1989.
2. Bernhard, H. B., and Cynthia Ingols. *Harvard Business Review*, September-October 1988.
3. "An Interview with Jack Bowsher." *ABTAC Newsletter*, August 1988.
4. *The 1988 Human Resources Management Survey*. Washington, D.C.: American Bankers Association, 1988.
5. "Getting Officers up to Speed in Capital Markets." *ABTAC Newsletter*, September 1989.
6. Head, Glenn E. *Training Cost Analysis: A Practical Guide*. Washington, D.C.: Marlin Press, 1985.

ADDITIONAL READINGS

Carnevale, Anthony Patrick. *Human Capital: A High Yield Corporate Investment*. Washington, D.C.: ASTD Press, 1983.

Craig, Robert L., ed. *Training and Development Handbook*. 3rd ed. New York: McGraw-Hill, 1987.

Kirkpatrick, Donald L. *More Evaluating Training Programs*. Washington, D.C.: ASTD Press, 1987.

Levin, Henry M. *Cost Effectiveness: A Primer*. Beverly Hills, Calif.: Sage Press, 1983.

Mitchell, Garry. *The Trainer's Handbook: The AMA Guide to Effective Training*. New York: AMACOM, 1987.

Robinson, Dana Gaines, and James C. Robinson. *Training for Impact*. San Franciso: Jossey-Bass, 1989.

CHAPTER 11

LEADERS AND VISIONARIES: WHAT MAKES THEM SUCCESSFUL

"I think that no one is going to succeed in managing human development with lip service from the top management. No one is going to succeed if the top management just writes an annual letter in support of corporate education."—*Ronald E. Compton, Aetna Life & Casualty.*

There's a certain feeling that once all the necessary adjustments have been made, we can just go about doing our job. We all expect that the rapid changes the banking industry has seen in the last 20 years will slow down, as if change will have found a water level. At that point in time, banks will be out of the raging white waters and into the placid pool. In a sense, there is good reason to expect that; after all, by 2000, a reasonable strategist might predict the following to have happened:

• Competition and the resulting mergers and acquisitions will have sorted out the major "players," creating a respite for those that survived. Managers will not have to be continuously struggling to create a better financial mousetrap.
• By then, banks should be up to speed technologically, which, combined with a reduction in new product development, will result in a relaxation of new development.
• Restrictive government regulations will be reestablished as a result of the banking debacles of the late 80s and early 90s. Banks will be limited in the type and extent of business that they can do, as well as the interest rates they can offer.
• The demand for baby boomers will lessen as they age, di-

minishing "the-grass-is-greener" job-hopping syndrome and engendering more acceptance of the status quo.

• Foreign competition will recede, reducing the threat of the United States becoming a second-rate nation, as the workers in Japan, et al. retreat from the frenzied pace and move into the more comfortable lifestyle of a mature, industrialized nation.

• Corporations have learned the value of the long-term banking relationship, having been stung by the now dormant junk bond market and other disappointing financial promises.

• The economic situation has leveled off; deficits have diminished; interests and foreign currency rates have stabilized.

• The organizational structure of the bank will have been completely revamped to conform to the workstyles of the 90s, such that it can accommodate all types of workers—undereducated non-native borns, women with young children who require flex-time, individuals working from home—as well as establish work teams, intrapreneurial departments, in-house franchises, and highly flattened hierarchies.

ON THE OTHER HAND . . .

The opposite might occur.

• Competition has become even more fierce as the survivors gear up for all-out battle.

• Deregulation extended "all holds unbarred": banks have invaded all the financial and some of the nonfinancial arenas, and vice versa.

• Product development departments are working overtime: new products are constantly being launched and often fail to meet expectations.

• Not only have the Japanese kept up their guard, but other newly industrialized countries, such as Korea, Taiwan, and Singapore have entered the global fray.

• The changing composition of the workforce has created havoc in the operational areas, and the professional staff is

job hopping as the stakes for experienced workers get bigger and bigger.
• The economy has been on a roller-coaster ride: even "two-handed" economists refuse to give predictions. Interest-rate and foreign-exchange trading have reached new heights, as well as new levels of risk.
• Companies are demanding more and more rate and risk concessions, making every new deal too risky, if profitable, or unrewarding, if safe.
• Lender-liability, wronged-employee, and bad-faith suits are piling up in the legal departments, threatening to undermine the very core of the bank.

In a recent strategic planning session, one human resources director commented that his bank decided to review the strategic plans it had completed 20 years ago and the ones it had completed 10 years ago. Neither plan came even close to projecting the way the bank eventually evolved.

> Everyone had done the usual straight-line annual growth projections: you know, this year we'll do 5% better than last year, ad infinitum. No one foresaw the radical changes in the business that ultimately occurred.
>
> The same thing is happening today. Even with the benefit of all the marketplace wisdom, we still have a hard time accepting the fact that change is upon us. No one reads or believes any of the workforce issues. I went to one key executive about a new program that was designed to address service quality in the bank. What was the response? "I'm 47, and I grew up in the industry; I don't want to change, so take this program and shove it."
>
> Of all the changes going on in this industry, the most disconcerting to most managers is that *they*, not the human resources department, will be responsible for the quality of the *people* under their command. In most organizations, managers only perceived them to be responsible for the quality of *work* that was generated. The fine distinction meant that as long as the work met the acceptable standards, the people were incidental. They only became relevant when there was a problem.

THE SENIOR MANAGER'S ROLE: THE TOP OF THE LINE

The problem with change is that it doesn't by itself cause instant adaption. People have to cause themselves to adapt, or, in the case of senior managers, cause others to adapt along with them. But many managers don't realize that is the role foisted on them. They often act like giant beings who don't understand the impact they have on the people around them.

For instance, ask anyone from the training and development area what was the most critical element in the success of their most recent undertaking. The answer *invariably* is "senior management commitment." Yet, in most of my interviews with senior managers, I asked if they felt that their commitment to the program under discussion played a critical role in its success. After a moment's reflection, the response was generally, "not really," or a shrug that conveyed "it never occurred to me before."

"I can understand where, without my directives, the program may have been less focused, but all the credit for making it work should be given to the guy in charge," noted one CEO. This comment reflects more than modesty or a desire to spread the goodwill around—*it indicates a lack of awareness of the importance of role of the senior management on the success of training endeavors within the organization.*

True, most of the CEOs were not directly involved in the actual management of the project, much less the implementation. That was accomplished by the subordinate ranks. But the leadership role, which goes beyond the more familiar management function, was consciously or unconsciously applied by the CEO and ultimately insured the program's success. One has to question whether the bank could achieve the same success with a program if the CEO had held back on the leadership qualities.

Warren Bennis, is his recent book *Why Leaders Can't Lead,* notes four qualities that were evident to some extent in every member of a group he had defined as true leaders:

- Management of attention through vision,
- Management of meaning through communication,
- Management of trust through constancy,
- Management of self through learning.

At the risk of oversimplifying, these qualities can be restated to mean that leadership encompasses having a vision or goal communicated in such fashion that it can be made meaningful to others. Further, those translating the vision into action can be assured there will be no reversals in thinking and that the leader's focus will always be on achieving the goal, not on the hindrances that are bound to occur.[1]

Management of Attention: The Visionary

Almost without thinking, we would list John F. Kennedy or Martin Luther King as visionaries and perhaps add some corporate leaders like Lee Iacocca to the list. But few of us would add our own names, not just out of a sense of modesty, but most commonly because we believe the concept of visionary can only apply to those who seek to achieve goals of great merit or social significance. The result is to diminish the value of the importance of leadership for lesser issues.

This is particularly true if the issue is not new or of recent notoriety, such as, say, the imminent collapse of the organization, but, instead, the issue has always been handled in a routine fashion by subordinates. It is usually easier to deal with a problem that is new or original than to do something that has the implication of "fixing what ain't broke."

John Connolly at National State Bank noted that the hardest problem he faced was to put into motion a vision that others could not perceive as necessary.

> Everything had worked fine up until that point in time. That the bank was headed for disaster was evident only to those who were in a position to have a macro view of the market changes, but few in the bank were involved in that, nor were there any immediate indications. Many in the bank could not understand the need for imposing management

training when everything up till that point worked perfectly well.

Then, the visionary elements are multiplied: first, the leader must not only perceive the problem but the leader must be willing to commit to an issue that is not of apparent major magnitude. Then, the leader must be willing to elevate the importance of a function, even one that has generally been deemed as working well or as relatively unimportant.

The Man with the Chisel

To see the unseen is the greatest aspect to the art of leadership. Richard M. Kovacevich, President of Norwest Corp., in paraphrasing the "seeing the unseen," noted that Michelangelo once said that "inside every piece of marble is a beautiful statue. All I have to do is chip away the excess marble." Kovacevich, who came in 1986 with the responsibility of reversing the sagging fortunes at Norwest, likens himself to that role.

> I'm the man with the chisel. I am simply there to allow the art to come out through the marble. In my mind, in every troubled organization, someone has the answer to the problem that is troubling it. My role is to be sensitive to the need for change and then find those people who can give me the answer. I'm not going around to people and "writing on their blank slates." Rather, it's more like "reading their book" and finding out the critical ideas of what's already inside.

> When I first told everyone that it was possible to determine the cause of our problems and fix it within 18 months, no one believed me—well, maybe .001% of the people did. After a year, 80% believed it. They saw the answer did exist, and it existed within us, the organization. All we had to do was draw it out.

Management of Meaning: The Communicator

It is almost universally accepted that the impact of training is greatly enhanced whenever the "message" of importance or the need for the training is first realized. Similarly, training failures have been attributed to the lack of such a message—that is, whenever employees wonder what the point of the training is. It's not that management doesn't attempt to communicate the importance of training; more commonly, management automatically expects that employees will appreciate its purpose. But the reality is far from the ideal.

"Actually, it's not a communication problem," noted Tony Terracciano, then President of Mellon Bank in Pittsburgh (now Chairman, President, and CEO of First Fidelity Bancorp in N.J.).

> It's a problem of translation. Senior management must bring the message from one level, where a problem or a strategy has been widely debated and understood, to another level that has considerably less familiarity with the issues. To reach them, the senior managers must first talk to their needs in their language.
>
> For instance, the question we are most frequently asked is, What is the new strategy all about? But that's not the real question. The real one, I discovered, has four separate parts.
>
> 1. Why is change necessary?
> 2. Why is this new strategy better or correct?
> 3. What makes you think that the strategy can succeed?
> 4. What makes you think that I can succeed?
>
> In fact, if you consider the fourth question alone, you have all the justification you need to do training. But it is in answering the first three questions that you can translate the real message of the training.

In short, simply providing the training does not make the participant *want* to apply the information learned. That can only be done if the importance of the training is communicated first. And the less concrete in nature the training, the more critical the need for explaining the reasons for learning. "But," cautions Terracciano, "you must give the answers in *their* vocabulary. They need to hear it, not as some platitude, but as a meaningful concept. In my mind, the real value of training is that it facilitates getting answers to those questions."

It's True: The Medium Is the Message

To say to the attendees that "the objective of training is to learn how to better service customers" does not convey the importance of why it should be learned. To have the presenter in the program provide a reason, such as, "We stand to lose business if we don't provide service" is a step forward, but still does not convey the immediacy of the problem.

Even if everyone in the room nods in agreement, the point is not necessarily internalized. Some level of force or power must underlie the statement. If the problem was so critical, they would have heard something from senior management. Consider this. How in the United States do we know that a political or economic problem is important? Answer: *Because the President personally announces it to the public.* The same is true with employees: if the issue is critical enough that it stands to impact the bank, surely the President would tell them. The medium is the message.

But, just as history distinguished Jimmy Carter from Ronald Reagan by the latter's ability to communicate in terms comprehensible to the electorate, so too must the CEO speak in terms comprehensible to the employees. The problem and the solution must be translated into concrete, readily understood terms.

"We deliver the message ourselves," added Terracciano. "I typically do a one and one-half hour introduction to our new wholesale training program, which is a requirement for everyone in the division. I address and answer the four questions and then discuss them with the attendees to make sure that they were translated into their language."

> Now, we could have had a more junior person do this introduction. Hell, we could have passed it out in a memo. But having our employees capable of carrying out our strategies is critical to our success. We're not just teaching them new skills: we are teaching them about a whole new cultural ap-

proach to the banking business. If that doesn't warrant our time and effort, what does?

Say It Like It Is

John Sponski, Corporate Executive Officer at Sovran Financial in Norfolk, experienced a communication gap when he tried to articulate his intense interest in improving the quality of the support and operations group under his control.

> I kept telling everyone that I wanted them to aim for perfection. They kept telling me that it couldn't be done. We had the training in place, and I was sure that they could meet the new standards; nonetheless, I met quite a bit of resistance.
>
> I finally realized that part of the problem was in the way I was communicating my goal. I was using a word *perfection* that was conceptual and full of biases rather than action oriented. So, to create a more concrete goal, I put it into a 12-word action statement: *Our mission is to exceed expectations for quality, cost-effectiveness, and timely service.* We later refined that to two words, which we even put on buttons: *Wow customers!* The message got through. I think we have the finest back office of any major bank in America.
>
> Now, whenever there is an issue or a problem, I ask myself: Is my message really getting through, and, if not, what are the barriers? Is it because we are not saying correctly, not supporting our words with deeds, not reiterating it enough, or doing anything else that causes messages to go astray. We know that if we truly value something, everything we do will reflect that. We must make sure our values match our goals—that they are communicated in everything we do and say.

Let's Go to the Videotape

Norwest Corp. took the concept of *TV* and *everyday* literally and combined the most communicative elements of the two. They picked up soap operas and the MTV scene to translate them into dozens of sales and training videos. Staff, employees, senior managers, even Richard Kovacevich, the President, dressed up in all types of outfits to make the point.

"In the early efforts, I was involved in every aspect," noted Kovacevich.

> I helped write the video scripts. I was particularly interested that their tone and design carried the message and supported the changes we wanted to make. The words and visuals had to make sense to them as much as it entertained them.
>
> Did it work? Absolutely. The care we put into those early efforts was not wasted. In fact, the approach proved so successful that now I don't need to be as involved; the others in the bank know which messages need supporting and can translate them into the videos. I only view them after they're made, and I think they've all been great.

Direct Bullet

Senior managers who wonder how they can best impact the cultural mores of the organization have found an ideal medium in the classroom. Addressing a whole group dramatically short-circuits the time-consuming "management-by-walking-around" approach. If anything, the process is accelerated, since a frank interchange on the platform floor is less likely than one in the classroom where open commentary and two-way discussions are encouraged.

"It's like shooting a direct bullet," noted Bill Plechaty, EVP from Southeast Bank in Miami. The bank had a situation that needed fast attention. Since 1973, it grew by absorption and acquisition, leaving them with a conglomerate of cultures and systems.

> It was like a fresh stew—all onions and lumps. It would take years of simmering before it would boil down to the type of bisque the more established banks have.
>
> Besides, we needed to establish an altogether different culture. The training arena is wonderful. First of all, people are of a mind to expect and to accept something different. So you can sledgehammer in changes that you typically whisper about in corridors.
>
> But it must be the senior managers who tell them and

teach them how they're going to be different if the culture is to flow through the whole organization. You can't put a notice on the bulletin board and hope that it sinks in. If that's what you want, you must make it happen.

In our case, we needed to get away from the elitist commercial-lending culture and create a people-oriented team-playing organization. Too many banks have created the cult of the M.B.A., only to find out that many were excellent with sophisticated spreadsheets, but terrible dealing with other people. We decided we needed to get away from the narrow approach of a few superior analytical types and develop a broad-based customer-oriented superiority among all our employees. What could be a better forum to achieve that than the classroom?

The senior managers at Southeast regularly show up in the classroom to forward their ideals. The bank's president will drop in on training classes held around Florida, not to preach, but to actually teach whatever the topic of learning is. All the senior managers show up at different training sessions, especially the one informally entitled "Welcome to the Real World," which is given to the management trainees as they complete the formal training program.

We don't expect anyone to be able to guess at what our needs and values are. We go in and tell them. We have the perfect vehicle to shape the culture we want this bank to have, and we use it. We rely on training 100% to communicate our message.

"How much training is necessary?" commented Bill Plechaty at Southeast Bank. "You never know. It's like polishing a rough stone. You can't tell ahead of time when it will be smooth and shiny; you only know that if you keep at it long enough, rubbing and burnishing, eventually you will have a beautiful specimen."

Management of Trust: The Commitment

"It's easy to start the process of getting everyone committed," noted Kovacevich, "but considerably more difficult to implement."

In my case, I felt that in order to get at the basic problem, I had to go into the field and find out what the issues were. It would have been a lot easier to ask just a couple of people nearby, but that would not have helped get to the full depth of the problem. You've got to be out there where the rubber meets the road.

I personally visited all but one of the subsidiary banks. By now, I can tell the attitude of the employees within one minute—60 seconds. It completely shows through. And I know that if *I* can sense it, so can the customer.

"But going to practically every location and talking to the employees was the most critical aspect of finding and fixing the bank's problems." Kovacevich identified, among others, attitude and knowledge issues that up till then had been ignored or not quite perceived as problems. "You can have all kinds of bells and whistles on your products, but, in the end, the customer is most impacted by the professionalism and the attitude of the contact person. And, in my mind, attitude is number one." To Kovacevich, his commitment to getting into the employees' heads was one of the key reasons for ultimately being a success in changing their attitudes, with its impact on the bank's fortunes. "It's not magic; it's not even luck. Anyone can do it, but you've got to be willing to go through all the steps."

Going through All the Steps
This sentiment was shared by everyone interviewed: the commitment must exceed words. "You hear from everyone," commented Terracciano, then from Mellon, "that to be successful, any training effort needs the backing of the top management. But it needs more than the backing; it needs the *involvement* of management."

And I mean *involvement* in all aspects—the design, the development, and the delivery. Top managers must get out there and *teach*. We all do it here—from Frank Cahouet (Mellon's Chairman) on down. And not just an introductory phrase or two. Really teach.

In addition to the kick-off on wholesale banking, I also personally do credit training, sales training, training in the private banking area. We also run informal training sessions on such topics as the differences between leadership and management and on developing corporate and individual strategies.

Why? Not because we're such superb teachers, but because we have developed a strategy and created a culture and a vocabulary around it. If you want it to stick, you must be constantly reinforcing that culture, that vocabulary.

Not only do we teach, we also take the time to read the evaluation reports and participants' feedback. Those provide clues to where the information fell short or where it wasn't translated clearly enough. I always pick up an idea or two to refine the next presentation.

In short, commitment is not represented in fleeting memoranda or cavalier actions. It requires more than a stroke of the pen or a slap on the back. It involves time, interest, and a steady commitment of resources.

Commitment of Resources

A decline in earnings usually precedes a general "belt tightening," translating for the most part into cutbacks in nonessential items. But what truly is nonessential?

Business schools and textbooks tell us the areas that tend to be the most vulnerable are the advertising budget, capital expenditure, and R&D. In the face of declining revenues, shouldn't advertising be stepped up? By the same token, should a company diminish its long-term chances of success by scaling down the new assets and product development foundation that the bank's future will rest on? Typically, the Japanese, whose focus is predominantly on the long haul, are revered for their business philosophy of long-term survival—and are notably successful at achieving it.

If the long haul is the focus, what then is the value in slicing the HR development budget? Granted, every budget has its fat. But the rationale for more aggressive pruning is usually done through a comparison of the "need-to-know" and "nice-to-know" courses: the latter is knocked out while the former is retained or compressed. But consider the message conveyed when the training budget is cut:

• Only certain aspects of HR development are significant. The implication is that the cut programs had little or no validity; otherwise, they would have been retained.
• The bank's present decline in earnings is not related to the job performance of the employees; clearly, if it were, training would be given more, rather than less, emphasis.
• The bank's future course will not be dependent on the quality of the employee base; therefore, the current skills and knowledge base of the employees must be adequate for the future.

Much worse, then, must be the message sent when management pulls back on a program heralded to be one designed to improve a problem or assure the success of a new strategy. The credibility factor is so diminished as to become negligible.

Management of Self: The Right Focus

The management of self is perhaps the least intuitively obvious of those discussed, because it relates to the manager's own level of self-confidence in achieving the goal. According to the author, Warren Bennis, it goes beyond "commitment": it is the ability to see beyond the mistakes likely to be made—keeping a fixed focus on the end goal.

The lack of it perpetuates a vicious cycle among subordinates, especially among those in training who are generally reliant on managers to provide support.

- Typically, line management requests a training program to meet a perceived need.
- The training department produces one based on their best understanding of the situation.
- For some reason, the program has mediocre reception or is under pressure costwise. Line support begins to evaporate.
- Training eventually drops the program. New programs are not recommended nor are others created without the training department's involvement.

- The training department's credibility is diminished; its function is given low priority and visibility.

The problem here is that the focus was the process, not the end payoff. Had the focus remained on the goal, the effort to assure that the process succeeded would be increased, not diminished.

John Connolly of National State noted that their "support must be consistent."

> If we changed our course, we knew we stood to ruin the employees' belief in our mission. Credibility lags the environmental situation; it takes a long time before management's actions are truly absorbed. A switch in your commitment midway will cause your credibility on that issue to be lost, and it will take even longer to gain it back on the next tour. Once we set the path to achieving a training program that focused on rewarding management skills, we never varied our attitude.

PART 2—LINE MANAGER'S ROLE: THE SOFT UNDERBELLY

Communication problems or, as Tony Terracciano put it, translation problems occur between groups at all levels—certainly between the executive office and the rank and file, but just as much between the executive office and the line manager.

"I'm not sure that we could have done what we did," added Terracciano, referring to the major overhaul of the strategic approach and the subsequent all-out training efforts that followed, "if this bank were not going through a problem period. During such a period, the culture unfreezes, leaving an open window for senior management to come in and shake things up. It will become more rigid again as things settle down, but, if management is quick, they can mold it to be better."

Getting the rank and file to change is often the easiest. Many are new and still impressionable. Their relationships with others at the bank are still being formed. However, it is presumptive to think that a whole culture can be changed in a few months, particularly among the middle-to-upper level executives who have been at the bank for many years. Their thoughts and habits will remain largely the same, as will their interactions with their colleagues and subordinates. Line management is a fulcrum on which major changes balance, yet often the most intractable to deal with.

Staff Is Line

Banks are starting to shift more HR functions to the line managers, primarily in an effort to reduce overhead expense. Thus, it will be the manager who will be asked to lead, coach, develop, and refine the skills of his or her staff and solve the problems, whatever employee relations problems arise, and not rely on HR to handle that function independently. Are most managers ready for it?

"Managing Problem Employees has always been one of our most successful management skills programs because it impacts the level of productivity," noted one training manager who had just come from a round of meetings with line managers, trying to convince them of the value of a new series of management skills training programs.

> But many managers grouse at having to attend less "productivity" focused programs. This is HR's function; why are we here?—we hear that all the time when we do programs dealing with improving managing styles or managing change. To them, programs on goalsetting for asset volume make sense; programs on career development for employees are useless. Many of them still hate to do performance appraisals, which are among their best tools to improve performance. They still see themselves as work-flow managers, not people managers.

Where'd They Get That Idea
That emphasis has been so heavily on productivity management is not the fault of the managers. (See Chapter 2 on Managerial Skills.) It's been the focus of the whole corporate

structure since the 50s, when management by objectives (MBO) first became the new buzzword at the watercoolers. The MBO process is a simple one and theoretically should involve the subordinate: both determine the job responsibilities, the standards of performance, and the general work plan for achieving the goal.

Over the years, the theoretical MBO process was modified considerably by other management theories. The degree of subordinate input increased in the participative management, which generally recommended the creation of a team to make decisions and define the desired result. The participative theory, in turn, was superceded by Theory Z, which placed greater emphasis on the creation of quality circles that would identify problems and determine solutions.

In reality, most managers revert back to the simplest of systems: the manager determines what should be done, tells the subordinate what to do, and does the appropriate monitoring to make sure it is done. The process, no matter how it is ultimately interpreted, is directed towards achieving a tangible goal—one that impacts the bottom line.

Typically, managers work up plans in the fall for the following year. Discussions center around how realistic the plans are, what additional resources are required, fall-back positions, and so forth. Bonuses to managers are rewarded, based on the achievement of the plan.

Issues that do not directly impact the realization of the plan are rarely discussed. Why should they be? They would only distract the manager from the goal at hand. Every basic and reinforcing element within the organization is one that supports achieving the goal—that is, *productivity management.*

More Work, Less Reward

That managers should hate the additional responsibility of *people management* is understandable. For the extra effort, they get little reward; in fact, many see it only as a penalty. They are charged with developing people, who, because of their identified superior skills, are then transferred into other areas. The mediocre workers typically remain—leaving the manager with a sense of eternally struggling to pull together a workable team.

Moreover, many managers feel that they will be forced to attend a slew of management skills programs that embody dubious management fads. "I don't ever want to be lost in the woods again," commented one disgusted manager, "and then asked how I felt about it. I hated it; that's how I felt about it." It is true, that in the search for truth, organizations (although banks tend to be the least of the prime offenders) have subjected themselves to a variety of managerial theories that have not proven to be the ultimate answer, from inward contemplation to wandering in the woods.

Trickle Down Hasn't Trickled Down Yet

"It may be out there, but it hasn't hit here yet," commented the head of corporate training at one large bank that had undergone a rapid change of management and attitudes.

> We know that the senior executives are preaching a new gospel of managing people, but our clients—the line managers—still see our game being one of productivity. Since the reorganization two years ago, our training has been 80% job skills training —no, make that 90% job skills and 10% managerial skills and professional development.
>
> We'd like to reach senior management to tell them that we want to help them. We know that the several new programs that they initiated really delve into the cultural change and the need for better managerial skills. Some executives are even doing the training themselves. However, we're so involved in the day-in, day-out skills training, we're stymied from addressing those issues.
>
> In fact, the way our training budget was laid out, we were practically precluded from doing any managerial development training at all. We literally kept those programs rolling by begging and borrowing funds from unused sources. What happened to our budget? Well, the chaos stemming from the pressure to have a successful turnaround caused a knee-jerk reaction.
>
> Ultimately, the line managers became so focused on

new product and sales training, they simply reallocated all the funds from development training into it. Senior management's full message never really "got" to them: sure, we need profits, but we'll also need a new type of leader and manager to achieve the full measure of the strategy. As a result, the line manager's immediate focus is strictly bottom line. It was an extension of their old-time culture—manage productivity, not people.

Our direct boss at the time, the head of Human Resources, was a replacement from the line area, so he parroted that attitude. Since then, we've had different HR bosses—three in two years—yet we're still not getting the necessary attention to managerial needs. In fact, the talk now is to use a CBT program for supervisory training as a cost-saving measure! CBT has many good aspects. But if you're trying to make a cultural change, how do you do that with CBT? That's a message that must be personally delivered.

As far as I'm concerned, we're missing—missed—an opportunity to do what senior management wants most to achieve: create a more dynamic culture. The perfect media for that message is right here, in our regular management and supervisory programs. Yet line management is so entrenched in short-term productivity, that the long-term issues are being overlooked.

What Must Middle Management Do

Leadership roles are not the exclusive domain of the executive office. Middle managers must also bring in their own elements of broad-minded thinking if the overall plan is to be successful. Some particular aspects middle managers should focus on include:

• *Whole-bank attitude.* The management by objective system has many strong points: it places a very specific focus on the goal line, and makes the manager directly responsible for achieving it. The contribution to U.S. industry has been undisputed. Since its introduction several decades ago, there has been a major shift in the mind-set of the middle manager from passive to active.

On the negative side, MBO forces the focus of the manager to be short term. The manager is rewarded when his or her department has an immediate impact on the bottom line. The long run is being ignored. But the basis of presumption is linear in thinking: if all the quarterly profits are good, then all those quarters strung together must therefore create a long line of success.

The MBO system has led, in some cases, to superior results and, in some cases, to unfortunate decision making—when long-term needs are sacrificed for short-term results. Many banks, such as Bank of America, experienced this when they allowed investment in technological equipment to slide, only to find the cost of upgrading the computer system to be overwhelming.

Managers have a vested interest in expenditures that have the greatest likelihood of increasing revenue. They also have the least vested interest in substituting certainty for uncertainty.

Unfortunately, most managers do not have the "right" to act independently of other managers or the corporate entity as a whole. Managers who go out on the corporate limb risk being treated as pariahs by their peers and as upstarts by their superiors. A well-known example is Lee Iacocca's tenure at Ford, where his actions, however well intended, had so irritated Henry Ford III that his success with the Mustang could not salvage his career there.

The pressure to conform to company policy means that any manager must choose his or her fights very carefully. The variant activities must prove successful in order to justify breaking with tradition.

• *Champion the cause.* In many banks, training and development suffer from numerous disadvantages. With the notable exception for sales training, most training programs do not go through the rigors of a cost-benefit analysis, so they are last to be considered when funds are allocated and the easiest prey when cost-cutting is required. Alternatively, managers could champion the cause of training without the benefit of cost analyses, but that leaves them without the ability to definitively justify the expense or prove their success.

Longer-term developmental training, such as a stint at a banking school, is even more exposed to manager rejection than knowledge or skills-based training because the definition of success is less tangible. Further, the impact of developmental efforts is *meant* to be felt in the future, so current expenditure is certain to appear wasted on the bottom line. Many banks have brought developmental training under the corporate wing to combat the managers' natural disinclination to shell out current funds for future needs.

But managers still must nominate the candidate and allocate time for the training. A manager may well see good reason to groom the candidate, but why have it done while the candidate is in the manager's particular department. If the potential candidates are so good, they probably will be transferred anyway—or so their managers may reason. Therefore, let the next department deal with the development issue.

In fact, the whole developmental issue runs contrary to the managers' preference, which is to keep the good employees in the department as subordinates as long as possible. Certainly, they would prefer not to lose them to other areas only to be replaced by employees of unknown abilities, or, worse, have the candidate push them out of their own jobs. It's therefore in the managers' best interest not to reveal the employees as stars—highly competent employees, perhaps, but not stars.

• *Focus on the future.* Experts assure us that the managers of the future will be different. They will be more cognizant of the limitations of short-term thinking and more influenced by the Japanese approach of deferring earnings now for future gain. They will be more accepting of the one-bank concept and less territorial. They will see that, although funds must still be allocated, putting immediate gratification over future development only hurts their own institution in the long run, as the quality of the personnel diminishes through lack of attention.

Middle managers who can now see through the immediate situation into the future are clearly the ones who will be the senior managers of the future. Taking the long-term approach will pay off in long-term rewards: not only will those above eventually realize the value of long-term decisions, but those below will be as loyal and supportive of the middle manager through the years as the manager was as supportive of them.

THE TRAINING MANAGERS: THE CRITICAL LINK

The training industry, like the banking industry, has been evolving. It is amply clear that training is an integral part of many significant aspects of the human resources management area and no longer a stand-alone function. However, role *perception* doesn't always keep pace with role *need*. Where trainers before could easily satisfy the bank's needs by keeping pace with skills-training techniques, the needs have now changed to require a more sophisticated and involved trainer who can develop a more proficient and committed employee.

Trainers themselves are seeing their role expand beyond the mere confines of knowledge- and skills-transference techniques into areas such as:

Organization development—ensuring healthy and strong individual, team, department, and corporate relationships.

Career development—ensuring an alignment of individual needs and career needs.

Job design—defining how tasks and responsibilities will be organized and integrated.

Human resources planning—determining the institution's needs and implementing strategies.

Performance management systems—ensuring that the employee's contribution match the institution's needs and expectations.

Selection and staffing—matching individuals' abilities and needs with the institution's jobs and career paths.[2]

The training professionals who set their sights on the highest level will be the most successful in achieving the best for the organization. For the most part, that means moving from *doing* to *consulting* and ultimately to being a *change agent*. But to be accepted as a conceptual contributor requires a high degree of credibility on the part of the trainer—credibility that, unlike other functions such as senior credit officer, is not inherent in the position—credibility must first be earned.

Insider Moves

The training area is technically a staff function, but in many banks it is treated as a staff "outsider," not a staff "insider." As an outsider, it is deemed as only tangential to the operations of the bank. As such, it does not merit the privileges of the insider—that of regularly being involved in banking affairs. Such privileges generally come by invitation only: for instance, to strategic-planning meetings or line business projections discussions. While many trainers point with pride to the fact that they are invited to these meetings (at many banks, they are not), for the most part they remain auditors, not active participants. Their role is limited to taking notes of the plans and commenting on training's involvement in achieving the plan.

What's wrong with that? you may wonder. Isn't the point of being a training professional to provide advice about training and development? Certainly. Doing that should be their primary function. *But limiting the expectations has also led to a limited perception as the value of training.*

Not that all training professionals should be encouraged to be more active in corporate affairs. Many trainers are currently at the limit of their own capacity to contribute. Why? Because those involved in the training functions fall into two categories:

1. Those who primarily focused their careers in human resource development and happen to have a position at a bank.

2. Those who were primarily trained in banking and transferred into a training function somewhere in their career path. In some banks, the training area still is a great "pasture-land."

The greatest irony is that of all the professional areas within the banking industry, people in the training department are the least formally trained. The human resources professionals rarely receive formal training in banking principles; likewise, those originally trained as bankers are rarely formally trained in human resource development. Both types rely on OJT in the training department, which often results in great vacuums of knowledge.

Undoubtedly, the worst situation is the one in which a bank arbitrarily chooses someone from the line area to be the head of training without anyone within the bank being available to act as coach for that position. It both deprecates the value of training and is a prescription for comparative failure, yet ABTAC receives pleas of assistance all the time from these individuals.

Banks are often very cavalier about training personnel. They offer few or no directives on what is truly expected of the training professional. "It's like taking a test, but without knowing what the questions are," complained one trainer. "But if I fail, I'll be typed as a loser." Their careers are in a vicious cycle. No one takes them seriously, so no one provides directives, and, without the directives, they don't know how to get the necessary credibility to be taken seriously.

We Don't Count; We're Just Trainers

"Don't ask *me*—I just work here." This is a classic sour grapes reply of anyone who thinks that he or she is the outsider and has no hope of ever being anything else. "Training has never had any clout; we're lucky if we get invited to the annual picnic."

The responsibility for developing a higher level of professionalism lies with the bank and the training professionals themselves. Those in training must seek out the professional development that will help them reach the level of "management peer." In turn, the bank must hold out the reward that will motivate them to do so—the privilege of being an insider. In this case, *insider* would include:

- Involvement in strategic planning, discussions, meetings, and retreats.
- Attendance at regular-line division meetings addressing business advancements and problems.
- A regularly scheduled meeting with a senior executive and access to all senior executives, including the chairman.
- Arrangements for the professional trainers for rotations through various line positions, in order to acclimate them to the "real" world.
- Arrangements for the nonprofessional trainer to attend human resources schools and other educational conferences, to expose them to training and developmental theory.

Can We Talk?

For their part, trainers must actively seek out a new level of professionalism if they are to be taken seriously as insiders. They must break from the comfortable insularity common to this profession by "joining the real world." The greatest annoyance line managers have about professional trainers, as noted by another professional trainer, is that they "don't really converse. They just share 'ahas,' practice active listening skills, and act out desirable communication behaviors. They also find symbolic meaning in everything, no matter how trivial. A Hulk Hogan wrestling match becomes a workshop on alternative methods of conflict resolution." Or, as someone else complained, discussing the next year's budget with them "is not an arithmetic exercise, but a neo-zen experience."

Bob Hamilton, then Vice President in charge of operations training at Sovran Financial Corporation, noted that most trainers "simply do not speak management's language." To reach the intended audience, trainers must learn to understand management's business, he commented. For trainers who were not previously bankers, this often becomes the most challenging aspect. However, if this "language barrier" is ignored, the trainer will be viewed as "one of them."

He also suggests that it is necessary to educate management. To most managers, the training process is only vaguely understood. It needs to be clarified by more than cursory explanations of what can be done to help them improve their employees' performance and productivity. Even if suggestions are not implemented, both parties are brought closer towards understanding each other's interests. Hamilton emphasized that using the correct verbiage makes a big difference. Since bankers think in terms of products and services, he suggested substituting the former word for *programs* and the latter for *consulting*.

Formal communication should include an annual "state-of-training-and-development" report for presentation to senior management, covering the current costs, perceived benefits, specific recommendations for future programs, and new technology and processes. Hamilton's own group produced an annual product plan including a summation of the various products and costs, time line, statement of measurability, and related value of the products to the serviced department. In addition, the group prepared a monthly performance report with budgeted and actual results similar to those produced by the line departments.

"We try to think like a banker and talk like a banker," added Hamilton. "If that causes management to think we are bankers, well, that only contributes to our credibility."[3]

Four Ps
In essence, Hamilton was merely noting that the training department is a "business" and should act as one. Doing so forces training areas to treat products and services with the same consideration as would be offered an external customer. The same questions should arise as with any product

that hits the market (commonly called the four Ps of product management):

- Is the *product* or service well conceived and well executed?
- Is it *priced* correctly?
- Is it well *packaged* and well marketed?
- Is it correctly *promoted*?

However, the difference between the outside customer and the internal one is that the latter is a captive audience. While outsiders can simply stop using the product, internal customers generally are compelled to use the inside one. But to avoid friction, often internal customers do not voice complaints or note shortcomings in the product.

The training area should never get so involved with doing training that they lose sight of the customer's goals—to support the bank's goals and strategy. The signs of becoming sidetracked are sometimes subtle: slipping attendance, late arrivals, no invitations to meetings, and so forth. Often, formal and informal surveys done regularly can help the areas determine if they are missing the point. In any case, it's up to the training areas, not the line areas, to keep the focus fixed and the needs fulfilled.

Business Professionals

To really become adequately integrated into the corporate world of banking, trainers must act like corporate people. It's necessary for them to start viewing the department as a business entity, rather than as an adjunct department in a bureaucracy. It's easiest to assume that role when the departmental philosophy is articulated in terms of actually being a business: an entity with a specific mission, customers, products, and market differentiation, which requires promotion, development, analysis, and a profit margin.

Treating training professionals as independent business people, not aides-de-camp, can make a big difference in their own attitude. It imposes upon them new "business disciplines" of responsibility, productivity, and goals-orientation. In other words, it empowers.

Trainer, Train Thyself

For trainers, unfortunately, it's not quite enough to meet the basic requirements of running a business. Like minority groups, they must really be outstanding to be awarded the basic degree of credibility. The outsiders must, in essence, become better trained in the aspects of business than the natural insiders in order to get a ticket to the inside. To do that, trainers should:

• *Learn about the banking industry and the bank.* Bank trainers should be able to converse with any and all as if they were "bankers," not "trainers." Bob Albright, the Vice President in charge of organizational development and training at The Huntington National Bank in Columbus, Ohio, has a specific regimen for his staff members. To begin, they are assigned two texts on banking principles to read within the first 90 days of hire. They then have a one-week rotation through one of the banking offices. In addition, all staff members are expected to read *The Wall Street Journal*, the *ABA Journal*, and the *BAI Magazine*, so that they are prepared to talk on banking issues at the monthly and biweekly meetings. After a year or so, the professional staff will also attend the Ohio Bankers School for the commercial banking curriculum. The department regularly brings in outside speakers to make a presentation exclusively to the Huntington Bank's training staff.

• *Learn financial analysis.* The training area staff should take it upon themselves to do cost-benefit analyses—not wait until they are asked by management. The best approach is to select the most costly programs first, and set out to determine the exact impact on the bottom line. Then, sort, using a matrix approach, choosing the most complex, most expensive programs, and ignoring the easily delivered and inexpensive ones. In this way, efforts are placed where management will be most impressed by the changes or savings.

• *Learn accounting systems.* Then use the information to create a budgeting system that is most effective in terms of "managing numbers and impressing the boss." Typically, it is a zero-based budgeting system, in which every program is automatically eliminated each year during the budgetary exercise and then brought back in accordance with "client" requests. It forces a closer review of each item, generally resulting in a leaner budget.

• *Learn about technology.* Determine which technological aids would be most useful, and seek funding for their incorporation. CBT and interactive videos may cut down on the expense of conventional training and cost of employee time away from the job. Computer systems allow for superior data maintenance and analysis. Trainers should be able to justify additional capital outlays which serve to reduce costs, especially labor costs, over time as well as improve the quality of information.

• *Learn politics.* Unfortunate as it is, corporations are political entities. As in Washington, the programs that are supported are not necessarily those which are the best, but those that have the most support. Trainers must be able to get out and sell, sell, sell the long-term value of their efforts. They should always have statistical data handy, such as the cost-benefit analyses, and sprinkle them around generously, so that the line managers can, in turn, justify their support.

THE ETERNAL TRIANGLE

In most corporations, the training function used to be far removed from the executive's office. (See Figure 11–1 below.) But in companies such as IBM and others, training is part of a triangle: three groups must interact to effectively meet all the needs and goals of the bank. (See Figure 11–2.)

Senior Management—to perceive the need and determine the training solution.

Line Management—to accept training solution and insure its implementation.

Training and Development—to enhance the implementation and assist in further need and solution determination.

FIGURE 11–1
Typical Current Structure

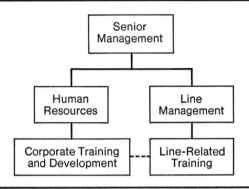

FIGURE 11–2
Recommended Structure

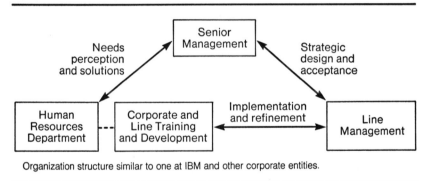

Organization structure similar to one at IBM and other corporate entities.

If one side is removed from this triangle, the whole structure succumbs. Similarly, if all three groups offer greater support in conjunction with each other, the structure becomes stronger.

Listen to what Edward F. McDougal, Jr., an Executive Vice President in charge of human resources at National Westminster Bancorp, holding company of National Westminster Bank USA in New York, says. In 1983, when he became a candidate for the position, his then-to-be boss, William Knowles, made a statement to McDougal: "I am the chief human resources officer and the chief morale officer of the bank. You would work for me."

McDougal accepted the job *because* of those terms.

> When people hear that story, they ask me if I feel threatened. Hell, no—just the opposite. I *want* to work in an institution where the senior management directly takes responsibility for what happens with the employees. It guarantees me access to the senior levels. With management support behind me, I knew that I would do the best job I could—not constantly struggling for resources and policy changes.
>
> Knowles made his attitudes known to the line managers. We, in turn, made it known to the line managers that they were our (HR's) customers: we're here to help them achieve their goals. The impact on attitude and our success has been enormous.

The human resources area defined its own mission in a "Statement of Values," a lengthy proclamation that starts out by noting that it is committed to "support the bank in achieving its business goals by serving, influencing, and leading it in attracting, managing, and developing its employees."

The bank also set up committees to translate its overall philosophy into written policy, with every employee group within the bank—officers to clerical staff, male and female, white and minorities—being represented. The committees set forth a *bankwide* "Statement of Values," essentially stating that the maintenance of the customer base, contribution to the community, and reputation are of critical importance. On an equal footing, the statement notes that the bank also values "ourselves"—the employees.

Most noteworthy is that the language in the statement does not distinguish between management and employees, but rather makes it apparent that it is everyone's responsibility within the bank to maintain the philosophy.

Excerpt from the National Westminster Bancorp's Statement of Values:

> **Ourselves:** We, the employees, are the strength of the Bank and the sources of its character. We work together to foster an open environment where trust and caring prevail.

Pride and enjoyment come from commitment, leadership by example, and accomplishment. We encourage personal growth and ensure opportunity based upon performance.

REFERENCES

1. Bennis, Warren. *Why Leaders Can't Lead: The Unconscious Conspiracy Continues.* San Francisco: Jossey-Bass, 1989.
2. McLagan, Patricia A. "Models for HRD Practice." *Training & Development Journal,* September 1989.
3. Keene, Margaret. "As I See It." *ABTAC Newsletter,* November 1988.

ADDITIONAL READINGS

Schein, Edgar H. *The Art of Managing Human Resources.* New York: Oxford University Press, 1987.

Vogt, Judith F., and Kenneth L. Murrell. *Empowerment in Organizations. How to Spark Exceptional Performance.* San Diego: University Associates, 1990.

APPENDIX

CURRICULA GUIDELINES FOR SELECTED CAREER TRACKS

A committee of bankers, trainers, and consultants formed by AB-TAC, The Association of Bank Trainers and Consultants, recently created curricula designs for several major career tracks:

Branch Management
Retail Lending
Private Banking
Commercial and Middle Market Lending
Corporate Relationship Management

The ultimate purpose of these curricula is to provide guidelines to financial institutions in the establishment of their own programs to train employees.

Each curriculum covers a wide range of skills and knowledge, including banking basics, credit and analytical skills, selling skills, and product knowledge. Specific areas of expertise are addressed at each level; from bookkeeping and credit inquiries at entry level to managing loan portfolios at the more advanced levels. The curricula also present recommendations on professional growth, which emphasizes basic communication skills at the lower levels and managerial skills at the more advanced levels. Comprehensive in scope and providing clearly defined objectives, these curricula should aid financial institutions in creating programs to meet their individual needs.

ABTAC Guideline Curriculum
BRANCH MANAGEMENT

(Note: Retail lending addressed in separate curricula guideline)

Banking Skills	Product Knowledge	Functional Skills	Selling Skills	Professional Growth
ENTRY/TELLER LEVEL: (within six weeks of hire):				
Overview of Financial Institutions & the Bank/1	**Depository Accounts/1**	**Teller Transactions/3 (or 3 week OJT)**	**Basic Selling Skills/1**	**Speaking & Listening Skills/1**
Basic Computer Skills/1	**Investment & Retirement Products/1**	**Spotting Fraud/1**	**Customer Service/2**	Basic Writing Skills/1
Bank Secrecy Act/1	Other Product Knowledge/1	**Emergency Situations/1**		Basic Numbers Skills/1
Expedited Funds/1		Head Teller/1 week OJT		Career Planning/1
Deposit Operations/1 (or 1 week OJT)				Professional Appearance/¹⁄₂
CUSTOMER SERVICE REPRESENTATIVE (Nonlending Responsibilities—See Retail Lending/Personal Banker Curricula):				
Overview of EDP & Operations/1 (or 1 week OJT)	**Advanced Deposit Account Knowledge/1+**	**Platform Services/3 (or 1 month OJT)**	**Customer Profiling/1**	**Interpersonal Skills/1**
Fraud Prevention and Bank Security/¹⁄₂	**Advanced Retirement Products/1+**	**Accounting/ Bookkeeping/2+**	**Advanced Sales Skills/2**	Persuasive Writing/1
ATM Operations/¹⁄₂	Small Business Services/1	**Loan Support/1**	**Advanced Customer Service/1**	Presentation Skills/1
Safe Deposit Operations/1	Overview of Credit Products/1 (including Mortgage Financing)			Ethics/¹⁄₂

ASSISTANT BRANCH MANAGER (Within two years):

Financial Markets and Investments/2

Bank Investments/1 (or 1 week OJT)

Financial Planning/2

Trust Services/1

Direct Lease Financing/1

Credit Card Operations/1

Brokerage Activities/1

Documentation & Compliance/4

Overview of Commercial Credit Analysis/3+

Overview of Marketing/2

Supervisory Training/2

On-the-Job Training Skills/1

Conflict Resolution/1

Time Management/1

Managing Stress/1

BRANCH MANAGER (Basic management skills immediately after attaining managerial status; others within five years):

Budgeting and Profit Planning/2

Strategic Planning/1

Asset/Liability Management Issues/1

Bank Simulation Game/3+

Managing Noninterest Expense/2

Compliance Management/1

Overview of Bank's Nonretail Products/1

Customer Profitability Analysis/2

Sales Management/3

Pricing Retail Bank Services/2

Developing Marketing Strategies/1

Management Skills/3

Team Building/1

Coaching & Counseling Skills/1

Compensation & Human Resources Issues/1

Note: Bold face denotes program of critical importance. Number after program is length in terms of days, but is intended only as a guideline. Delivery methods might include instructor-led, computer-based, self-study, audio, or video methods and done in-house, off-site, or at a professional school.

©ABTAC, the Association of Bank Trainers and Consultants, 1989.

ABTAC Guideline Curriculum
RETAIL LENDING

Banking Skills	Product Knowledge	Credit/Analytical Skills	Selling Skills	Professional Growth
ENTRY LEVEL (Within six weeks of hire):				
Overview of Financial Institutions & the Bank/2	**Depository A/Cs/2 +**	**Bookkeeping/ Accounting/3**	**Basic Selling Skills/3**	**Listening Skills/1**
Business Math/1	**Investment & Retirement Products/2 +**	**Credit Inquiries/$^1/_2$**	**Customer Service/2**	**Writing Skills/1**
Consumer Banking Compliance/1	**Other Product Knowledge/2 +**		**Telephone Sales/1**	
PREOFFICIAL LEVEL (Within six months prior to becoming an officer):				
Overview of EDP & Operations/1	**Installment Loans/2**	**Consumer Credit and Income Tax Analysis/3 +**	**Advanced Sales Skills/2**	**Interpersonal Skills/1**
Computer Skills/1	**Home Equity Loans/2**	**Lender Liability/1**		**Persuasive Writing/1**
Fraud Prevention and Bank Security/1	**Residential Mortgage Financing/3**	**Documentation/1**		**Presentation Skills/1**
	Small Business Financing/2	**Loan Policy and the Approval Process/1**		Ethics/1
	Advanced Deposit A/C Knowledge/3 +			
	Titled Vehicles Loans/1			
	Credit-Insurance Products/1			

OFFICIAL LEVEL (Within three years after becoming an officer or just prior to "need-to-know"):

Asset/Liability Management Issues/1	Credit Card Operations/1	**Small Business Tax Return Analysis/1**	**Negotiation Skills/1**	Managing Stress/1
Secondary Mortgage Markets/2		**Loan Agreements/2**	Overview of Marketing/2	Time Management/1
		Collections & Bankruptcy/2		

MANAGERIAL LEVEL (Basic management skills immediately after attaining managerial status; others within five years):

Budgeting and Profit Planning/2	Commercial Mortgage Transactions/2	**Commercial Credit Analysis/2**	**Sales Management/3**	**Management Skills/3**
Monetary Economics/1			**Pricing Retail Bank Services/2**	**Team Building/1**
Bank Simulation Game/3+			Developing Marketing Strategies/1	**Training & Coaching Skills/1**
Managing Noninterest Expense/2				
Human Resources Issues/1				
Compliance Management/1				

Note: Bold face denotes program of critical importance. Number after program is length in terms of days, but is intended only as a guideline. Delivery methods might include instructor-led, computer-based, self-study, audio, or video methods and done in-house, off-site, or at a professional school.

©ABTAC, the Association of Bank Trainers and Consultants, 1989.

ABTAC Guideline Curriculum
PRIVATE BANKING

Banking Skills	Product Knowledge	Credit/Analytical Skills	Selling Skills	Professional Growth
ENTRY LEVEL (Within six weeks of hire):				
Overview of Financial Institutions and the Bank/2	**Deposit Accounts/2+**	**Accounting/3**	**Basic Selling Skills/3**	**Listening Skills/$\frac{1}{2}$**
Business Math/1	**Investment & Retirement A/Cs/2+**	**Credit Inquiries/$\frac{1}{2}$**	**Telephone Sales Skills/1**	**Basic Writing Skills/1**
Consumer Compliance/1	**Other Basic Product Knowledge/2+**	**Loan Interviewing/1**	**Customer Service/2**	
		Consumer Credit Analysis/3		
PREOFFICIAL LEVEL (Within six months prior to becoming an officer):				
Overview of EDP & Operations/1	**Installment Loans/2**	**Commercial Credit Analysis/5+**	**Advanced Selling Skills/3**	**Interpersonal Skills/1**
Computer Skills/1	**Home Equity Loans/2**	**Documentation/1**		**Persuasive Writing/1**
	Small Business Financing/2+	**Loan Policy and the Approval Process/1**		**Presentation Skills/1**
	Credit-Insurance Products/1	**Income Tax Analysis/3**		Ethics/1
	Residential Mortgage Financing/3	**Credit Analysis for the Upscale Individuals/3**		
	Investment Product Knowledge/3	**Loan Agreements/1**		
		Lender Liability/1		

OFFICIAL LEVEL (Within three years after becoming an officer or just prior to "need-to-know"):

Securities Markets/3	**Securities and Asset Management Products/2**	**Small Business Tax Return Analysis/2**	**Negotiation Skills/1**	Managing Stress/1
Monetary Economics/1	Personal Trust Products/1	**Loan Agreements/2**	Marketing Concepts/2	Team Building/1
Asset/Liability Management Issues/1		Collections & Workouts/1		Time Management/1

MANAGERIAL LEVEL (Basic management skills immediately after attaining managerial status; others within five years):

Budgeting and Profit Planning/2	Commercial Mortgage Transactions/2	**Loan Portfolio Management/1**	**Sales Management/3**	**Management Skills/3**
Managing Noninterest Expense/2			**Pricing Retail Bank Services/2**	**Team Building/1**
Banking Simulation Game/3+			Developing Marketing Strategies/1	**Training & Coaching Skills/1**
Human Resources Issues/1				
Integrating Internal Controls and Policy/1				

Note: Bold face denotes program of critical importance. Number after program is length in terms of days, but is intended only as a guideline. Delivery methods might include instructor-led, computer-based, self-study, audio, or video methods and done in-house, off-site, or at a professional school.

©ABTAC, the Association of Bank Trainers and Consultants, 1989.

ABTAC Guideline Curriculum
COMMERCIAL/MIDDLE MARKET LENDING

Banking Skills	Product Knowledge	Credit/Analytical Skills	Selling Skills	Professional Growth
ENTRY LEVEL (Within six weeks of hire):				
Overview of Banking and the Bank/2	**Overview of Bank Products/1**	**Accounting/3+**	**Basic Selling Skills/2+**	**Listening Skills/1**
Business Math/1		**Basics of Credit Analysis/5+**	Overview of Marketing/1	**Report Writing Skills/1**
Basic Economics/3		Credit Inquiries/¹⁄₂		
Compliance/1				
PREOFFICIAL LEVEL (Within six months prior to becoming an officer):				
EDP & Operations/1	**Applied Credit Product Knowledge/2**	**Documentation/2**	**Consultative Selling Skills/3**	**Interpersonal Skills/1**
Computer Training/1	**Noncredit Product Knowledge/1+**	**Lender Liability/1**	**Negotiation Skills/2**	**Persuasive Writing/1**
Monetary Economics/1		**Loan Policy/Approval Process/1**	Marketing Planning/1	**Presentation Skills/1**
Asset/Liability Management Issues/1		**Loan Structure/Pricing/2**		Ethics/1
		Monitoring Credit/1		
		Problem Loan Workouts/1		

OFFICIAL LEVEL (Within three years after becoming an officer or just prior to "need-to-know"):

Money & Capital Markets/3	Cash Management Services/2	Advanced Credit Analysis/5+	Complex Account Management/2	Interpersonal Skills/1
Bank Simulation/5	Commercial Real Estate Lending/2	Industry Analysis/2	Marketing Strategy/1	Team Building/1
		Applied Corporate Finance/3		
		Asset Based Lending/2		

MANAGERIAL LEVEL (Basic management skills immediately after attaining managerial status; others within five years):

Budgeting and Profit Planning/2	Managing the Loan Portfolio/3	Sales Management/3	Basic Management Skills/3
Integrating Technology Issues/1	Secondary Markets/1	Developing Marketing Strategies/2	Training & Coaching Skills/1
Managing Overall Bank Risk/3	Interest Rate Swaps and Options/1		Decision Making and Problem Solving/2
Compliance Management Issues/1	Applied Merchant Banking/2		Managing Change/1
Integrating Internal Controls and Policy/1	Managing the Credit Function/2		Human Resources Issues/1

Note: Bold face denotes program of critical importance. Number after program is length in terms of days, but is intended only as a guideline. Delivery methods might include instructor-led, computer-based, self-study, audio, or video methods and done in-house, off-site, or at a professional school.

©ABTAC, the Association of Bank Trainers and Consultants, 1989.

ABTAC Guideline Curriculum
CORPORATE RELATIONSHIP MANAGEMENT

Banking Skills	Product Knowledge	Credit/Analytical Skills	Selling Skills	Professional Growth
ENTRY LEVEL (Within six weeks of hire):				
Money & Banking/3+	**Overview of the Bank and Products/1**	**Accounting/3+**	**Basic Selling Skills/2+**	Listening Skills/1
Computer Training/1		**Commercial Credit Analysis/5+**	Overview of Marketing/1	Report Writing Skills/1
Business Math/1		**Loan Documentation/2**		Ethics/¹/₂
Compliance Issues/¹/₂		Personal Financial Statement Analysis/1		
PREOFFICIAL LEVEL (Within six months prior to becoming an officer):				
Financial & Capital Markets/3	**Applied Credit Product Knowledge/2**	**Intermediate Credit Analysis/5**	**Consultative Selling Skills/3**	**Interpersonal Skills/1**
International Financial Markets/2	**Cash Management Services/2**	**Loan Agreements/3**	**Negotiation Skills/2**	**Persuasive Writing/1**
Asset/Liability Management Issues/1	**Other Noncredit Products/1**	**Loan Policy/Approval Process/1**	Marketing Planning/1	**Presentation Skills/1**
	Interest Rate Risk Management/1	**Loan Structure & Pricing/2**		
	International Banking Products/1	**Lender Liability Issues/1**		
		Corporate Finance/3		
		Monitoring Credit/1		
		Problem Loan Workouts/1		

OFFICIAL LEVEL (Within three years after becoming an officer or just prior to "need-to-know"):

Bank Simulation/5	**Investment Banking/ Capital Market Products/2**	**Advanced Credit Analysis/5+**	**Complex Account Management/2**	Decision Making and Problem Solving/2
Interest Rate and Currency Swap Markets/1	Commercial Real Estate Lending/2	Basics of Corporate Taxation/2		
Foreign Exchange Markets/1	Asset-Based Lending & Securitization/2	Advanced Corporate Finance/2+		
		Accounting/Other Technical Knowledge Update/1+		

MANAGERIAL LEVEL (Basic management skills immediately after attaining managerial status; others within five years):

Budgeting and Profit Planning/2	**Industry Analysis and Product Needs/2**	**Managing the Loan Portfolio/3**	**Sales Management/3**	**Basic Management Skills/3**
Managing Overall Bank Risk/3	Risk Issues in Noncredit Products/1	**Corporate Restructuring/3+**	Developing Marketing Strategies/2	**Coaching Skills & Counseling/1**
Compliance Management Issues/1		Tax Implications of Mergers & Acquisitions/2		**Team Building/1**
Integrating Internal Controls and Policy/1				Managing Change/1
				Compensation & Other Human Resources Issues/1

Note: Bold face denotes program of critical importance. Number after program is length in terms of days, but is intended only as a guideline. Delivery methods might include instructor-led, computer-based, self-study, audio, or video methods and done in-house, off-site, or at a professional school.

©ABTAC, the Association of Bank Trainers and Consultants, 1989.

INDEX